VERBAL KNOWLEDGE
IN
PRĀBHĀKARĀ-MĪMĀṀSĀ

SRI GARIB DASS Oriental Series No. 60

Verbal Knowledge in Prābhākara-Mimāṁsā

Dr. Rajendra Nath Sarma

SRI SATGURU PUBLICATIONS
A Division of
Indian Books Centre
Delhi-India

Published by :
SRI SATGURU PUBLICATIONS
Indological & Oriental Publishers
A Division of
Indian Books Centre,
40/5, Shakti Nagar,
Delhi-110007
INDIA

First. Published : Delhi, 1990

ISBN-81-7030-194-7

Printed at : Print India, A-38/2 Mayapuri-I, New Delhi-110064

CONTENTS

Preface

I had the pleasant opportunity of being initiated to the study of Mīmāṁsā system of Indian Philosophy when I had been a student in the Darśana group of the M.A. class in Sanskrit of the University of Gauhati during the period 1972-74. My acquintance with the Mīmaṁsā works in that period resulted in developing a keen interest in me for making a critical study on the Prābhākara-mīmāṁsā, especially in the context of verbal knowledge.

Later on, when I joined the Deptt. of Sanskrit, Gauhati University as a Lecturer in 1978. Professor Dr. Mukunda Madhava Sharma, M.A., Ph.D. D. Litt. Kāvyatirtha. the then Supervisor of mine suggested me to make a critical exposition of the *Vāyārthamātṛkā* of the *Prakaraṇa-Pañcikā* and according to his valuable suggestion, I prepared my doctoral thesis under the supervision of Dr. Ashok Kumar Goswami Reader, Deptt. of Sanskrit, Gauhati University for which I have been awarded the Ph.D. degree by the University of Gauhati in 1984. The present work is the thesis itself under new title, "*VERBAL KNOWLEDGE IN PRĀBHĀKARA-MĪMĀMSĀ*.

It may be mentioned here that I have also given the English translation of the *Vākyārtha-Mātṛkā* in my thesis which has been already published by Indian Books Centre, earlier.

The scheme of the present work is unusual as the usual chapterwise division is not maintained in it. It is in the form of a commentary in English. The original text presented piecemeal has been critically exposed and a comparative study of it with other systems of thought such as Bhāṭṭa school of Mīmāṁsā, Nyāya Vedānta and Vyākaraṇa has also been made in it.

I like to add here that the present work is devoted to the issue on the Śābdabodha (Verbal knowledge) according to the Prābhākara school of Mimāṁsā.

I am very much indebted to my revered teacher Dr. Ashok Kumar Goswami under whose supervision, this work was completed.

I shall also remain ever grateful to my teacher Professor Dr. Mukunda Madhava Sharma who was kind enough to supervise my work initially.

I am also grateful to my teachers Dr. Priyamsu Prabal Upadhyaya and Dr. Apurba Chandra Barthakuria. M.A,, Ph.D. for their fruitful suggestions offered to me.

I also put on record the help I received from late Acharya Manoranjan Shastri in respect of understanding some passage of the *Vākyārtha-Māṭrkā.*

I express my gratefulness to my wife Smt. Jamini Devi; M.A., Kāvya-Śāstri, for ungrudgingly relieving me of the domestic responsibilities during the period of the preparation of the present work.

To Indian Books Centre, Delhi, are my sincere thanks due for bringing out this work.

As I conclude, I am really concious of the probable shortcomings. However,

"आपरितोषाद्र विदुषां न साधु मन्त्रे प्रयोगविज्ञानम्"

12th October, 1989 R.N. SARMA

Scheme of Transliteration

आ	ā
ई	ī
ऊ	ū
ऋ	ṛ
ऌ	ḷ
ए	e
ऐ	ai
ओ	o
औ	au
ङ	ṅ
च	c
छ	ch
ञ	ñ
ट	ṭ
ठ	ṭh
ड	ḍ
ढ	ḍh
ण	ṇ
व	v
श	ś
ष	ṣ
क्ष	kṣ
ं	ṁ
:	ḥ

Abbreviations

As	Arthasaṁgraha
ASP	Aṣṭādhyāyī-sūtrapāṭha
AVM	Abhidhāvṛttimātṛkā
BK	Bṛhaṭṭīkā
BP	Bhāṣāpariccheda
BR	Bṛhatī
BS	Brahmasiddhi
BV	Bhāvanāviveka
CS	Citsukhi
DOP	Discourses on the Pūrvamīmāṁsā.
EBM	Epistemology of the Bhāṭṭa School of Pūrvamīmāmsā.
IDM	In Defence of Mimāṁsā
IP	Indian Philosophy
IPM	Introduction to Pūrvamīmāṁsā
ITK	Indian Theory of Knowledge
ITM	Indian Theory of Meaning
JNM	Jaiminīyanyāyamālāvistara
K	Kārikā
KM	Karma-Mīmāṁsā
KP	Kāvyaprakāśa
KPS	Kāvyatattva-Samikṣā
LC	Literary Criticism in Ancient India.
MAI.S	Maitrāyaṇa-Saṁhitā
MB	Mahābhāṣya
MD	Mimāmsā-Darśana
MK	Mīmāṁsā-Kośa
MM	Mānameyodaya
MNP	Mīmāmsā-Nyāka-Prakāśa
MP	Mimāṁsā-Paribhāṣā
MS	Mīmaṁsā-Sūtra
MT	Manu-Saṁhitā
NK	Nāyakaratna

NKK	Nyāyakaṇikā
NKM	Nyāyakusumāṁjali
NM	Nyāyamañjari
NPS	Nayanaprasādinī
NRM	Nyāyaratnamālā
NS	Nyāya-Sūtra
NSM	Nyāyasiddhāntamuktāvalī
NTK	Nyāya Theory of Knowledge
NVTT	Nyāyavārttikatātparyaṭīkā
PIS	Pūrvamīmāṁsā in its Sources
PLM	Parmalaghumañjuṣā
PP	Prakaraṇa-Pañcikā
PR	Puṇyarāja's Commentary on Vākyapadiya
PSP	Prābhākara School of Pūrvamimaṁsā
PV	Prabhākaravijaya
PWM	Philosophy of Word and Meaning
RVL	Ṛjuvimalā
SB	Śābarabhāṣya
SDK	Śāstradīpikā
SKD	Śabdakalpadruma
SP (I)	Śṛṅgāraprakāśā (ed. by V. Raghavan)
SP (II)	Śṛṅgāraporakāśā (ed. by G.R. Joshier)
SSP	Śabdasaktiprakāśikā
TAI.S	Taittiriyasaṁhitā
TB	Tattvabindu
T. BRA	Tāṇḍyabrāhamaṇa
TC	Tattvacintāmaṇi
TP	Tattvaprakāsīkā
TR	Tantrarahasya
TS	Tarkasaṁgraha
TV	Tantravārttika
V	Vṛtti
Vā. P.	Vākyapadīya
Vār	Vārttika
VB	Vātsyāyanabhāṣya
VBS	Vaiyākaraṇabhūsaṇasāra
VM	Vākyārthamātṛkā (ed. by H. Subrahamanya Sastri)
VM(d)	Vākyārthamātṛkā-dīpikā (Hindi ed.)
VP	Vedāntaparibhāsā
VV	Vidhiviveka

INTRODUCTION

The schools of Indian Philosophy are classified into two types namely, the Āstika or Orthodox schools and the Nāstika or Heterodox schools. While the former type accepts the authority of the vedas, the latter does not. The Āstika or Orthodox schools are six in number. These are Sāṁkhya, Yoga, Nyāya, Vaiśeṣika, Pūrvamīmāṁsā and Uttaramīmāṁsā or Vedānta. The Nāstika or the Heterodox schools are mainly three viz., the Bauddha, Jaina and Cārvāka.

The Pūrvamīmāṁsā or Karmamīmāṁsā system of Indian Philosophy is ascribed to the great sage Jaimini who wrote the *Mīmāṁsā-Sūtras*. Śabarasvāmin wrote the major commentary known as *Śābarabhāṣya* on Jaimini's *Sūtras*. He was followed by a long line of commentrators and independent writers of whom Kumārila Bhāṭṭa and Prabhākara Miśra deserve special mention. These two scholars founded the two chief branches of Pūrvamīmāṁsā known after their names, viz., the Bhāṭṭa school and the Prābhākara school.

Prabhākara Miśra composed two commentaries namely, *Bṛhatī* and *Laghvī* on the Śābarabhāṣya. The reputation enjoyed by Prabhākara among scholars was mainly due to the subsequent contribution of Śālikanātha Miśra, a first-rate scholar and an independent writer of the Prābhākara system. Among other writers of this school are Bhavanātha Miśra, author of the *Nayaviveka*, Nandīśvara, author of the *Prabhākaravijaya* and Rāmānujācārya, author of the *Tantrarahasya*. They are the only ancient writers of the Prābhākara system. Of the modern scholars writing on this system, the names of Dr. Ganganatha Jha and M.M. Kuppuswami Shastri deserve to be specially mentioned. It may perhaps be deduced from the length of the list of scholars of this system, both traditional and modern, that there were only a few scholars who were interested in the study of the Prābhākara school and as such, this school unlike the Bhāṭṭa school was not so popular among the students of Indian Philosophy. It will, however, be wrong to conclude that as the Prābhākara school of Pūrvamīmāṁsā was not popular and not widely studied, so it has no importance as a system of philosophy. Rather it can be said that the school of Prabhākara is more important than the Bhāṭṭa school despite its wide popularity. Dr. Ganganath Jha is of the view that Prabhākara is more faithful to the Bhāṣya of Śabara than Kumārila. According to Professor Hiriyanna, the original teaching of the Mīmāṁsā is better preserved in the writings of Prabhākara than in those of Kumārila.[1] Prabhākara, however, was a more original thinker than Kumārila and he will always be remembered as the author of a peculiar theory of knowledge known as Tripuṭīpratyakṣavāda or the theory of triple perception and a theory of error called Akhyātivāda or the Vivekākhyātivāda.[2] To understand the Mīmāṁsā-system fully and precisely, one must go through the works of the Prābhākara system. S. Subrahmanya Sastri maintains the view that though many theories of this school are criticised in other Darśanas particularly in the Nyāya and although the Advaitins are wedded to the Bhāṭṭa school in matters of phenomenol Reality ('vyavahāre Bhāṭṭanaya'), the Prābhākara school commands respect from and is actually made use of by reputed scholars. The Viśiṣṭādvaita school of philosophy follows the Prābhākara school in matters regarding the categories of the world.[3]

It may be added here that the study of the system of Prabhākara is indispensable even for acquiring a clear knowledge of the Dharmaśāstras and the *Sāyaṇabhāṣya* of the vedas as well. The Bhāṭṭa and the Prābhākara schools differ in certain points. There is wide difference between both the schools in the exposition of the process of Śābdabodha centering round the concept of Bhāvanā. Some important points of difference between the two systems may be mentioned here :

(i) The Prābhākara school recognises only five pramāṇas, viz., Pratyakṣa, Anumāna, Śāstra, Upamāna and Arthāpatti. But the Bhāṭṭa school recognises six Pramāṇas including Anupalabdhi.

(ii) While the Prābhākaras admit eight Padārthas namely,

Dravya, Guṇa, Karma, Sāmānya, Śakti, Sādṛśya, Sāṁkhya and Samavāya, the Bhāṭṭas recognise only five Padārthas, viz., Dravya, Guṇa, Karma, Sāmānya and Abhāva.

(iii) The school of Prabhākara advocates the theory of Anvitābhidhāna, while that of Kumārila advances the theory of Abhihitānvaya.

(iv) While the Bhāṭṭa school accepts the theory of Anyathākhyāti, the Prābhākara advocates the theory of Akhyāti.

(v) The Prābhākaras admit the theory of Niyogavākyārtha, while the Bhāṭṭas accept the theory of Bhāvanāvākyārtha.

(vi) While the Bhāṭṭa school admits importation of words (Śabdādhyāhāraḥ), the Prābhākara school recognises the importation of ideas (Arthādhyāhāraḥ).

These are only the most important points of difference between the two sister schools of Pūrvamīmāṁsā.

In addition to the aforesaid two schools of Mīmāṁsā, one more school is found to exist, known as the 'Miṣramata' initiated by one Murāri Miśra. This school, however, is not known except through some references in other works. He appears to have given birth to a new school within the Mīmāṁsā system, which had led to the saying—

'Murārestṛtīyaḥ panthāḥ' (the third path i.e., school initiated by Murāri). But materials for preparing a full account of this 'Miśramata' are not yet available to the scholars.[4]

Dr. Umesh Misra, however, wants to identify the founder of the 'Murāri-mata' as the Murāri Miśra II. He also observes[5] that 'Murārestṛtīyaḥ panthāḥ' has become a proverb in Sanskrit which has got its origin in Murāri Miśra II. He was one of the greatest Mīmāṁsakas who held independent views on several topics of Pūrvamīmāṁsā. His views were so distinct and convincing that he was regarded as the founder of the third school of Pūrvamīmāṁsā.

An Exhaustive note on the Prakaraṇa-Pancikā with reference to the Vākyārthamātṛkā

The *Prakaraṇa-pañcikā* is the most celebrated independent

treatise of the Prābhākara school of Pūrvamīmāṁsā. It is a primer of the Prābhākara system and deals with very important tenets such as Pramāṇa, Prameya and other subjects which distinguish the system from the other systems including its sister school i.e., the Bhāṭṭa school.

The *Prakaraṇa-pañcikā* is a large volume in fourteen chapters called 'Prakaraṇas'. It is in a mixed form of prose and verse i.e., certain Prakaraṇas are composed in prose contatning also some qouted verses, while certain 'Prakaraṇas' are presented entırely in verse. Of the fourteen 'Prakaraṇas', the second (viz., the 'Nītipatha') the third (viz., the 'Nayavīthī'), the fifth (viz., the 'Amṛtakalā') the eleventh (viz., the 'Vākyārthamātṛkā') and the fourteenth (viz., the 'Atideśapārāyaṇa') are written in verse and the remaining nine 'Prakaraṇas' viz., the Śāstramukha, Jātinirṇaya, Pramāṇapārāyaṇa, Vimalāñjana, Tattvāloka, Nyāyaśuddhi, Mīmāṁsājīvarakṣā, Viṣayakaraṇīya and Aṅgapārāyaṇa are presented in prose.

In these Prakaraṇas, the author has dealt with all topics of the Prābhākara system such as the validity of non-vedic texts, the theory of error known as 'Akhyāti', nature of Pramāṇas, their number and definitions, Padārthas, relation of word and its meaning as eternal, existence of Ātman, refutation of the existence of Īśvara, refutation of the Buddhists' theory of momentariness, establishment of Anvitābhidhāna, establishment of Apūrva as the meaning of vedic optatives etc. The author explains and criticises the other systems of Indian philosophy particularly the system of Kumārila Bhāṭṭa so far as the topic selected by him are concerned.

The very title of the book viz., *Prakaraṇa-pañcikā* shows that it is an exposition of the views of the Prābhākara system. It solves logically the problems both minor and major arising out of the Śāstras. The woad 'Prakaraṇa' means a context i.e., a topic which is useful in determining the sense of a word. It is a process towards the part of the Śāstras and the word 'pañcikā' means exposition.[6]

The Prakaraṇas are introductory manuals. The literature of the philosophical works like the *Mīmāṁsā-sūtras* and the *Vedānta-sūtras* etc. had become so vast that it was not practically possible on the part of an ordinary student to have sufficient knowledge of logic within a sort time for the pursuit of his studies in other branches. Teachers in various subjects must have realised this situation and to avert the same summarised the principles of the systems in simpler language. These summaries came to be known as prakaraṇas. We may resonably add here that the word 'pañcikā' is generally found elsewhere in the sense of five. As for instance, the five chapters of the *Aitareya Brāhmaṇa* are traditionally referred to as prathama pañcikā etc.

The word 'pañcikā' as used in the name of *Prakaraṇa-pañcikā* may, therefore, sometimes create a wrong notion that the present work consists of five chapters. But as rightly pointed out by PT. A Subrahmanya Sastri, the word 'pañcikā' in the present context is to be understood as derived from the root 'pac' in the sense of 'to elaborate'.

The *Prakaraṇa-pañcikā* is a very important work as it gives the views of the Prābhākara system on almost all the relevant topics. In fact, it is indispensable for a comprehensive study of the Prābhākara Mīmāṁsā, It has been often quoted as authoritative work and referred to for crtticism of the Prābhākara thought by some prominent scholars in their works. For over thirty pages, Bhoja clearly follows the *Vākyārthamātṛkā.* In Chapter VIII of the *Śṛṅgāraprakāśa* of Bhoja, Śālikanātha is reproduced verbatim on the issues like Ākāṁkṣā, Sannidhi, Yogyatā and the theories of verbal comprehension viz., the Abhihitānvayavāda and the Anitābhidhānavāda which Śālikanātha deals with in the *Vākyārthamātṛkā.*[7]

Some of the works wherein we find ample quotations from and references to the *Prakaraṇa-paācikā* may be mentioned as follows :

(i) *Tantrarahasya* of Rāmānujācārya.
(ii) *Nayaviveka* of Bhavanātha Miśra.
(iii) *Prabhākaravijaya* or Nandīśvara.
(iv) *Nyāyaratnamālā* or Pārthasārthi Miśra.
(v) *Citsukhī* of Citsukhācārya.
(vi) *Tattvabindu* of Vācaspati Miśra.
(vii) *Tattvacintāmaṇi* of Gaṅgeśopādhyāya.
(viii) *Nyāyakusumāñjali* of Udayana.
(ix) *Bhāṣāpariccheda* of Viśvanātha.

(x) *Sarvadarśanasaṁgraha* of Mādhavācārya.
(xi) *Śṛṅgāraprakāśa* of Bhoja.
(xii) *Locapa* of Abhinavagupta, etc.

As is rightly observed by Professor A.B. Keith, the author of the *Prakaraṇa-pañcikā*, dealt with the important epistemological and metaphysical views of Prabhākara Miśra.[8] M.M. Kuppuswami Sastri also points out to the scholarly character of this great work of the Prābhākara school.[9]

The *Prakaraṇa-pañcikā* deals not only with the facts relating to the epistemology found in the Tarkapāda (i.e., the first pāda of the first Adhyāya of the *Sābarabhāṣya* of Śabara), but also all the topics of the twelve chapters of the *Śābarabhāṣya* wherein Prabhākara does not agree with Kumārila. Moreover, it establishes the tenets of the Prābhākara school very clearly. An acquintance with the contents of the *Prakaraṇa-paācikā*, makes one believe that without a faithful study of the work, none can have a clear and complete knowledge of the Prābhākara system.

The *Vākyārthamatṛkā* known as the *Vākyārthamātṛkāvṛtti* is the eleventh prakaraṇa of the *Prakaraṇa-pāñcikā*. It is a cluster of verses on which the author was written the vṛtti. As has been admitted by the author himself, this Prakaraṇa was written in order to facilitate dispassionate understanding of the system in accordance with the views of the teacher Prabhākara.[10] This Prakaraṇa has two sub-sections namely, prathama pariccheda and dvitiya pariccheda of which the first one serves as an introduction to the second. The prathama pariccheda of the *Vākyārthamātṛkā* consists of twenty two Karikās besides ten collected verses (samgraha ślokas) pertaining to the same author. The topics and problems dealt with the kārikās have been explained by the author in the subsequent vṛtti texts. In the first section of the said Prakaraṇa, the author has established Anvitābhidhānavāda (the theory of expression of the co-related) and in doing so, he has criticised and refuted Abhihitānvayavāda (the theory of expression of the co-relation) of the Bhāṭṭa Mīmāṁsakas, and also the theory of Sphoṭa of the Grammarians.

The author has also discussed in this chapter, the three factors that lead to the comprehension of the total meaning of the sentence namely, Ākāṁkṣā (expectancy), Sannidhi (contiguity) and Yogyatā (compaṭibiliṭy).

In the second section of the said Prakaraṇa, the author of the *Vākyārthamātṛkā*, has established Niyoga (moral imperative) as the meaning of the optative case-endings, Apūrva (unique result) as the meaning of the vedic operatives and the effect of the actions as the meaning of non-vedic optatives and in this section, he has refuted the views of Maṇḍada Miśra, who has, in his *Brahmasiddhi*, strongly criticised and discarded the views of the Prābhākara school regarding Niyoga prompting as the meaning of the vedic optatives. In this second pariccheda, there are forty six Kārikās of which the last Kārikā gives the name of the *Vākyārthamātṛkā*, its author and the purpose of writing the *Vākyārthamātṛkā*.[11]

The name 'Vākyārthamātṛkā' comprises of two parts, viz., 'Vākyārthā' and 'mātṛkā' which may be analysed as 'vākyārthasya mātṛkā'. The word 'vākyārtha' again may be expounded as 'vākyasya arthaḥ' (the meaning of a sentence) and the word 'mātṛkā' may be derived as mātṛ+ivārthe kan+'tāp'.[12]

By way of explaining the title of the *Vākvārthamātṛkā* as shown above, it may be humbly observed here that the *Vākyārthamātṛkā* serves as the source of the theories of meaning i.e., in comparison to the other prakaraṇas of the *PP*, this prakaraṇa is directly concerned with the Vākyārthabodha (i.e., the knowledge of the meaning of the sentence). Here again, we shall have to record another observation in this connection made by PT.A. Subrahmanya Sastri who has edited the *Prakarṛṇa-pañcikā* with introduction and notes, the very name 'vākyārtha-mātṛkā' signifies that it is the very basis of all the speculations of the Prābhākara system.[13] Of all the fourteen Prakaraṇas of the *Prakaraṇa-pañcikā*, the *Vākyārthamātṛkā* is considered to be the most important and that is why, the author has written a vṛtti on it and not on the other Prakaraṇas. It is believed that the *Vākyārthamātṛkā* aimed at defending the doctrine of Niyoga against the onslaughts that came from the critics like Maṇḍana Miśra, the author of the *Brahmasiddhi*.

Author of the Prakaraṇa-pancikā

Śālikanātha Miśra is the author of the *Prakaraṇa-pañcikā*. Scholars do not differ regarding the authorship of the *Prakaraṇa-pañcikā*. Śālikanātha Miśra is also known as Śālikanātha and

Śārikānātha. That the name is 'Śālikanātha' and the *Prakaraṇa-pañcikā* is composed by him is clearly mentioned by Rāmānujācārya in his *Tantrarahasya.*[15] Kṛṣṇa Miśra, author of the *Prabodhacandrodaya*, has mentioned Śālikanātha as Śārikānātha[16] That the *Prakoraṇa-pañcikā* is composed by Śālikanātha is also clear from certain lines of Rāmānujācārya's work.[17] Mādhavācārya also mentions Sālikanātha as the author of the *Prakaraṇa-pañcikā.*[18] It is, therefore, an established fact that Sālikanātha is the author of the *Prakaraṇa-pañcikā.* As we have already stated, Sālikanatha is the first rate scholar among the Prābhākaras and the reputation that his teacher Prabhākara Miśra enjoyed among scholars was mainly due to his contributions. In this context, some observations of some modern scholars like K.S. Ramaswami Sastri and PT. A Subrahmanya Sastri deserve notice.[19]

Other works of the Author

In addition to the *Prakaraṇa-pañcikā*, two works ascribed to him are *Ṛjuvimalā* and *Dīpaśikhā* both being the commentaries on Prabhākara's *Bṛhatī* and *Lāghvī* respectively. The author himself makes a reference, in his *Prakaraṇa-pañcikā*, to these commentaries which he calls pañcikādvaya.[20] We are tempted here to refer to a popular saying that no dullared person like Śālikanātha was born or will be born, who composed the *Dīpaśikhā* only to popularise Prabhākara.[21] One can easily understand that the popular saying under reference is nothing but an indirect appreciation of the *Dīpasīkhā* as a great work of merit. Another work that stands to the credit of Śālikanāta is the *Mīmāṁsābhāṣyapāriśiṣṭa*, a commentary dealing with certain difficult passages of the first chapter of the *Śābarabhāṣya*. According to Candibhaṭṭa. the author of *Prakāśikā*, a commentary on Keśava Miśra's *Tarkabhāṣā*. Śālikanātha wrote, besides the works on Mīmāṁsā, a commentary on *Praśastapādabhāsya* of Praśastapādācārya.[22] Professor A.B. Keith also corroborates the above view.[23]

First Chapter entitled "Introduction" of the Vākyārthamātṛkā along with the Commentary

Śālikanātha Miśra has begun his Vṛtti (V) on the *Vākyārthamātṛkā* (*VM*) with the verse cited above, wherein he has stated the purpose of his writing the Vṛtti. The author is confident that he has written the Kārikās (*K*) without much elaboration so that readers can follow with ease. Yet in apprension of some readers failing to grasp the ideas maintained in the Kārikās, the author has composed the Vṛtti so as to facilitate the easy understanding of such readers. By way of stating the purpose of writing the Vṛtti, the author has satisfied a traditional requirement that one should be clear in mind regarding the purpose or utility of a work before he starts the same.[25]

In the *V* text "tatrakārya etc.," Śālikanātha refers to the three views of three different scholars regarding their concept of Vākyārtha (sentence-meaning). These three sects of philosophers are commonly known as Kāryavākyārthavādins. But they differ from one another in respect of their idea regarding what generates or gives rise to a vākyārtha. The kāryavākyārthavādins are namely, the vaiyākaraṇas, the Bhāṭṭa Mīmṃṁsakas and the Prābhākara Mīmāṁsakas. According to the Vaiyākaraṇas, Bhāva (activity) is vākyārtha. Bhāva is the activity denoted by a root when it is conceived without any regard to its continuation or progress when is effected by different instruments of action or kārakas. Though Bhāva and Kriyā are almost used as synonyms denoting the sense of a verb or a verbal derivative, still it can be said that Bhāva shows a completed activity, while kriyā shows activity in progress.[26]

The followers of Kumārila Bhaṭṭa accepted Bhāvanā (urge) as the vākyārtha and as such they are called Bhāvanāvākyārthavādins and their theory is known as Bhāvanāvākyārthavāda. Bhāvanā is a stimulating activity for that which is to take place.[27] In course of our exposition of the *VM*. II, we will deal with Bhāvanā and Bhāvanāvākyārthavāda at length.

The Prābhākaras, however, admit Apūrva (unseen potency) as the vākyārtha. According to them, Apūrva (unseen potency) Niyoga (prompting) and Kārya (performable) are synonyms.[28] Because of their admitting Apūrva or Niyoga or Kārya as the vākyārtha, they are known as Apūrvakāryavākyārthavādins or

Niyogavākyārthavādins and their theory comes to be known as Niyogavākyārthavāda. In course of our exposition of the text of the *VM*.II, we will have scope to deal with these two theories namely, Bhāvanāvākyārtha of the Bhāṭṭas and Niyogavākyārtha of the Prābhākaras. In the *V* text, 'atra ye pratyastamita. . . .' etc., Śālikanātha refers to the view of the Grammarians according to whom, a vākya is an indivisible unit presenting the meaning as a unit which, for convenience, is further divided into separate meanings of individual words which have a phenomenal existence.[29]

Again with the expression, 'ye ca vākyântyavarṇa eveti. . . .' etc., in the *V* above, the author of the *VM* refers to the views of Śabaraswāmin and the Naiyāyikas. According to Śabara, the antya varṇa (last letter) along with the impressions of each of the preceding letters brings about the knowledge of the vākyārtha (the meaning of a sentence).[30] Some of the Naiyāyikas also contend that the carama varṇa (last letter) combined with all those words revives (the collective impressions) and thus give rise to the knowledge of the vākyārtha.[31]

In the V text, 'ye ca padairanavitāḥ . . .', Śālikanātha refers to the view of Vārttikakāra Kumārila who contends that the meanings of the Padas (words), not syntactically connected are conveyed by respective Padas and thereafter give rise to the knowledge of the mutual connection, i.e , the Vākyārtha.[32]

The three views referred to above shall come to be criticised by Śālika, in *V* text under *K*(6). So, we shall have the opportunity to discuss these views again in the succeeding pages.

In 'padebhya . . .' etc., of the *K*(1) and *V* above, Śālikanātha has laid stress in establishidg the view of Prabhākara Miśra, according to which the knowledge of the vākyārtha is from the padas (words) only. The inclusion of the emphatic particle 'eva' in *K* and *V* above, indicates that it is only the Padas that give rise to the knowledge of the vākyārtha and thereby the author discards the views held by other thinkers, viz., the view of the vaiyākaraṇas, according to which the knowledge of the vākyārtha is due to the sentence as a whole; the view of the Bhāṣyakāra, i.e., Śabara who contends that the antya varṇa (last letter) along with the impressions of each of the preceeding varṇas brings about the knowledge of the vākyārtha.[33]

Śālikanātha also refutes the view of the Bhāṭṭa Mīmāṁsakas

who assert that the knowledge of vākyārtha or verbal comprehension arises from the padārthas (meanings of the words).[34] While the Bhāṭṭas regard padārthas as the Śābdabodhakāraṇa (cause of the verbal comprehension), the Prābhākaras regard pada as such.[35] In other words, they contend that the vākyārtha is denoted by padas. As we have already stated, we shall discuss these views again in context of ouɪ exposition of *V* under *K*(6).

In the *V* text, 'vākyārthapratipattau . . . ātmānaṁ labhhnte' etc., the author of the *VM*, discards totally the view of the vaiyākaraṇas who contend that the vākya denotes tne vākyārtha. But in comparison to the view of the Grammarians, Śālikanātha prefers the view of Śabara and in comparison to this view of Śabara, he prefers the view of Kumārila. But, on the whole, he rejects these aforesaid views and forwards the view of Prabhākara. The emphatic particle 'tu' is used in the *V* in order to eliminate the views of other philosophers. It has also been stated by Śālikanātha that if his view (i.e., the view, according to which, the padas denote related meanings) can be established, then the aforesaid three views do not stand to reason. We have already stated that Śālikanātha discards these views in his *V* text under *K*(6) and as such we do not want to discuss here the refutations of these views by Śālika. We shall dlscuss the same there in context of the exposition of *V* under *K*(6).

In 'pradhāna . . .' etc., of the *K*, Śālikanātha forwards the view of the Prābhākaras who consider the vākyārtha as constituted by the Padārthas and who understand the two viz., the Padārtha and the Vākyārtha in a relation of Pradhāna (principal) and Gauṇa (secondary). According to the followers of the Prābhākara, the Padas constitute a Vākya and the Padārthas give rise to a Vākyārtha. The Prābhākaras contend that the Vākyārtha is the Pradhāna and the Padārtha is the Gauṇa, because the Vākyārtha is the whole, while the Padārthas are its parts. It is the parts that make the whole. It may be stated here that the phala (result) is the Pradhāna and the means of attaining it is the Gauṇa. For instance, svarga (heaven), the phala is the Pradhāna while its mecns, i.e., the yāga (sacrifice) is the Gauṇa.[36]

The inclusion of the particle 'eva' after the word 'Padārthān' in *K* above, is for laying stress on the view of the Prābhākaras that the Padārthas that have already attained a mutual relationship give rise to the vākyārtha. We have already stated that in the view of the Prābhākaras, the Padas constitute a Vākya and as such the meanings of the Padas constitute the meaning of a Vākya. But mere association of the Padārthas can never give rise to the Vākyārtha but the syntactically related meanings of the Padas give rise to Vākyārtha.[37]

In *K* viz., 'bhūyāṁso . . .' etc., the author proceeds to remove the misgiving expressed earlier that as there are many meanings of the Padas and as such many meanings of Vākyas, the Vākyas will also come to be many. Śālikanātha cotends that though there may be many meanings of the Padas, still there becomes one Vākyārtha only and as the knowledge of the Vākyārtha leads to a single Kārya (performable), the Vākya is also stated to be one necessiated by the unity of purpose of the word-meanings. The Prābhākaras as the advocates of the Anvitābhidhṇnavāda, contend that a Vākya has a unitary meaning of its own, the constituent Padas possess meanings only as they are related to the unitary sentence-meaning. Thus, in the expression, 'gāmānaya' (bring the cow), the word 'gau' (the cow) means not the isolated meaning of 'gotva' (cowness), but 'gau' as related to the act of 'ānayana' (bringing), so also the word 'ānaya' means the act of 'ānayana' as related to the 'gau'. The Padas give their own meanings and their syntactical relation to other Padas in the Vākya so that the Vākyārtha is directly conveyed by the Padas themselves.

It is also indicated in the *K* above, that a group of Padas serving a single purpose, forms one Vākya, but only if any one of these Padas on being disjoined from the rest makes it wanting or defective. Moreover, the *K* texts above, have a reference to 'ekavākyatā' (principle of unitary passage) of the Mīmāṁsakas. We shall have scope to discuss this principle in course of our exposition of the relevant *V* text later on.

In 'pratipattirguṇānāṁ hi . . . etc.' and 'yaddhi pradhāna-bhūtaṁ . . . etc.' in *K*(5B) and *V*(5) respectively above, Śālikanātha states that the knowledge of the principal meaning is the only purpose of the secondary meanings. In reply to an objection as to how that which is the Pradhāna artha (principal meaning) can be known specially, the author of the *VM*, states that it is the Gauṇa artha (secondary meaning) in the intentness of which lies the Gauṇa artha or in other words, the Gauṇa arthas are intent on bringing about the Pradaāna artha i.e., the Vākyārtha. The Vākyārtha which is the Pradhāna artha is ihe Prameya or the object to be known. It is because of the fact that Śabda as Pramāṇa is admitted only with reference to Tātparya (the intentional meaning). This Vākyārtha cannot be understood by one Pada only. The Vākya itself, is, therefore, is the source of Śābdabodha, i.e., the Vākyārthajñāna (or the knowledge of the sentence-meaning). This is, as it appears, from the present context, the view of the Grammarians who accept Vākya as the cause of the knowledge of the Vākyārtha.

In the *V* above, we find a quotation viz., Ṣṣṭhādye ca padaṁ nāma . . .' etc., which is stated in the *VM* as being taken from the *BK* of Kumārila. We regret our inability to find out the same as the work viz., the *BK* is not available in print.[38] Moreover, the word'Ṣaṣṭhādye' (i.e., the beginning of the sixth chapter) must refer to the sixth chapter of the *SB*, because the *BK* is a commentary on the *SB*. But the contents in the quotation are not found in the beginning of the sixth chapter of the *SB* (Śābarabhāṣya) and the quotation, as it appears from the context, is in support of the view of the Grammarians.

In the *K*(6) the author, explains how a Śakti (denotative power) is ascertained and again in *V* under *K*(6), he rejects the view of the Grammarians who contend that a Vākya is the denoter of the Vākyārtha and the view of Śabara and a section of Naiyāyikas who contend that the Antya varṇa is the denoter of the Vākyārtha.

It is stated in the *K* above, that Śakti of the Padas is ascertained through a process of inclusion and exclusion in the usages subsequent to the hearing of sentences by elderly persons. The author here refers to the Vṛddhavyavahāra (usage of elderly person) which is, in the view of the Prābhākaras,[39] thē most important method of learning the words. There are eight methods of learning the words. These are Grammar, Comparison, Dictionary, Statement of trustworthy persons, Usage of the elderly persons, Supplementary statement, Paraphrase and the contiguity of a well-known word.[40] Though the number of methods suggested for acquiring the knowledge of new words varies from school, to school itis interesting to find that Vṛddhavyavahāra (usage of elderly persons) is invariably recognised by almost all the scholars of various schools and as such it deserves to be admitted as the most important of all the methods suggested in this regard. It is why we find Nāgeśa referring to (Vṛddha) Vyavahāra as Śaktigrāhakaśiromaṇi, the chief (lit. the crest jewel) of the factors determining the Śakti (of words).[41] This singular position is given to Vṛddhavyavahāra in all the chief schools including Mīmāṁsā.[42]

The Naiyāyikas have also given due recognition to this Vṛddhavyavahāra. Gaṅgeśa comes to admit that the knowledge of all words primarily results from Vṛddavyavahāra. He understands the other ways to be dependent on the baeic knowledge of meanings of words derived through Vṛddhavyavahāra.[43] It is only from the sentences in the imperative mood that we can observe some kind of visible activity on the part of the listener. Hearing the utterance of a sentence by a prayojaka vṛddha (directing elderly person) to prayojya vṛddha (directed elderly person) and observing the consequent activity on the part of the listener, a child gets the idea that the activity of the directed elderly person is based on his undstanding the meaning of a sentence. At this time, the whole activity of the directed elderly person is understood as the meaning of the whole utterance of the directing elderly person. From several such observations of various utterances and their meanings, the child is able to understand the meaning of single words through a process of inclusion and exclusion.

In the *V* text above, Śālikanātha refutes the view of the Vākyavādins, i.e., the Grammarians who contend that it is the Vākya that denotes the Vākyārtha. But according to the Prābhākaras who are known as the Padavādins, it is the Pada that denotes the Vākyārtha.[44]

In the *V* text above, Śālikanātha, with a view to giving us thc way haw a *Śakti* is ascertained, again states that though the knowledge of Pada can be acquired by Vṛddhavyavahāra and the Vṛddhavyavahāra is through the Vākyas, yet the vāccka-śakti (denotative power) is ascertained in respeci of that meaning the inclusion of which is due to the inclusion of the Pada and the exclusion of which is due to the Pada. It cannot be said that because of admitting the Śakti in respect of a pada, there will be no knowledge of the Vākyārtha. For, the principle is being stated here after in *SK*(11) of the *VM*. According to this principle, because of their denoting the meaning first and of their conveying the tātparya (intention of the speaker), it is better to admit Śakti in respect of the Padas.[45] We shall deal with the principle, at length, in course of our exposition of the relevant (*K*) text.

Śālikanātha, again in the *V* text above, explains both the views of the Vākyavādins, i.e., the Grammarians and the Padavādins i.e., the Prābhākara Mīmāṁsakas (strictly) regarding their admission of Śakti in a Vākya and in a Pada respectively. In the eight expressions as cited by Śālikanātha in the *V* text above, viz., 'Śiśo; gāmānaya; Śiśo. gāṁ badhāna; Vatsa; gāmānaya; Vatsa! gāṁ badhāna; Arbhaka; gāmānsya; Arbhaka; gāṁ badhāna; gāmānaya; Dimbha Ḍiṁbha; gāṁ badhāna', the Vākyavādins shall have to admit eight Śaktis (i.e., the denotative powers). It is because of their admitting the Śakti in a Vākya. But the Padavādins because of their admitting the Śakti in a Pada, will admit only seven Śaktis. They count only seven Padas from the above eight expressions. They are Śiśu, Vatsa, Arbhaka, Ḍiṁbha. gām, ānaya and badhāna. Thus, on the part of the Padavādins, there is simplicity in the matter of assumption of the Śakti and as a rule, it is better to support or accept the view where there is simplicity in the matter of assumption and to discard the view which involves prolixity in the matter of assumption.[46] Moreover. if another Pada as an adjective to the noun 'gām, is added, then the Vākyavādins shall have to admit another eight Śaktis in the aforesaid eight expressions, while the Padavādins will admit only one Śakti. Thus, in the view of the Padavādins there will be only eight Śaktis, while in that of the Vākyavādins, there will be sixteen Śaktis.[47] Again, Śālikanātha rejects the view of the Vākyavādins who contend that the division of Pada and Padārtha is unreal. By means of raising doubt 'apāramārthike ca . . .' etc. in the *V* text above, he wants to assert that in the event of admitting the division of Padas and Padārthas as unreal, the knowledge of the Vākyārtha will be without something to which it may belong.

In the *V* text, viz., 'ye punaḥ . . . .' etc., above, the author discards the view of Bhāṣyakāra Śābara and a section of Naiyāyikas like Vātsyāyana who maintain the Vākyāntyavaraṇa (the last letter of a sentence) as the Vācaka of the Vākyārtha. Śabaraswāmin states that what brings about the knowledge of the meaning of a Vākya is the Antya varṇa along with the Saṁskāras (impressions) of each of the preceding letters.[48] Each component Varṇa, as it is uttered, leaves a Saṁskāra behind and what brings about the knowledge of the denotation of the Vākya is the last component Varṇa along with the Saṁskāras of each of the preceding component Varṇas. In actual experience, the composite word-unit is never found ro be anything entirely different from the component Varṇas and as such there can be no Pada apart from the component Varṇas. This is a much simpler hypothesis than that of the Vaiyākaraṇas who have to postulate the 'Sphoṭa' which is completely different from the component Varṇas.

Vātsyāyana states that through a process, one can acquire the knowledge of the Vākyārtha. The process is like this—every varṇa in a Vākya is heard after it is uttered, then the varṇas heard, be it one or many are joined together in the form of Pada and then it comes to be understood as Pada. After ascertaining the Padas, one understands, through Smṛti (recollection), the corresponding Padārthas. Thus the Padas being known, came to be understood as a Vākya and by taking the ɹelated Padārthas, one understands the Vākyārtha.[49] It appears from this view of Vātsyāyana that he is perhaps influenced by Śabara in this regard. It may be added here that aceording to the Nyāya thinkers, the Antyavarṇa of the series of words, only as aided by the accumulated Saṁskāras corresponding to the very words, serves as the Udbodhaka (reviver) of the knowledge of the total meaning that amounts to the knowledge of Vākyārtha. The power of the Carama varṇa (last letter) to serve as such an udbodhaka need not be doubted. otherwise, it will be difficult to explain the knowledge of a single word that consists of only several letters. It is because, as held by the Naiyāyikas, the Carama varṇa combined with the Saṁskāras of all those words revives the collective impressions of the preceding Varṇas which come to perish after their utterance.[59]

In the V text above, Śālikanātha asserts that even in the views of both Śabara and the section of the Naiyāyikas as already discussed, because of the division of the Padārthas as real, the vyutpatti (denotativeness) is possible. It may be urged here that only the ascertaining of the relation that subsists between the Vācya (conveyed) and the Vācaka (conveyor) is what is called vyutpatti. Moreover, because of their admitting the Antya Varṇa as the Vācaka of the Vākyārtha, the Pada cannot be accepted as the Vācaka of the Padārtha and as such Vyutpatti is, in their view, something without a Viṣaya (subject) to which it belongs.

It is replied here that Vyutpatti cannot be said to be nirviṣaya (without being a subject), because a relation of Nimitta (cause) and Naimittika (effect is admitted between the Pada and Padārtha (i.e., a Pada is a cause and the Padārtha is an effect). There will, again, be no fault if it is questioned as to what is this Nimittatā (causeness) of that which is not the Vācaka. It is because in a Vākya, that Pada, even not being the Vācaka of the Vākyārtha becomes the Nimitta of that Padārtha, which Pada being used and which Padārtha being syntactically related, the Vākyārtha comes to be conveyed, The word 'vākyāt' (from a sentence) in *V* text, is to be understood in the sense of 'Vākye' (in a sentence). Thus Śālikanātha rejects the views of Śabara and a section of the Nyāya philosophers inasmuch as these views also like that of the Vaiyākaraṇas, involve prolixity in the matter of assumption in respect of Śakti, and thereby, he asserts that it is preferable to admit Śakti in respect of the Padas.

In the *V* text, 'ye'pyāhuḥ . . . etc. Śālikanātha refutes the view of a section of Mīmāṁsakas who opine that only the Vākya conveys the Vākyārtha attained through Smṛti (recollection). According to Śālikanātha, this view of these Mīmāṁsakas also cannot avoid the same demerit i.e., prolixility in the matter of assumption of Śakti as is also seen in the views of Śabara and a section of Naiyāyikas. It is because, in the view of this section of the Mīmāṁsakas, there is the contention of Saṁskāra as the word 'Smṛti' is accepted by them and where there is question of 'Smṛti' the Saṁskāra is also there *in as much* as Smṛti is the knowledge which is produced by Saṁskāra.[51] It may be noted here that Śālikanātha categorically rejects the view of Śabara and as such he observes that the statement of Bhāṣyakāra Śabara viz., "what brings about the knowledge of the Vākyārtha is the Antya Varṇa along with the Saṁskāras of each of the preceding varṇas," is without any base whatsoever. Moreover, he comments that the simultaneous recollection of a Mahāvākya (great sentence) is not possible. The idea is this. In a smaller sentence like 'svargakāmo yajeta', it may be possible for the Antya varṇa of the series of varṇas, constituting the vākya to revive the impressions of the preceding varṇas. But in case of larger sentences like "tat siddhikāraḥ iti sarvo hyātmanaḥ kāryasiddhiṁ karoti, anyo'pi yaḥ tasya kāryasiddhi karoti, sa tasmin uccarite hṛdayamagacchati, yathā rājā pattigamakaḥ iti, pattiganako rājñaḥ kāryaṁ sādhyati, sa rajaśabde uccarite pratīyate, evamihāpi yajamānakāryaṁ prastaraikakapālau sādhayataḥ tau yajamāne pratīte, tasmāttau yajamānaśabdena pratyayyete", it is impossible to think of the Antya varṇa as capable of reviving the impressions of the preceding varṇas in order to convey the Vākyārtha. Under these circumstances, Śālikanātha concludes that the Vācaka Śakti is to be admitted in respect of only the Padas.[52]

In the *V* text, 'atra keciccodayanti . . .' etc., the author of the *VM*, proceeds to refute an objection raised by a section of thinkers who argue that in a vākya used by an elderly person, the Vācaka-Śakti in respect of the Padas cannot be ascertained. It is because, they contend, the Padas are admitted as the source of the meanings of the Vākyas of the elderly persons as Liṅga (indicator). It is, again, because of the fact that, the previous knowledge of the Vaktā (Speaker) as known from the Vākya in the form of some Kārya inferred as the cause of the Vākyārtha. They also assert that due to there being invariability of the previous knowledge in respect of the knowable objects, there arises the ascertaining of the meanings of the knowable objects and hence, the Vācaka Śakti cannot be understood. In this way, these thinkers do not recognise Pada-śakti (denotative power of the words) of the Prābhākaras. They accept Padārtha-śakti (denotative power of the meanings of the words) which they contend does not involve the prolixity in the matter of assumption, rather it involves simplicity.[53] Here, Śālikanātha prepares to reply to the said objection and comments that certainly he (i.e., the opponent) has not properly understood what has been stated by Śālikanātha in the chapter called 'Nītipatha prakaraṇa' of his *Prakaraṇa-pañcikā*. As we have stated in the introduction of the present work in the said Prabaraṇa, the author refutes the Buddhist theory that words have no connection with meanings and establishes the validity of non-vedic texts through Anumāna.[54] It is also stated there that the non-vedic sentence which is always under control of a person does not ascertain the meaning.[55] Now Śālikanātha proceeds to assert how the Vācaka-śakti of the Padas can be ascertained from the Vākyas used by the elderly persons. In this context, he explains how a child, while learning new words, comes to acquire knowledge of the meaning of words by way of inference from a particular effort of the Prayojya Vṛddha, subsequent to hearing of the words uttered by the Prayojaka Vṛddha and then he comes to ascertain word as the cause of knowledge of the meaning. He who has understood thus, again ponders as to how this Vākya composed of the Padas with possibly unrelated meanings conveys the meaning to the Prayojya Vṛddha. Even, in the use of a Vākya being under control of a person, the apprehension of the meaning which is constructed with the Padas with unrelated meanings, may arise to the Prayojya Vṛddha as does it to the the child. Thus doubt having occured to the child in this way, he comes to ascertain it again—the Prayojya Vṛddha thus understands that surely the Prayojaka Vṛddha uses the Padas with related meanings. This discussion on the learning of the new words from Vṛddhavyavahāra, is also made in simpler way by the author in the Śāstraparicceheda of the chapter called pramāṇapārāyaṇa of the *PP*.[56]

The rule governing the use of the Padas in a Vākya does not occur in case of not ascertaining the syntactical relation and, therefore, by way of inferring the obtainment of the syntactical relation in this manner, the child ascertains the syntactical relation. The syntactical relation being ascertained, the Vākya comes to be the Anuvāda (restatement) of the meaning Śālikanātha explains Anuvāda (restatement) in the Nītipatha prakaraṇa. It is stated there that when the syntactical relation is ascertained, then the Vākya comes to have Anuvādata of the meanings.[57] Thus if it is so that the Vākya comes, on the strength of being Anuvāda of the meaning, to denote the meaning, then it is considered that the previous knowledge of the Śakti is true and thereby the view that the Vākya denotes the Vākyārtha comes to be untrue. Moreover, if the Prayojya Vṛddha does not understand the ascertaining of the meaning of the Vākya preceded by Anumāna and the syntactical relation of the meanings not being ascertained, that Anumāna which is the specific knowledge of the speaker, does not occur from the knowledge of the Padas as they are (i.e., from the Padas themselves), but from the knowledge of the specific ones (i.e., the meanings of the Padas). The words viz., 'svarupa' and 'viśeṣa' in the *V* text, mean the Padas as they are and their meanings respectively. And without the Śakti of the Padas, the meanings of the Padas cannot be ascertained. Therefore, like the

Prayojya Vṛddha, the child also ascertains the Vācaka-śakti of the Padas. In this way, the child, because of using the Padas as denoting the relation of the meanings, inferred the previous knowledge of the Prayojaka vṛddha regarding the Vācaka-śakti of the Padas. The rules relating to the Vācaka-śakti of the Padas, are so intricate that the author compares them to a big and deep lake.

In 'atra kecidācakṣate . . .' etc. of the *V* text, Śālikanātha presents the view of the Bhāṭṭa Mīmāṁsakas who oppose the *Anvitābhidhānavāda* (the theory of expression of the correlated) of the Prābhākaras and advocate the *Abhihitānvayavāda* (the theory of correlation of the expressed). The word 'kecit' in the *V* text, refers to the followers of Kumārila.[58] We have already stated that the Prābhākaras admit Śakti in respect of the Padas. Here the Bhāṭṭas argue that though the knowledge of the Śakti of the Padas may be there in respect of the Padārthas, yet the Anvitābhidhāna of the Prabhākaras cannot be accepted. They argue that the Pratiyogins (i.e., the counter-corrective-meanings) are innumerable and as such the syntactical relations also come to be innnmerable and because of the innumerability of the syntactical relations, the related meanings also come to be innumerable. As a result, it becomes difficult to ascertain the relation between the Pada and the Padārtha. In the *V* text, the word 'Protiyogī' means the meanings of other words to be correlated with the meaning of a word i.e., counter-correlating to a meaning. Again, if it is accepted that a Pada, the relation of which with the Padārtha is not ascertained, denotes the Vākyārtha, then only from one and the same word, the meanings of all the words will be understood. Moreover, in the event of admitting the Vākyārtha by the denotation of the Padas as they are and also in the event of simultaneous acceptance of the Anvitābhidhāna, there will arise the prolixity in the matter of assumption of the Śakti in respect of the Padas.

Similarly. the question may arise as to whether the related meaning which is being denoted by the Pada, is related by the expressed meaning of the other Pada or by that which is unexpressed. Now, this is to be ascertained by discussing both the alternatives. If it is said that the meaning of a Pada is denotated as related with the undenoted meaning of the other Pada, then there will arise uselessness in respect of the use of other Pada. Moreover, only one Pada will lead to the knowledge of the syntactical relation of the meahings of all the Padas. If again, it is said that the related meaning is denoted by the expressed meaning of other Pada, then it will involve the fallācy of mutual inter-dependence. For, the Pada because of its denoting the related meaning needs, for its denotation, the meaning to be attained from other Pada. We find, this discussion, by our author in his *Ṛjvuimalā* (RVL) also.[59]

Thus the Padas denote only the Padārthas as they are, without the denotation of other Pada. The Padārthas again, give rise to the knowledge of the Vākyārtha aided by three factors namely Ākāṁkṣā (expectancy), Sannidhi (contiguity) and Yogyatā (compatibility) which are regarded as the causes in understanding the vākyārtha.[60] It is also not to be doubted that the Padārthas have the necessity for ascertaining the syntactical relation, because, this (i.e., the denotation of the Padārthas) is the function of the Padas and not of their Arthas. In their view, the individual word-meanings come to serve as the Kāraṇa in the matter of bringing about the corresponding Vākyārtha with the aid of the aforesaid three factors. The Padārthas are independently apprehended (i.e , abhihita) until all the words are heard: then there is a simultaneous recollection of various meanings so as to form the Vākyārtha. Thus, as held by the Bhāṭṭas, the mutual relation comes to take place simultaneously at a later stage in respect of all the meanings irrespective of the sequence in which the corresponding Padas appear.

In support of their explanation, the Bhāṭṭas refer to the view of Śabara who states that the Padas conveying their own meanings refrain from funciioning and then the Padārthas being understood, give rise to the knowledge of the Vākyārtha. This is stated by Śabara in his Bhāsya under *MS. 1.1.25*.[61] Thus the followers of Kumārila do not accept the Anvitābhidhāna of the Prābhākaras and prefer their theory, i.e., the Abhihitānvayavāda. We may add here a note on both the theories under discussion.

According to the Anvitābhidhānavāda, word expresses its meaning as connected with some act to be done (Kārya). The words in a sentence convey their meanings in relation to the meanings of other words. Thus, according to the Prābhākaras, the words of a sentence have the double function of giving their individual as well as the constructed meanings. In other words, the theory of the Prābhākaras contends that both the individual word-meanings and their mutual relation are conveyed by the words constituting a sentence. It is meant that a word has no separate existence and it always conveys a complete meaning only in relation with the other words. Every word, therefore, expresses its meaning as connected with an action which is denoted by other word, and these cumulative expressions of all the words in a sentence are called Anvitābhidhāna.[62] Thus in an expression, viz., 'gāmānaya' (bring the cow), the word 'gām' does not properly mean 'gotva' (cowness), ānayanānvita *gotva*' i.e., the genus cow as connected with the act of bringing.

The theory called Abhihitānvayavāda is advocated by the Bhāṭṭa Mīmāṁsakas. According to this theory, the words convey only the individual word-meanings which, in their turn, come to be mutually related.[63] Though the meanings of individual words can also be comprehended separately as far as the sentence-meaning is concerned, it results from the association of word-meanings constituting the sentence. This makes it clear that the meanings of all the words are responsible for the total meaning of a sentence. When we read or hear a sentence, we have first an understanding of the separate meanings of the words one after another. Then by way of putting together the meaning of all the words in accordance with their Ākāṁkṣā, Sannidhi and Yogyatā, we arrive at the construced meaning of the whole sentence. According to this theory of Abhihitānvaya, the expression of the meanings of words leads to a relational thought, i.e., Vākyārtha. The Abhihitānvaya view is also shared by the Naiyāyikas and the vedāntins, We shall present a comparative dlscussion between these two theories in subsequent pages.

In *K*(7) (and corresponding *V* texts viz., 'atrā'h . . .' etc.), the author asserts that the Śakti of the Padas is understood in respect of the related meanings and in the *V* text viz., 'atrā'ha . . .' etc., makes a reference to an apprehension by Vārttikakāra Kumārila in this regard. According to Kumārila, although thc inclusion and exclusion correspond to the Padārthas as syntactically related, yet the Anvitābhidhāna theory of the Prābhākaras does not hold good. It is because, Kumārila asserts the inclusion and exclusion are obtained through indirectncss. For, the meanings denoted by by the words even though not related come to be the cause of understanding the related meading and hence indireetly the Padas are admitted as the cause of the related meaning. The Padārthas are the cause that give rise to the Vākyārtha and the Padārthas again are conveyed by the Padas and as such while the Padārthas are the direct cause of the Vākyārtha, the Padas are the indirect cause of the same. In support of this view, a verse from the *Śiokavārttika* (SV) of Kumārila is referred to here. It is stated in the verse that in the view of the Bhāṭṭas, the Padas do not abandon their capacity even at the stage of Vākyārtha being conveyed. The Vākyārtha is understood from the Padārthas when the dircct functiod of the Padas cease their individual denotation. What is implied in the verse is that the Padas are indirectly responsible for giving rise to a Vākyārtha.

Moreover, the conveying of the meanings of the Padas is the intermediary function of the Padas which are used in order to understand the Vākyārtha and the Padas are used for this reason. In this context another verse from the *SV* is referred to what is stated in the verse is this—

For the purpose of bringing about the knowledge of the meaning of the Vākyas, there is no obstruction in the functioning of the Padas. The Padas are as necessary for the Vākya as for anything else. With the help of a simile, it is explained by the the author i.e , Kumārila. Just as the burning is a necessary accompaniment of the fuel for the purpose of accomplishing the cooking, so also the conveying of meanings of the Padas is a necessary accompaniment of the Padas for the purpose of conveying the Vākyārtha. The Padas, Padārthas and Vākyārtha are compared to the fuel, burning and cooking respectively.

In 'ākāṁkaṣā . . .' etc., and 'yattāvaduktam . . .' etc., of *K* and *V* text respectively, Śālikanātha refutes the faults that may arise out of innumerableness and violation in respect of assuming the Śakti of the Padas. We have already discussed that the Bhāṭṭas object to the view of the Prābhākaras in their admitting the Śakti in respect of the Padas. According to the Bhāṭṭas, if Śakti is admitted in respect of the Padas, then it will lead to the assumption of the innumerable Śaktis. But Śālikanātha refutes this objection raised by the Bhāṭṭas. According to Śālikanātha, when knowledge arises that the Padas convey their own meanings related to other compatible meanings aided by Ākāṁkṣā and

Sannidhi, there will be no fault arising out of innumerableness. And what has been stated that, in the event of admitting the denotativeness of the Pada with relation not being comprehended, there lies the possibility of understanding all the meanings of all the Padas from one and the same Pada and thus it will lead to fault arising out of violation is not tenable. It is because, the syntactical relation can be understood by means of resorting to the upalakṣana (secondary function) also, one is to take resort to the knowledge that the Pada conveys its own meaning syntactically related with another meaning aided by Ākāṁkṣā, Yogyatā and Sannidhi. In order to explain this view of the Prābhākaras clearly, Śalikanātha presents a Saṁgraha Śloka (collected verse) with states thus—

A Pada conveys ints own meaning as related with that meaning, whatever meaning has Ākāṁkṣā, Yogyatā and Sannidhi. This verse is also found in the *Siddhāntamuktāvalī* (NSM), but the second line has a variant reading.[64]

The Saṁgrahasloka above. is obviously in reference to the theory of Anvitābhidhāna of the Prābhākaras. According to the Prābhākaras, the Padas can denote their respective meanings only when they are syntactically related. A Pada conveys a meaning only as Yogya (compatible) in relation to other word-meanings, Sannihita (contiguous) to word-meanings with which it is intended to be related and only as having Ākāṁkṣā (expectancy). It comes to be clear that in the opinion of the adherents of the view, Abhidhāna (denotation) is preceded by Anvaya (Syntactical relation).

In the *K* above, we come to have the mention of three factors viz., Ākāṁkṣa, Sanniddhi and Yogyatā which are accepted by all as the causes of understanding the Vākyārtha.[65] We shall take up elaborate discussion on these three factors in subsequent pages in connection with Śālikanātha's treatment of the aforesaid factors.

In Kā Punariyamākaṁkṣā . . .' etc of the *V* text, the author presents the view of the Naiyāyikas on Ākāṁkṣā and rejects the same. Śālikanātha says that Ākāṁkṣā being the curiosity on the Part of the listeners has been explained by the Naiyāyikas on the basis of invariable concomittance. The word 'kecit' in the *V* text refers to the Naiyāyikas Viśvanātha, a Naiyāyika states that

Ākāṁkṣā of a particular word exists with that very Pada without which it cannot lead to the idea of the desired syntactical relation. As without a Kriyā (verb), a kāraka (case) cannot give rise to the apprehension of a syntactical relation, there is Ākāṁkṣā of the Kāraka with that Kriyā.[66] Thus in the view of the Naiyāyikas, the invariable concomitance is the basis of Ākāṁkṣā. But this view of the Naiyāyikas regarding Ākāṁkṣā is considered improper by Śālikanātha and so he proceeds to reject it in the *V* text above. Śalikanātha does not believe that Ākāṁkṣā is enquiry (curiosity) on the part of a listener and that this enquiry is due to a relation of invariable association (avinābhāva). For there will be no end of the enquiries on the part of a listener. Thus when there is enquiry into the Kāraka, then there will also arise the enquiry into the cause of the Karaka, its guṇa (attribute), its Kriyā and other Kāraka. If it is said that because of there being no necessity, nothing additional to the Kāraka is sought to be known, then where is no necessity of the knowledge of the Kāraka even in understanding the Kriyā only, there should be no enquiry into the Kāraka. For, a Kriyā is known because of its necessity of being performed. It is also because of the fact that there can be no performance of a Kriyā without a Kāraka. But according to the Prābhākaras there is no necessity of the knowledge of a Kāraka for the knowledge of the Kriyā because of its not being performed due to the imposition of the present tense on it. The word 'na' after the word 'nā' sti' in the *V* text above is, actually, 'naḥ' (our). The *VM* (D) shows the correct reading. Moreover, where a Vākya is deemed to be incomplete and that the incompletenss arises due to its denoting the expectant meaning, the Prābhākaras accept Adhyāhāra (importation) for the of completing a Vākya.

In the *V* text above, we find Śālikanātha's reference to *Adhyāhārna* of the Mīmāṁsakas. As we know, both the schools of Mīmāṁsā accept Adhyāhāra which arises as a result of there being incompleteness in a Vākya. But there is difference between these two schools in respect of their treatment of Adhyāhāra. while the Bhāṭṭas accept Śabdādhyāhāra (importation of words), the Prābhākaras advocate Arthādhyāhāra (importation of ideas). Thus, because of their admitting Śabdādhyāhāra, the Bhāṭṭas are known as Śabdādhyāhāravādins and because of their recognising Arthādhyāhāra, the Prābhākaras come to be known as the

Arthādhyāhāravādins. In the utterance of a word like 'dvāraṁ' (door), the Bhāṭṭas import a word like 'Pidhehi' (shut). But the Prābhākaras import a meaning like 'shutting'.[67] But this view of the Prābhākaras on Adhyāhāra is not accepted by the Naiyāyikas and the Vedāntins. They prefer the view of the Bhāṭṭas. According to the Naiyāyikas, where the word 'dvāram' is uttered, verbal comprehension takes place from the apprehension of a word such as 'Pidhehi' and not from the apprehension of its meaning such as 'Pidhāna'—as held by the Prābhākaras. For, the apprehension of particular meanings of words, which is generated by those words, is the the cause of particular verbal comprehension.[68]

The vedāntins also admit 'Śabdādhyāhāra. According to them, even in the case of vedic sentences, there is importation of the Padas. Thus in the utterance of the word 'iṣetvā' (oh ! the Palāsābranch, the), (I), the word 'chinatti' (cuts) is imported.[69]

Again in the *V* text above, Śālikanātha states that where the Kriyā to be performed is known, there will also be enquiry into all the Kārakas. As for instance, the expression viz., 'Devadatta! gāmānayā (oh! Devadatta, bring the cow), will be incomplete because of there being no use of the Karaṇa Kāraka (instrumental case). If it is said that as the performance of a Kriyā takes place by knowing a single Kāraka, there will be no enquiry into any other Kāraka, then in the expression, 'Devadatta! gāmānaya daṇḍena' (oh! Devadatta, bring the cow with the stick), though the word 'daṇḍa' (stick) is used, there will arise no Ākāṁkṣā towards the word daṇḍa. And as there is no Ākāṁkṣā to wards daṇḍa, so the meaning of the word 'daṇḍa' will have no syntactical relation in respect of the Vākyārtha. Therefore, the Ākāṁkṣā towards the word 'daṇḍa' is assumed from the utterance of that very word. If it is not assumed like this, then due to lack of syntactical relation of the meaning of the word 'daṇḍa' in the context of the Vākyārtha, the utterance of the word'daṇḍa' will come to be meaningless. Likewise, in the vedic expressions like 'aruṇayaika-hāyaṇyā piṅgākṣyā somaṁ kriṇāti' (one purchases the soma creeper with the exchange of one red coloured, tawany-eyed and one year old cow) also, there will be no scope of the syntactical relation. It is because there is no proof to assert that there should be no meaninglessress by the utterances of the Vaidika Padas. Therefore, there is no cause in the arising out of Ākāṁkṣā towards the uttered vaidika Padas. Thus there will be no syntactical relation of the meanings of the words additional to Somaṁ kriṇāti' i.e., the words 'aruṇayā', 'ekahāyanyā' and 'pingākṣyā' will have no syntical relation in the Vākya. Moreover, the Kriyā and Kāraka being laukika (popular) and as on the presentation of these two vedic kriyā is accompalished, there is not so much special enquiry. It is because desire to know something exists in that which is not known and not in that which is already known.

The expression viz , 'aruṇayā . . .' etc. is found in the context of Krayaṇa-prakaraṇa (context regardtng purchase of sacrificial material) in connection with Soma-yāga.[70] Thus, Śālikanātha rejects Naiyāyikas' view that Ākāṁkṣā is the enquiry on the part of the listeners.

In *V* text viz., 'atrocyate . . .' etc., Śālikanātha explains Ākāṁkṣā in his own way. We have already stated that Ākāṁkṣā is one of the three factors in understanding the Vākyārtha. It is stated by Śālikanātha that Ākāṁkṣā is the enquiry of a person into another meaning and that enquiry arises due to the non-completion of the entire denotation or sometimes, only of a denotable. It is because of the fact that when only one Pada is used like 'dvāram' (door), there will be no denotation at all. If the Pada that presents the meaning of the protiyogī, is not uttered, then there can be no expression of the correlated. As it is ascertained from the Vṛddhavyavahāra that the Padas tend to denote the co-related meanings, it is, indeed, proper to enquire into the Pratiyogī. Even in the view of the Abhihitānvayavādins who contend that there can be no syntactical relation of a Padārtha without another Padārtha, the enquiry into the Protiyogī in order to attain the syntactical relation is deemed proper. It is known in the common parlance that when there is Ākāṁkṣā, there is Adhyāhāra and the appropriate Pratiyogī (meaning of a word) is imported through Prakaraṇa etc. By the inclusion of the word 'ādi' in the word 'Prakaraṇādivaśena' in the text, Śruti, Linga, Sāmākhyā etc., are also included. The word 'Prakaraṇa' means mutual expectancy[71] We have discussed earlier the Adhyāhāra of the Mīmāṁsakas. It may be repeated here that while the Bhāṭṭas accept the Adhyāhāra of the Padas in an incomplete Vākya, the Prābhākaras accept Adhyāhāra of the Arthas (ideas or meanings). The Prābhākaras accept Arthādhyāhāra (importation of ideas) because of their advocating the theory of Anvitābhidhāna.

In the *V* text, again, it is stated that as in the popular sentences, there is Adhyāhāra, so in the vedic sentences also, there is Adhyāhāra. As for instance, in the Injunctive sentence viz., 'amāvāsyāyāmaparāṇhe piṇḍapitṛyajñena caranti' (one should perform the Piṇḍpitṛ sacrifice in the afternoon on the New-moon day) the word conveying the Niyojya (prompted person) i.e., a person like Devadatta who desires the heaven is imported. The Niyojya is imported as there arises enquiry into it, because the Kārya cannot take place without a performance and without a kartā there can be no performance and without the Adhikāra, the Kartā is improper and without a Niyojya (prompted person) there will be no assumption of the Adhikāra and thus arises the enquiry into the Niyojya compatible for having a syntactical relation.

In the *V* text we find Śālikanātha's reference to certain terms such as Kārya, Apūrva, Kartā, Adhikāra and Niyojya etc., which are important in connection with the performance of a particular Vedic rite. Here, it may be mentioned that in the view of the Prabhākaras, Apūrva and Kārya are one and the same thing. They are known as Niyoga. This Apūrva and Kārya or Niyoga (prompting) is a force which mediates between a yāga (sacrifice) and its resultant benefit and which cannot be known by any other source of valid knowledge.[72] A Kartā is one who actually performs the action indicated by the principal root in a Vidhi. Adhikāra (right) is one's ownership to a result.[73] Adhikāra accures always to him who is stated as the Niyojya. One who understands the Kārya (performable) as allotted to him is a Niyojya and the Kārya is known as the Niyoga (prompting).[74] In some Vidhi vākyas, a svargakāma (one who is desirous of heaven) is the Niyojya as he understands that Kārya is allotted to him or in other words, he is directed to perform the Kārya.[75] We shall take up these terms elaborately in connection with our exposition of the text of the second sub-section of the *VM*.

It is also stated in the *V* text that Niyojya is not imported in case of the performance done by other Agent in respect of the Adhyayana Vidhi (the Injunctive Sentence regarding the study of the veda viz,, 'svādhyāyo' dhyetavyaḥ'). This Vidhi is considered by the Prābhākaras as incapable of imposing the study of the

Veda as a Kārya, because the Niyojya is not mentioned there and there can be no Adhikārī to undertake the study of the Vedas.[76] Because of its being a Vedic rite, without the Adhyāhāra of the Niyojya. Ākāṁkṣā does not stop in respect of the Apūrvakārya.

Śālikanātha discards the objection that may arise as to how there can be Anvitābhidhāna, while in an expression like 'gāmānaya śuklām' (bring the white cow) etc. There arises no Ākāṁkṣā because of there being impossibility in respect of the Syntactical relation of the two Kārakas like 'gām' and 'śuklām'. It is because, the completeness of the Vākya may lie with the portion of 'gāmānaya' only. But Śālikanātha says that the objection is correct only in the event of the other pada not being uttered i.e., the 'Śuklām', but in case of its utterance, because of its having the contiguity with the verb 'ānaya', the Ekavākyatā (unitary passage) is understood and as such it denotes its own meaning only as related to the verb 'ānaya' and because of there being no Ākāṁkṣā, the Ākāṁkṣā towards the verb 'ānaya' is assumed. In support of his argument, Śālikanātha, refers to the statement of Śabara, which is as follows : 'bhavati ca raktaṁ pratyākāṁkṣā' iti (and there is expectancy for the red). This is stated by Śabara under *MS. 1.2.7.*[77] Śabara states that in a sentence like, 'paṭo bhavati' (here is a piece of cloth), there are two unexpectant padas and as soon as another pada like 'rakta' (red) is heard, then arises the Ākāṁkṣā towards the word 'rakta'.[78]

It is said in *V* under exposition, that *Ākāṁksā* is admitted only in order to attain the Advitābhidhāna. In support of his view, Śālikanātha refers to his own Saṁgraha Śloka wherein the purpose of admitting Ākāṁkṣā is stated by him. Ākāṁkṣā is the enquiry into the counter co-rrelative meaning which is for the sake of Anvitābhidhāna or for the consistency of the meaning already stated.

This Ākāṁkṣā is, says Śālikanātha, admitted as an upalakṣaṇa (auxiliary cause) in understanding the Vākyārtha. Śālikanātha also solves the objection as to why Ākāṁkṣā is admitted as an auxiliary cause in understanding the Vākyārtha, while Sannidhi and Yogyatā alone can be accepted as such. In his reply to the said objection, Śālikanātha says that there can be no syntactical relation without Ākāṅkṣā even if Sannidhi and Yogyatā are present. In order to explain it clearly, he cites an example viz., "am yameti putro rājñaḥ, puruṣo'yama-panīyatām" (here comes the son of the king, let this person be removed), wherein the word 'rājā' (the King) being unexpectant because of its relation with the word 'putra' (the son), is not Syntactically related to the word 'puruṣa' (the person). This expression is also cited by Viśvanātha. Of course, his explanation is something different from that of Śālikanātha and he uses the verb as 'apasāryatām' instead of 'apanīyatām'. According to Viśvanātha, since there is apprehension of the Tātparya (intention of the speaker) that the word 'rājā' is to be related to the word 'putra', its relation is understood to be that alone. But if the Tātparya were so apprehended that it was to be related to the word 'puruṣa' then it would certainly be understood as related with that.[79]

It is also stated in the *V* text that Ākāṁkṣā does not arise, at once, in respect of all the Pratiyogīs, but it arises according to the particular order in which the causes occur. In this context, Śālikanātha refers to three essential psychological Ākāṁkṣās which are towards—(i) Viṣaya or the act enjoined; (ii) Karaṇa or the means of performing it (i.e., the act) and (iii) Niyojya who performs it (the act). Thus, in an expression like, 'Viśvajitā yajeta' (one should perform the Viśvajit sacrifice), as there is no mention of the Niyojya, the expression i.e., the sentence is incomplete and as such there arises Ākāṁkṣā towards, a word conveying the Niyojya i.e., a person like Devadatta etc., who is desirous of heaven, without whom, the act cannot be performed. Śālikanātha also states that the Anvitābhidhāna takes place in the same order as in which Ākāṁkṣā also occurs. It is clearly explained by Śālikanātha in a Saṁgraha Śloka which states—

As the enquiry of the listeners arises into the related meanings, so also the state of denoting the related meanings by the padas. In the *V* text 'atha sannidhiḥ kaḥ' . . .' etc., the author of the *VM*, describes *Sannidhi* (contiguity). Sannidhi is the transformation of the intellect from a meaning subsequent to the hearing of a meaning to another meaning with the help of Ākāṁkṣā and Yogyatā. But this transformation of the intellect is not based on words only. It is because, in common parlance, Anvitābhidhāna is seen to attain by means of Adhyāhāra also. But it should be borne in mind that, in the present context, by Adhyāhāra, Adhyāhāra of ideas or meanings and not that of Śabdas or words is meant. For Adhyāhāra is resorted to when there is incompatibility of the Anvitābhidhāna. Although Adhyāhāra is based on Arthāpatti, (postulation), yet the assumption of Śabda is inconsistent.

In the *V* text above, we come to have two types of Arthāpatti namely, Dṛṣṭārthāpatti (postulation from the seen) and Śrutārthāpatti (postulation from the heard). While both the Arthāpattis are accepted by the Bhāṭṭas, the Prābhākaras accept only Dṛṣṭārthāpatti and not Śrutārthāpatti. It is because, they contend, what is to be assumed is only the meaning of closing etc., in the utterance of the words like 'dvāram' (door) etc., and as such there is no assumption of word.[80] The Bhāṭṭas accept Śrutārthāpatti where, however, in an incomplete sentence there takes place the Adhyāhära of the Śabda in order to make the syntactical relation.[81]

In the *V* text, it is also stated that where the word 'dvāram' (door) is imported, there also the Arthāpatti cannot lead to the assumption of the Śabdas like 'āvriyatām' (let it be open) and 'saṁvriyatām' (let it be shut). It is for this reason that the Arthāpatti is the cause of the assumption in general. Therefore, in common parlance, there is the importation in order to complete an incomplete sentence. Because of its possessing Yogyatā and on the strength of the Prakaraṇa and due to its ascertaining the particular meaning, the meaning comes to complete the incomplete sentence. Thus the Anvitābhidhāna holds good by the Niyojya in the sacrifices like 'Viśvajit' etc., and by the use of the means and by the meanings corresponding to the Prakṛti yāgas (Achetype rites) in the context of Vikṛti yāgas (Ectype rites) though not presented by the words. In the *V* text, we find Śālikanātha's reference to the Prakṛti and Vikṛti yāga. There are many sacrifices with regard to which the Veda does not prescribe all the necessary details; but lays down simply that such and such a sacrifice is to be performed in a manner similar to such and such another. For example, with regard to the Iṣu sacrifice, after having mentioned what is peculiar to it, the texts declare—'the rest is like the Śyaṇa sacrifice. In such cases the Śyeṇa would be called the Prakṛti yăga and the Iṣu is called the Vikṛti yāga. The Vikṛti yāga is to be performed in the manner of Prakṛti yāga.[82]

Śālikanatha also stated in the *V* text that as in the case of

Ākāṁkṣā, Sannidhi works step by step in the order in which the words are cognised and in this way the Anvitābhidhāna is also to be understood. From the Saṁgraha Ślokas in the *V* text above, it is clear that Sannidhi is only the contiguity of cognition of the of the meaning and not necessarily of words actually uttered· It may be mentioned here thai the Prābhākaras understand Sannidhi as the immediate association of the idea of the meaning of a related word. They do not favour the definition of Sannidhi as the proximity of words. In their concept of Anitābhidhāna, it is an accepted fact that the Śakti conveys only the related meanings of the words. Only an 'artha' (the meaning of a word) can have a relation with another 'artha'. For one who believes in the concept of 'Anvitābhidhāna'. 'Abhidhāna' succeeds 'Anvaya'. As such, one is to accept the position that there is always the 'Abhidhāna' of the 'Anvitārtha'. Hence the school of Prābhākaras contends that if by Sannidhi, we meet the immediate need of something to complete the relation of an expression, then that 'something' is invariably an 'artha' and not merely a Śabda. Here lies the difference between the Bhāṭṭas and the Prābhākaras. While the Bhāṭṭas understand Sannidhi as the contiguity of a word or of the idea of a word, the Prābhākaras accept it only as the contiguity of the idea of the meoning of a word.

In the Schools of Nyāya and Vedānta and in the circle of the Ālaṁkārikas Sannidhi is known as Āsatti.

In the *V* text 'kiṁ punaridaṁ yogyatvaṃ nāma. . . . . .' etc. quoted aboee, Śālikanātha elucidates his concept of *yogyatā*. yogyatā as stated by Sālikanātha is that which is capable of making a relation. The Prābhākara Mīmāṁsakas understood yogyatā as the suitability of Padas to have Syntactical relation with other Padas of the same Vākya. The knowledge of this yogyatā occurs in the mind of the speaker and the listener in a particular context on the strength of the previous experience of seeing the words to be in such relations. In the sentence, 'payasā siñcati' (he sprinkles it with water), here is yogatā of meaning, since secena (sprinkling) is generally done with a liquid like water and there is nothing incompatible between the idea of secana (sprinkling) and that of water. But a sentence like 'vahninā siñcati' (He sprinkles it with fire) has no yogyatā since the idea of sprinkling is something incongruous with that of fire.

In the *V* text, Śālikanātha also rejects an objection that if yogyatā is accepted as making a relation, then in the veda, how there can be Anvitābhidhāna in case of the Apūrvakārya (unique result) as no relation of it with anything else is seen. In his reply to this objection, Śālikanātha says that there will be no fault in admitting yogyatā as a factor in bringing about a relation between Padas. For the knowledge of yogyatā in general is the means of understanding the yogyatā in particular. As the Apūrva is also Kārya (performable). so its relation with Kārya is seen and as such it has yogyatā. In his Saṁgraha śloka, Śālikanātha explains yogyatā clearly. It has been stated there that yogyatā which is ascertained in common parlance, is the auxiliary cause in understanding the Anvitābhīdhāna.

It may be mentioned here that the Bhāṭṭas admit yogyatā as an essential factor for understanding the Vākyārtha as they hold that there can be no knowledge of a Vākyārtha in sentence like 'Agninā siñcati' obviously for lack of yogyatā between the words 'Agninā' and 'Siñcati'.[83]

In 'anye tu yadayogyatayā. . . . . .' etc., of the *V* text, quoted above, the author of the *VM*, refers to the view of some thinkers regarding yogyatā and then refutes the same. According to these thinkers, yogyatā is that which is not ascertained as being incompatible. In other words, those meanings of words may be said to be capable of making a relation, in which the lack of yogyatā is not ascertained. Thus in their view, the Anvitābhidhāna holds good through the meaning of even the Vidhi vākyas. This view is of the Navya-Naiyāyikas. These Naiyāyikas do not believe in the knowledge of yogyatā as a necessary condition for the knowledge of Vākyārtha. As they hold, it is actually the knowledge of the Ayogyatā (incompatibility) between two concepts that stands in the way of understanding of a Vākyārtha. As for instance, the knowledge of Vākyārtha does not occur from a sentence like 'Vahninā siñcati' only being prevented by the ascertainment of the Ayogyatā existing in the form of the absence of the instrumentality of fire in respect of sprinkling.[84] Śālikanātha rejects this view of the Navya Naiyāyikas as he thinks that the view carries no sense. For, as in the case of certain object not known by any other source of knowledge; the Yogyatā of anything cannot be ascertained, the Ayogyatā also cannot be ascertained. Thus there may be, by all means, the Syntactical releation of all in respect of that object even in its being not known.

In 'padārtheṣvapi............' etc. and 'yasyā'pi mate.........' etc. of the *K* and *V* text respectively, Śālikanātha discards the objection according to which there will be the involvement of prolixity even in the theory of Anvitābhidhāna if the auxiliary cause is accepted for understanding the Vākyārtha. This is an objection that is raised by the advocates of the Abhihitānvaya theory. In reply to the objection, Śālikanātha contends that even in the event of admitting the theory of Abhihitānvaya, one must accept that only those Padārthas aided by Ākāṁkṣā, Sannidhi and Yogyatā give rise to the knewledge of the Vākyārtha. But the Padārthas devoid of these three factors cannot lead to the knowledge of the Vākyārtha, For. it is seen in the Vṛddhavyavahāra. There is no way to avoid these three factors in case of Abhihitānvaya also. Thus Śālikanātha asserts that as the demerit is common to both the theories of Abhihitānvaya and Anvitābhidhāna, so, the fault should be connived at the same should not be repeatedly questioned.[85]

In "kintu teṣām..........." etc., of the *K* and "padārthānaṁ hi........." etc., of the *V* text respectely, Śālikanātha puts forward the view of the Bhāṭṭas who contend that the conveying of the mutual relation by the Padārthas cannot be known by any other source of knowledge except Śabda (i.e., the verbal testimony). Therefore, to them, the power of conveying that mutual relation is to be assumed in respect of the meanings denoted by the words and the association of the words is the cause of producing the power. The words are not capable of conveying the Vākyārtha directly and so they involve the meanings of the words as intermediate cause. It is also stated in the *V* text that the word has a power called Ādhāna Śakti corresponding to the power of the meaning of a word in respect of conveying the mutual relation.

In order to strengthen their view that the conveying of the mutual relation by the Padārthas can be known only from the verbal testimony, the Bhāṭṭas refer to the peculiar instance of the running of horse viz., the verse 'paśyataḥ etc.' of the *Ślokavārttika* of Kumārila. In a situation where one sees a white figure without noticing its special features and hears the neighing sound and the noise of hoofs, the knowledge 'a horse is running' at once occurs in one's mind. The combination of different facts is governed by the factors viz., Ākāṁkṣā, Yogyatā and Sannidhi, though there is no word known to denote any one of these facts. From this it is clear that the meanings which are the facts meant by the words much have the capability to combine with one another.[86]

The word 'Śvetamārūpam' in the verse, 'paśyataśvetamārūpam etc.' as quoted in the *V* text above, is found as 'Śvetimārūpam' in many works. Even in the Ślokavārttika to which the verse belongs, the word is found as 'Śvetimārūpam'.[87] Again the word 'Ārūpam' in the said verse, is used by some as 'Arūpam'.[88]

It may be pointed out here that while in most of the works, we find the word 'Śvetimārūpam' in the verse 'paśyataḥ.........?' etc. as stated in the *V* text, In the *VM* and in the *Tantrarahasya* of Rāmānujācārya. the word is used as 'Śvetamārūpam'. The word Śvetimārūpam' is, however, considered appropriate.

In the *V* text viz., 'atrocyate.......' etc. of the *VM*, Śālikanātha rejects the view of the Bhāṭṭas who contend that it is only the verbal testimony from which one can understand the mutual relation from the Padārthas. He also rejects the Bhāṭṭa's explanation of the verse viz., 'paśyataśśvetamārūpam............' etc. which states that the knowledge viz., 'a white horse is running' occurs in one's mind through verbal testimony. But according to the Prāhākaras, the peculiar instance of the running horse is the cases of Anumāna and Arthāpatti.[89] Śālikanātha states that due to the repeated sound of the hoofs of the horse, the person comes to know that the sound belongs to the horse and then infers the running of the horse. Thus having ascertained that there is no animal but the horse, the person ascertains the horse-hood as pertaining to the same substratum in common with the neighing sound and whiteness. And thus it is a case of Arthāpatti which is the source of the person's knowledge of that "which is white is the horse" like one's knowledge of another's being outside by not seeing him in the house. Thus according to the Prābhākaras the knowledge of the mutual relation conveyed by the Padārthas cannot be attained without Anumāna and Arthāpatti.

In ihe *V* text, Śālikanātha rejects the view of the Bhāṭṭas that the mutual relation is understood from only the Padārthas and he also objects that if this is so, then it is to be stated as to in which

Pramāṇa the knowledge of the mutual relation is included. According to Śālikanātha, it cannot be included in the Śabdapramāṇa because of there being no word that preceeds the knowledge of the mutual relation. It is again because, in the view of the Bhāṭṭas, that is Śabdapramāṇa where the knowledge of the mutual relation arises from the words with the involvement as the intermediate cause. of the denotation of the Padārthas. Therefore, the knowledge of the mutual relation cannot be said to be included in the verbal testimony. If again it is said that the mutual relation of the meanings of words can be understood from other source of valid knowledge, then the verbal testimony is to be excluded. For, if the meaning of a word known from other source is admitted as the verbal testimony, then other source will be known from the meanings of words known from verbal testimony i.e., there will be violation of the rule that meaning which is known from which source of valid knowledge, will be the object of that source of valid knowledge. As a result, the power of conveying the Vāyārtha in respect of the Padārthas that are denoted by the words is to be imagined. For, this power is not seen elsewhere. This power is the producing capacity, i.e., the Ādhāna Śakti and it belongs to the words only and as such there is the simplicity of assumption and because of there being the simplicity, it is proper to assume the power in respect of the words only, i.e., the words denote the related meanings. In this way it is discarded that the Padas have the power in respect of the related meanings indirectly.

In the *V* text viz., 'nanvanantapratiyogya. . . . . .' etc., above, the author of the *VM*, refers to an objection raised by some of the followers of Kumārila and discards the same. According to the view of these Bhāṭṭas, in the theory of the Anvitābhidhāna of the Prābhakāras, innumerable Śaktis of a single Śabda shall have to be imagined in favour of conveying its meaning as related with its innumerable counter-co-rrelative meanings and thus the Anvitābhidhāna of the Prābhākaras involves the demerit of having innumerableness and as such this view of the Prābhākaras cannot be accepted. But in the case of the theory of Abhihitānvaya of the Bhāṭṭas, only one power of a word is assumed in respect of one meaning only and as such because of its (of the view) having simplicity in the matter of assumption i.e., because of there being no assumption of innumerableness in respect of the view of the Bhāṭṭas, it is better to accept the Abhihitānvaya of the Bhāṭṭas. But Śālikanātha states that the objection raised by the followers of the Abhihitānvaya does not stand to reason. According to him, by only the Abhidhāna Śakti of a Pada denoting its meaning as related with the meanings having Ākāṁkṣā, Sannidhi and Yogyatā as in the case of sense-organs like eye etc., in respect of the actions by the difference of the counter-positives may be obtained. With the help of the example of the sense-organ like the eyes, Śālikanātha explains the function of the Abhidhāna Śakti of the Padas. Just as the eyes with the single power of seeing produces different cognitions on the basis of the difference in contact with the counter positives such as jar etc., so also a Pada by its single Abhidhāna Śakti produces the knowledge of the related meanings with the difference of the counter-co-rrelatives. Here, a Pada is compared to an eye, the Abhidhāna Śakti of the Pada is compared to the Darśana Śakti or the power of seeing of the eyes and the Padārtha is compared to a jar which is the Protiyogı or the counter positive of the knowledge of a jar.

In this way, Śālikanātha asserts that there will be no assumption of innumerable powers of a Pada as the Bhāṭṭas object to and thereby, he rejects the same.

In the *V* text viz., 'anye tvāhuḥ...........' etc., Śālikanātha rejects the view of some thinkers who contend that the Padārthas having Ākāṁkṣā, Sannidhi and Yogyatā become (i e., transform into) the Vākyārtha and do not give rise to the knowledge of the Vākyārtha. But Śālikanātha considers this view as the worst. For, there will be no cause of understanding the Vākyārtha. But it is known to all that most of the thinkers of the systems of Indian Philosophy and also of the Alaṁkāra Śāstras, accept that Ākāṁkṣā, Sannidhi and Yogyatā are the causes of understanding the Vākyārtha.[90] If Pada or Padārtha is not accepted as the cause of giving rise to the Vākyārtha, then one will have to admit that Vākyārtha can be understood without any cause. But this cannot be said so.

In the *V* text again, Śālikanātha puts forward another view which states that the expectant meaning having been denoted either by the Kriyāpada or by the Kārakapada, whichever counter co-rrelative meaning is conveyed in contiguity by another Pada, then that meaning becomes related to the other meaning. Śālikanātha says that, no doubt it may be true, but it is to be stated as to what is the basis of the knowledge of that relation. If it is said, the earlier expectant meaning of the Pada having been denoted, whichever other Pada is uttered, that Pada brings about its own meaning only as related to the other meaning as in the case of a Pratyaya. Just as the meaning of the Prakṛti having been known earlier, the Pratya that is uttered, denotes its own meaning only as qualified by the meaning of the Prakṛti. Same is the case with the other Pada also. In this context Śālikanātha refers to the view of Patañjali that Prakṛti and Pratyaya together denote the meaning of the Pratyaya. But this is also found in the *Bhāṣya* of Śabara under MS. 11.1.22.[91] of the meanings of the two viz., Prakṛti and Pratyaya, the meaning of the Pratyaya is more important.[92] Prakṛti transforms its own meaning to the meanings of the Pratyaya as a Viśeṣaṇa (qualification) of the Pratyaya and as a result of that, it is Pratyaya that denotes the meaning of the Prakṛti and as such the meaning of the Pratyaya comes to be the Principal one. The quotation from the *Mahābhāṣya* viz., 'prakṛti-pratyayau pratyayārthaṁ sahabrūtḥ' occurs under Sūtra 3.1.68 of the *Aṣṭādhyāyī* of Pāṇini.[93] By the word 'Sahabrūta', mutual non-abandonment of Prakṛti and Pratyaya is to be understood.

In the *V* text viz., 'aṅgikṛtam tarhi . . . etc., the author refutes an objection that though the Anvitābhidhāna of the second pada is possible, yet that of the first pada cannot be accepted. But according to Sālikanātha, the Anvitābhidhāna is possible even in respect of the first Pada, because there is no rule regarding the particular order in respect of the use of the Padas in a Vākya. The Anvitābhidhāna is possible in respect of all the Padas in a Vākya, because a Pada is sometimes used first in a Vākya and sometimes not i.e., a Pada may sometimes be the first and sometimes the second in a Vākya. An Abhihitānvayavādī admits the Abhihitānvaya only in respect of the Prakṛti and Pratyaya possessed of an additional Śakti which is ascertained by means of concomittance and non-concomittance as he does in the case of the Padas in a Vākya. In order to strengthen his explanation against the followers of the Abhihitānvaya, Śālikanātha quotes two verses viz., 'prakṛtipartyayau . . .' etc., in the *V* text. The idea of the verses is like this—Prakṛti and Pratyaya together denote the meaning of the Prtyaya and it is stated on the strength of importance of the Pratyaya in spite of there being the denotation of the both (i.e., the Prakṛti and the Pratyaya) with a difference. It is because the Dhātu 'Pac' denotes Pāka (cooking) and the Pratyaya 'Nvul' or 'Aka' denotes the Kartā and again the Kartā connected with Pāka (cooking) is not denoted by one alone of the two i.e., it is neither denoted by the Prakṛti alone nor by Pratyaya alone. According to K.S. Rāmaswami Shastri these two verses, quoted by Śālikanātha, are, from the *Bṛhaṭṭīkā* of Kumārila.[94] It has been stated by Śabara that the Dhātu i.e., the Prakṛti refers to the Kriyā and the Pratyaya refers to the Kartā[95] and the Kartā is Pradhāna or the Principal and the Kriyā is Upasarjana (i.e. Gauṇa) or the Subordinate and as such Pratyaya is the Pradhāna and the Prakṛti is the Gauṇa and this is what is stated in verses quoted above.

In the *V* text again, Śālikanātha refutes the view of the followers of the Abhihitānvaya who contend that the Pratyayas denote the related meanings and not the Padas. But Śālikanātha argues that as the Padas do not differ from the Praryayas, so the Padas also denote thc related meanings as such the followers of the Abhihitānvayavāda should admit that the Padas denote related meanings. If again, it is admitted that Prakṛtis and Pratyayas also have the Anvitābhidhāna, then there will be no Adhyāhāra of the verbs like 'Vivriyatām' (let it be) open or 'Samvriyatām' (let it be shut) in respect of the utterence of the Pada viz., 'dvāram' (the door) by means of Ākāṁkṣā which is due to the non-attainment of Anvitābhidhāna. It may be stated here that according to the system of Mīmāmsā, Adhyāhāra plays an important role in understanding the Vākyārtha; but both the schools of Mīmāmsā differ in admitting Adhyāhāra. We have already stated that while the Bhāṭṭas accept Śabdādhyāhāra, the Prābhākaras admit Arthādhyāhāra. The objection raised may be met thus—in the expression, 'dvāram', the firse case-ending denotes the meaning not different from the meaning of the Prātipadika. Therefore, with which can there be Anvitābhidhāna i.e., Anvitābhidhāna cannot take place. Thus the Abhihitānvayavādins contend that while the Pratyaya denotes a meaning different from that of the Prātipadika, the Adhyāhāra such as 'praviśa' (enter) involves no fault as in the case of the Viśvajit sacrifice etc., for removing the inconsistency of the denoted meaning. In the sentence, 'Viśvijitā yajeta' (one should perform the sacrifice), a Pada like 'Svargakāma' (one who desires heaven) is to be taken by means of Adhyāhāra in order to obtain the complete sense of the sentence. For, without the Agent, a sacrifice cannot be performed and as such there is the Adhyāhāra of the Pada i.e., 'Svargakāma'.

In the *V* text viz., 'vārttikakāramiśrāstu . . .' etc., Śālikanātha presents the view of Vārttikakāra Kumārilā who contends that the words give the Vākyārtha through Laksaṇā (implication) i.e., Kumārila accepts Lakṣaṇā in each and every Vākya. Therefore, he repudiates the assumption of Śakti in respect of the understanding of the Syntactical relation of the Padārthas. It is because the Padārtha which is in an unrelated condition, when denoted indicates the related condition of its own. The relation between a condition and that having the condition is permanent and as such when that having a condition is denoted, the condition is also recollected. Therefore, there is no assumption of Śakti in respect of the Padas in understanding the Syntactical relation.[96] This is the view of Kumārila and in order to assert his view, he states in the Vākyādhikaraṇa of his *Ślokavārttika*[97] that the Vākyārtha is indeed, indicated in all cases. Rāmānujācārya, in his *Tantra-rahasya* mentions the expression 'vākyārtho laksamāṇo hi . . .' etc., as belonging to the *Bṛhaṭṭīkā* of Kumārila.[98] This view of Kumārila is merely the development of the idea contained in the Sūtra of Jaimini.[99] The Sūtra is explained by Śabara in his Bhāṣya thus—the Padas perform the task of denoting their own meanings and cease functioning; when this task is finished and the Padārthas thus conveyed later on give rise to the knowledge of the Vākyārtha.[100] But this view of Śabara is not totally accepted by Kumārila, because in his view, Abhidhā (primary denotation) alone cannot establish the relation of the Padārthas in a Vākya. In order to establish this relation, he contends, one has to take resort to Laksaṇā. According to him, Laksaṇā is the function of the Padārthas and not of the Padas.[101]

Pārthasārathi Miśra, a staunch follower of Kumārila, concludes that neither Vākya nor the Padas directly give rise to the knowledge of the Vākyārtha. It is the Padārthas which by means of Laksaṇā convey the Vākyārtha. This view of Pārthasārthi is in conformity with that of Kumārila.[102]

Thus it is observed that a high status to Laksaṇā is given by Kumārila and his followers as they accept Laksaṇā in each and every Vākya.

In the *V* text viz., 'atrā' pare brūvate . . .' etc., Śālikanātha points out that *Laksaṇā* (by which, according to the Bhāṭṭas, the Vākyārtha is understood) cannot be recognised in respect of each and every sentence inasmuch as there is no necessity for giving up the primary meaning of a word or words in case of every sentence. In the expressions like 'gaṅgāyām ghosaḥ', there is Laksaṇā because of there being a case of discarding the primary meaning which is called Svārtha i.e., the own meaning. Śālikanātha contends, therefore that Laksaṇā occurs only where there is the question of Svārthaparityāga (i,e', the discarding of the primary meaning). Thus Śālikanātha refutes the view of Kumārila that every sentence meaning is a meaning denoted by Laksaṇā on the ground that there is no discarding of the primary meaning of a word or words in every sentence. But, according to the Bhāṭṭas this is not correct. For, sometimes, Laksaṇā conveys the meaning of a word without discarding its own meaning and sometimes by retaining the same. For instance, in the expression, 'sṛṣṭirupadadhāti' (he spreads the creation), there is Laksaṇā without the discarding of the primary meaning of the word 'Sṛtṣṭi. For, the secondary meanings of the words which are read in the class of the word 'Sṛṣṭi' are secondarily denoted even where the word 'Sṛṣṭi' is not clearly stated and because of there being the inclusion of the meaning of the word 'Sṛṣṭi' therein. Moreover, according to the Bhāṭṭas, in the Vedic expressions like *Paurṇamāsīṁ yajate*, because of there being inconsistency in respect of the singular number of the word *Paurṇamāsī*, it by means of Laksaṇā refers to the group of sacrifices. To be more clear it can be explained thus : In the expression, *paurṇamāsīṁ yajate*, the word *paurṇamāsī* is used in singular number and the primary meaning of this word is the *panrṇamāsa yāga* or full-moon sacrifice. But in Mīmāmsā, along with the *paurṇamāsa yāga*, another yāga called *darśayāga* or new-moon sacrifice is also to be performed. These two sacrifices cannot be performed separately. So one who performs the full-moon sacrifice must perform the new-moon sacrifice also. Hence, here in the expression above, the meaning of the word *paurṇamāsī* is *darśapaurṇamāsī* and as such the word should be used in dual number. As it is used in singular number, the syntactical relation is not consistent. As a result, accepting the inconsistency of the syntactical relation as the cause, Laksaṇā is resorted to and by means of it, the word *paurṇamāsī* refers to the group of the two sacrifices viz., the full-moon and the new-moon sacrifices.[103] And when the group is taken, that which has groups is not discarded. For, the whole is included in parts. Śālikanātha, in the *V* text above, refers to the *Niṣādasthapatyadhikaraṇa* in order to show that in each and every Laksaṇā, the primary meaning is not found to be discarded. In the said Adhikaraṇa, there is a Vedic injunction viz., 'etayā niṣādasthapatim yājayet' under MS : 6.1.51. In the Sūtra it is stated that there involves Laksaṇā if the word is compounded as a Tatpurusa. And in that case, the primary meaning of the word 'niṣāda' is not discarded.[104] The Mīmāmsakas give preference to the expression 'niṣādasthapatim' in the above vedic injunction, as a case of Karmadhāraya compound because of there being no function of any Laksaṇā in it. The word 'niṣādasthapati' may be compoundd as 'niṣāda eva sthapatiḥ' when it is taken as a Karmadhāraya compound. When the component parts convey the idea of 'niṣāda' and 'Sthapati', it becomes a case of Karmadhāraya compound. But when it is considered as case of Tatpurusa compound, the word 'niṣāda' cannot directly mean 'of the niṣādas' and as such it must be accepted as a case of Laksaṇā. As in the case of conflict between a primary meaning and a secondary meaning, the Mīmāṁsakas find it proper to admit the primary meaning and so they recognise the expression 'niṣādasthapati' as a case of Karmadhāraya compound which involves no Laksaṇā.[105]

Jaimini, the author of the *Mīmāṁsāsūtras*, prefers Karmadhāraya compound in the above expression because of there being no involvement of Laksaṇā. He observes that the word 'Sthapati' in the said expression refers to a 'niṣāda' by caste because it is the primary of the word.[106] This point is very clear in Śabara's Bhāṣya from which we know that the Mīmāṁsakas prefer the expression 'nisādasthapatim' as a case of Karmadhāraya compound because of its not involving a Laksaṇā and says that he who is a niṣada is a sthapati.[107]

Viśvanātha Nyāypañcānana, the author of the *Bhāsāpariccheda*, in order to show that there is no Laksaṇā in a Karmadhāraya compound, indirectly refers to the above position of the Mīmāṁsakas by illustrating their approach with the help of the said example i.e., the expression.[108] Likewise, in the expression like 'rathaghoseṇa Māhendra—stotramupākaroti' (i.e., with the rumbling of the chariot, Mahendra begins the stotra), the primary meaning of the word 'ratha' is not discarded. Here, the knowledge of the sixth case-ending of the word 'rathaghosa' (i.e., rathasya ghosaḥ) is obtained through Laksaṇā. For even after there being Ṣaṣṭhitatpuruṣa compound in the word 'rathaghoṣa', the word 'rathaghoṣa', the word 'ratha' becomes secondary and the word 'ghoṣa' becomes the primary and the case-ending always takes place in the primary one and the case-ending of the secondry word becomes hidden. As a result, the knowledge of the meaning of the sixth case-ending which is hidden, cannot be attained through Abhidhā but through Laksaṇā. So, the meaning of the Prakṛti characterised by sixth case-ending is not discarded. Hence, the meaning of the word 'ratha' of the word 'rathaghoṣa' is not discarded even though the sixth case-ending is understood through Laksaṇā.

The expression above is found used in a different word viz., 'rathaghoṣeṇa Māhendrasya stotramupākaroti'. There is another similar expression also viz.,—'dundubhighoṣeṇa Mahendrasya stotramupākaroti.[109] Though, the primary meaning of the word 'ratha' in 'rathaghoṣa' is not discarded, yet the meaning of the sixth case-ending is known through Laksaṇā.

Thus in the expression 'Meghapataye megham upanayata', singular number is used in the word 'Meghapati' and the relation of this case-ending is not with the word 'megha' and the knowledge of the relatedness of the word 'megha' cannot be gathered through Abhidhā, but through Lakṣaṇā. Along with the knowledge of the meaning of the word 'Pati', the knowledge of the relation between the meaning of the word 'megha' and that of the word 'pati' is attained through Lakṣaṇā. And thus in the expression, 'Agnisomau juhuyāt' (i.e., one should offer obltations to Agni and Soma), the word 'Agnisomau' being a word of Itaretarādvandva compound, the knowledge of the meanings of Agni and Soma is acquired through Laksaṇā. But the primary meanings of the word are not discarded. The name of the sacrifice of which Agni and Soma are the deities, is called 'Agnisomīya yāga' which is performed on the full-mood day.[110] Though in the expression above the Agnisomīya yāga is indicated through Lakṣaṇā the primary meanings of the words 'Agni' and 'Soma' are not discarded. From this discussion it appears that in case of Laksaṇā the discarding of the primary meaning is not a must and as such without the discarding of the primary meaning the knowledge of the meaning of a word can be acquired through Lakṣaṇā.

In the *V* text viz., 'atrocyate.........' etc., Śālikanātha defines and explains *Lakṣaṇā* in the light of his teacher Prabhākara. When there is the inconsistency in syntactical relation of the primary meanings of the individual words, then it is Lakṣaṇā that removes the inconsistency. Now what is meant by the Anupapatti (inconsistency) ? Along with the ancient Naiyāyikas and the later Ālaṃkārikas, the Prābhākaras say that this Aunpapatti is only the impossibility of establishing the logical connection in a Vākya. We have already stated that a Vākyārtha, according to Kumārila, is invariably a Lakṣyārtha. But Sālikanātha in support of Prabhākara's view points out that Lakṣaṇā cannot be recognised in each and every sentence because of there being no necessity for discarding the primary meaning of a word or words in every sentence. In the *V* text above. Sālikanātha has taken the expression 'gaṅgāyām ghosaḥ' as an example of Lakṣaṇā. In this expression there is the admission of Lakṣaṇā only because there is really a case of discarding the primary meaning which is termed by Sālkanātha as 'Śrauta Artha' (literally, the primary meaning). In the above expression viz., 'gaṅgāyām ghoṣaḥ', the immediate primary meaning of the word 'gaṅgā' cannot make a syntactical relation in the sentence and so it is discarded and the Kūla (bank) by the relation of proximity with the primary meaning is accepted so as to make a compatible syntactical relation in the Vākyārtha. Śālikanātha takes the expression 'gāmānaya' as a counter example to show that there is no obstruction in the expression to find a syntactical relation even with the meanings that are immediately and directly derived. The primary meaning (which Sālikanātha calls śrauta artha) of the word 'gām' suitable for relationship with 'ānaya'. The primary meaning of the word 'ānaya' is taken to be an Anvita one.

In the *V* text, we find that Sālikanātha accepts *Anupapatti* (inconsistency) and sambandha (relationship between the primary and the secondary meaning) as the two factors for determining the function of Lakṣaṇā. The Prābhākaras believe only in-anvayānupapatti (inconsistency in Syntactical relation) as the Lakṣaṇābīja (ground for Lakṣaṇā) and as such they find no reason at all of Lakṣaṇā as belonging to a single word. In place of Avinābhāvasabandha (invariable association) and Ekavākyatā (unitary passage) of the Bhāttas,[110] Śālikanātha recognises the above two factors for promulgating a new concept of Lakṣaṇā. The 'Anvayānupapatti of the Prābhākaras came up as a rival factor of 'Tātparyānupatti' of the Naiyāyikas and the Vedāntins, who accept 'Tātparyānupapatti' (i.e., the incansistency of the intention of the speaker) as the Lakṣaṇābīja.

Among the Naiyāikas, Gaṅgeśopādhyāya, the author of the *Tattvacintāmaṇi*, seems to follow the view of the Prābhākaras so far as the conception of Lakṣaṇā is concerned as he quotes the Samgraha śloka of the *VM* above.[111] He has discarded 'tātparyānupapatti' or the inconsistency of the intention of the speaker as the Lakṣaṇābīja. But later Naiyāyikas like Viśvanātha, the author of the *Bhāṣāpariccheda* do not seem to accept the view of Gaṅgeś in full In this *Siddhānta-muktāvalī* of the *Bhāṣāparic-cheda*, Viśvanātha while discarding the 'Anvayānupapatti' as the Lakṣaṇābīja, says that if 'Anvayānupapatti' is accepted as the Laksaṇābīja, then in the expression 'yaṣṭīḥ praveśaya' (admit the sticks), there would be no Lakṣaṇā; for, there is nothing inconsistent in sticks being related to admission. Hence, according to him, since the intention of the speaker, viz., feeding, is not consistent with the admission of sticks, Lakṣaṇā is with regard to persons who carry the sticks.[112] Thus the Naiyāikas assert that the 't ātparyānupapatti' paves the path for the operation of Lakṣaṇā and thereby discards the view that Anvayānupatti is the only ground that leads one to resort to Lakṣaṇā. Nāgeśabhaṭṭa also opines that 'tātparyānupapatti' is the Lakṣaṇābīja. Otherwise, he says, in the expression 'gaṅgāyām ghoṣaḥ', through Laksaṇā of the words 'makara' etc., place of 'ghosa', the inconsistency can be removed where in line the necessity of admitting Lakṣaṇā of the word 'gaṅgā' in the sense of 'gaṅgātīra' ? So, in order to avert these difficulties, the Naiyāikas say, the ground that paves the path for operation of Lakṣaṇā is not 'Anvayānupapatti' but its inconsistendy to bring out the intention of the speaker (tātparyānupapatti).[113]

The Vedāntins also do not accept 'Anvayānupapatti' as the Lakṣaṇābīja, but they accept 'tātparyānupapatti' as such like the Naiyāyikas. In the expression, 'kākebhyo dadhi rakṣyatām' (protect the curd from the crows), there is no inconsistency in the syntactical relation, i.e., 'Anvayānupaptti', but there is tātparyānupapatti. For, the word 'kāka' (crow) implies any creature that may spoil the curd. Here the intention of the speaker is about protecting the curd not only from the crow but from all creatures that may spoil the curd.[114]

Let us now discuss the Lakṣaṇā from the view point of the Ālaṁkārikas. Aecording to the Ālaṁkārikas Laksaṇā is imposed on a word, the primary meading of which is incompatible with the meaning of other words (in the sentence), whereby another meaning (than the primary), connected therewith, becomes apprechended, either through some motive.[115] From this definition, we get three requisites for the operation of Laksaṇā viz., (1) inconsistency (bādha) of the primary meaning, (2) some definite relation between the primary and the secondary meanings and (3) usage or purpose (ruḍḍhi or prayojana). Lakṣaṇā, the Ālaṁkārikas contend, is a function capable of making secondary meaning. An Ālamkārika does not define Lakṣaṇā in terms of relation existing between the primary ahd the secondary meanings but considers this relation as as a factor needed for the operation of Lakṣaṇā.

Viśvanātha, the author of the *Sāhitya-darpaṇa,* puts forward the expression, 'Kaliṅgaḥ sāhasikaḥ' as an example of Lakṣaṇā based on usage. In this expression which means 'the Kaliṅga is brave' the term 'Kaliṅga' is said to indicate through Lakṣaṇā the idea of a man living in Kaliṅga. Here the relation between the primary and the secondary meaning is that of a container and the thing contained. The particular term is used in the secondary meaning because it is the usual practice of the people to use that paɹticuiar term to convey the particular idea.

The expression 'gaṅgāyāṁ ghoṣaḥ' i.e., 'a cowherd colony on the river Gaṅgā' is cited by Mammaṭa, the author of the Kāvyaprakāśa as an example of Lakṣaṇā based on motive. Mammaṭa says that as logical connection of the flowing water (jalapravāha), the primary meaning of the term 'Gaṅgā' is not eapable of being established with a cowherd colony, Lakṣaṇā conveys the idea of the bank of the river Gaṅgā [116] This expression is also cited by Viśvanāiha as an example of Lakṣaṇā based on motive. According to the Ālaṁkārikas, Lakṣaṇā is a function belonging to the primary meaning. The Ālaṁkārikas seem to be influenced by the Mīmāṁsakas who consider Lakṣaṇā as a function belonging to the primary meaning conveyed through the function of Abhidhā. According to the Prābhākaras, the meaning of a w›rd is what is conveyed by Abhidhā. There is, they contend, no restriction for the Śakti of a Pada. In a sentence, a word conveys not only its own meaning, but also its relation to the other meanings of words in the sentence. But Kumārila does not accept this and says that Abhidhā alone cadnot establish the relationship of the meanings of the words in the sentence and for that purpose one has to resort to Lakṣaṇā.

The Naiyāyikas, however, do not admit Lakṣaṇā in a Vākya and they claim that it might belong to a Pada and Pada alone.[117] Gaṅgeśopādhyāya refutes the above view of the Mīmāṁsakas on vākyalakṣaṇā. According to him, the words 'gabhīra' and 'nādī' in the expression 'gabhīrāyām na 'yāṁ ghoṣah' first get themselves involved in a syntactical relation (Anvaya) and convey the meaning of 'a deep river'. Then either of the two words conveys the meaning of 'the bank of a deep river' as a Lakṣyārtha. Thus it is not the Vākya but the Pada only that conveys the Lakṣyārtha.[118]

In the Muktāvalī of the *Bhāṣāpariccheāa* of Viśaṅātha we find the refutation of Lakṣaṇā in a Vākya. Viśvanātha contends that owing to the absence of Śakti, there is the Lakṣaṇā in a Vākya, which is a kind of relation to the thing denoted by the primary meaning. He has also cited the expression 'gabhīrāyāṁ nadyām ghoṣḥ' above as an example. The word 'river' implies the bank of the river and the meaning of the word 'deep' is connected by a relation of ideality with the river; for, sometimes, connection with one part (of a word) is also admitted. Even if this sort of connection is not admitted here, then the word 'deep' indicates the intention of the speaker (tātparya).[119]

The vedāntins, however, accept Lakṣaṇā in both the Pada and the Vākya as well. They also cite the expression 'gabhīrāyām ghoṣaḥ' as ah example of Vākyalakṣaṇā, Here, the group conissting of the Padas deep' and 'river' refers by Lakṣaṇā to the bank of the river. Here the Naiyāyikas may urge since a group of Padas does not possess Śakti, how ean it have Lakṣaṇā which is a relation to what is conveyed by Śakti ? The vedāntins answer by saying that Lakṣaṇā is a relation to what is conveyed by Sakti, which is a relation of Padas with the Padārthas. Just as the meaning of a Pada is conveyed by Śakti, So also is that of a group of a Padas.[120] The deflnition of Lakṣaṇā of Sālikanātha is refuted by Vācaspati Miśra in his *Tattvabindu*. He follows the views of Kumārila and as Kumārila differs from Prabhākara Miśra in explaining the tenets of Mīmāṁsā, so automatically it is not surprising to have Sālikanātha's definition of Lakṣaṇā been refuted by Vācaspati. According to Vācaspati, there is no inconsistency of the relation of the primary meanings in the sentence-meaning as conceived by Śālikanātha in his definition of Lakṣaṇā and as such the word 'sambandhānupapattitaḥ' in the definition is improper. In the expression 'odanam pacati caitraḥ piṭhare' (i.e., Caitra cooks rice in the vessel), there is no inconsistency of the relation of the meanings of the words 'caitra' and 'piṭhare' etc. in the sentence-meaning nor there is other relation of the condition of the related attained through the relation of meanings of the words in any sentence-meaning. So, it canot be an instance of Lakṣaṇā.

Thus the word 'Sanbandhānupattitaḥ in the definitton, says Vācaspati, may be replaced by 'vācyānupapattitaḥ' and the words 'vākyārthe' and 'anvayāt' should not be used'.[21] The definition of Lakṣaṇā given by Sālikanātha is also refuted by Citsukācārya in his *Citsukhī* in the same manner as Vācaspati does.[122]

We have already said that Gaṅgeśopādhyāya seems to follow the view of the Prābhākaras so far as the conception of Lakṣaṇā is concerned. In this connection he has quoted Sālikanātha's definition of Lakṣaṇā in his *Tattvacintāmaṇi* (Vide, p. 660).

In 'prāthamyādababhhidhātṛtvāt.........' ......etc. and 'prathamabhāvini...........' etc. of the *K* and *V* texat respectively of the *VM* above Sālikanātha discusses the view of the Prābhākaras that as the Pada is the cause of understanding the Vākyārtha, Śakti must belong to the Pada and thereby refutes the view of Kumārila who maintains that the Padārtha is the cause of understanding the Vākyārtha. In the *K* obove, Sālikanātha gives three reasons for accepting Pada as cause of understanding the

Vākyārtha. These are—(1) the Padas appear first in a Vākya; (2) the Padas have Śakti (i.e., Abhidhā Śakti) and (3) the Padas lead to the purport of the Vākya. For these three reasons one has to admit the Śakti in respect of the Padas.

Regarding thc question as to whether the Padas or the Padārthas are the causes of understanding the Vākyārtha, the Prābhākaras contend that it is the Fadas and not the Padārthas as stated by the followers of Kumārila that are the causes of understanding the Vākyartha. The Padas, the Prābhākaras contend, denote the Vākyārtha in the form of an Anvaya (relation). That the Pada is the cause of understanding the Vākyārtha is stated by Sālikanātha in *K* (I) of the present work. Again that the Padārtha is the cause of understanding the Vākyārtha, according to the Bhāṭṭas, can be gathered from Pārthasārthi Miśa's explanation.[123]

According to the followers of Kumārilā, the meaning of the words directly becomes the Kāraṇa of Vākyārthabodha or vākyārthajñāna and as the supporters of the Abhitānvayavāda, they maintain that words denote unrelated meanings, Sālikanātha rejects the view of the Bhaṭṭas' regarding the cause of the Vākyārthajñāna and asserts that the Pada and not Padārtha should be regarded as the canse of Vākyārthabodha. The Prābhākaras contend that the Padas appear earlier to the meaning of the words ('padāni prathamabhāvini') and the Padas signify the meaning of them and come to determine the purport in the sentence. Hence, Sālikanātha contends that the Padas should be admitted to possess Sakti in producing the Vākyārthajñāna.

Sālikanā also in the *V* text above, rejects the view of those who after Kumārila's statement contend that the Pada is nothing more than what provides recollection i.e., the word does not differ from the means of recollection and if there is anything more that happens to be cognised, it cannot be denoted by the Pada. Since the Padārthas are mode out through recollection, there is no assumption of another Sakti as the Prābhākaras hold.[124] Moreover, Sālikanātha rejects when the Bhāṭṭas conted that the word signifying the Bhāvanā (urge) reminds us (i.e., gives us an idea) of the Bhāvanā (urge), just as in common parlance. And through positive and negative concomittanbe, Bhāvanā is taken to be the denotation of the affix. Thus the Bhāṭṭas hold that the act of denothing by the Padas is nothing but the recollection and as such the not have the Śakti. This view is discarded by Śālikanātha by using the expresssion 'tātparyāvgamādapi' *K* (II) above. As the Padas determine the purport of the sentence, the Sakti belongs to the Padas. According the Prābhākaras it is the padas that give rise to the knowledge of the puroport of the sentence. Hence, the particular Sakti should be admitted in respect of the Padas only and not in respect of the Padārthas.

Moreover, Sālikanātha objects that Bhāṭṭas who follow the Abhihitānvayavāda must admit three powers of the Padas viz., Abhidhāyakātvaśakti (the power of denoting the mutual relation of the Padārthas), Ādhānaśakti (the producing power) and Anvayajñāpana śakti (power to donvey the relation of the Padārthas). But the Prābhākaras, as the followers of the Anvitābhidhānavāda admit only two powers viz., Ādhāna śakti Anvayajāñpanaśkti and they do not accept Abhidhānakti. The Prābhākars are called Smārakatvavādins as they conted that Padas certainly make their meaning recllected separately and meanings this recollected are denoted again as related to the meanings of other Padas.[125] As the Prābhākaras admit two powers, so there is simplicity in their view and as such the Padas do not denote the unrelated meaning. This is their established doctrine.

The Bhāṭtas assert that the Prābhākaras also must admit three powers as stated above.[126] As a result, the views of both the Mīmāmsakas are not free from the fallacy of mutual inter-dependeedce. As we shall find in the explanation of the *K* (12) in subsequent pages, Śālikanātha refutes the same and asserts therein that it is the Padas from which we can acquire the knowledge of the Vākyārtha i.e., the Padas is the cause of understanding the Vākyārtha and not the Padārthas as the Bhāṭṭas contend.

Thus in the *V* text above, Śālikanātha establishes that the Padas denote related meanihgs.

In 'padajātam . . . .' ete. and 'yastāvadagrhīta-sambandhaḥ . . .' etc. of the *K* and *V* text respectively of the *VM above*, Śālikanātha explains how the Vākyārtha can be understood from the Padas. It is stated in the *K* above that the Padas that are heard and the menings of which are recollected as unrelated and of which the Vacana (number) and Vyakti (person) are khown through Vṛddhavyavahāra, give rise to the khowledge of the Vākyārtha. The compound word 'nyāyasaṁpāditavyakti' in the *K* above, indicates that so long as the 'Ekavākyatā' (unitary passage) and 'Bhinnavākyatā' (diversified passage) etc. are not known through Vṛddhavyavahāra, the Padas do not convey the Vākyārtha. The compound word 'nyāyasaṁpāditavyakti' has been well explained by Rāmānujācārya.[127] It may be mentioned here that we find variant readings of the *K* above. Pratyaksvarupa Bhagavan has quoted the *K* above as 'śrūyamāṇaṁ padam sarvam' instead of 'padajātam śrutam sarvam' as written by Śālikanātha.[156]

In the *V* text, Śālikanātha states that one who does not ascertain the relation between the Pada and the Padārtha and one whose impression for ascertaining the relation is not produced or destroyed after being produced, cannot understand the Vākyārtha. But on the other hand, one whose impression for ascertaining the relation is not disturbed, can recollect after hearing the Pada, that the Pada denotes counter-correlatives (i.e. meanings) which have Ākāṁkṣā, Sannidhi and Yogyatā. Moreover, it is not con sidered by anybody that by way of hearing a Pada one can have the knowledge of the Vākyārtha. Even in the theory of Abhihitānvaya, so long as another word does not present another meaning, these will be no knowledge of the Vākyārtha. It is because the meaning of a word depends on the meaning of another word in order to convey the svntactical relation and because of the syntactional relation being dependent on counter-correlative (meanings). Thus in the view of the Abhihitānvavādins, all the Padas dedote unrelated meanings. Then there takes place the ascertainment of the Vākyārtha from the meaninsg obtained from the recollections. In support of this view, Śālikanātha quotes a verse from the *Bṛhaṭṭīkā* of Kumarila, which states that the Padārthas if not recollected cannot give rise to the knowledge of the Vākyārtha and as such the validity of the Padārthas depends on their being united by recollection. In the *V* text, Śālkanātha also quotes the definition of a Vākya given by Śabara in the Balādhikaraṇa of his *Bhāsya*, which states that the Padas that unitedly give rise to the meanings constitute the Vākya.

In the *V* text viz., 'nanvanvitābhidhānavādinam . . .' etc., of *VM*, the author presents a query that may be made by the followers of the theory of Abhihitānvaya as to how the followers of the theory of Anvitābhidhāna understand the Vākyārtha. It is because, the meaning which is not conveyed by a Pada while being heard, canont appear while it is kept hidden. Now Śālikanātha, in order to meet this query contends that even in the theory of Abhihitānvaya, this is not a process that as soon as the Pada is heard the Antya varṇa along with the impressions of each of the preceding varṇas brings about the Padārtha. For, we see that the knowledge of the meanings of the vedic sentences arises through the recollection later on by means of the impressions caused bv the knowledge of the vedāṅgas although those sentences were not understood previously during childhood. With the knowledge of these viz vedāṅgas viz., Sikṣa, Kalpa, Vyākaraṇa, Nirukta, Chanda and Jyotiṣa the meaning of the venic sentences can be understood. We have already stated that the statement viz., 'pūrvapūrvavarṇajanitasamskārasahito'ntyo varṇaḥ padārthapratipādaka iti' as referred to by Śālikanātha in the *V* text above, is stated by Śabara under *MS. 1.1.5.*[128] Thus, there will be no fault in respect of understanding the Vākyārtha from the words attained through recollection. A Pada which depends on its countercorrelative and so long as there is no Anvitābhidhāna, does not convey its own meaning withaut an auxiliary cause and comes to canvey its meaning later on when there is the Anvitābhidhāna. Thus Śālikanātha asserts that there is noting inconsistency in respect of the theory of Anvitābhidhāna with regard to the understanding of the Vākyārtha.

In the *V* text viz., 'ye'pi vādina evamāhuḥ. . . . ' etc,, Śālikanātha presents the view of the Vaiyākaraṇas according to whom either the first Pada or the Pradhāna Pada (i e , the Pada which is more important) constitutes a Vākya and then he refutes the same. In the *V* text, Śālikanātha makes a reference to the verse No. 2 of the *Vākyapadīya* of Bhatṛhari by way of mentioning only the first Pada of the verse.[129] In stead of reproducing verbatim, he simply presents the idea of the first Pada which is, according to Bhartṛhari, one of the eight alternatives that constitute a Vākya.[130] The word 'Pradhāna' as stated by Śālikanātha in the *V* text, is perhaps, added by Bhartṛhari to mean the first Pada as such. It may be mentioned here that the Prābhākaras advocating the Anvitābhidhāna, accept only three alternatives that constitute a Vākya viz., Ākhyāta pada, Ādya pada and Pṛthaksarva pada.[131]

Śālikanātha does not accept the view of the Vaiyākaraṇas and that is why he uses the word 'Sarvam' (i.e. all the Padas) in *K* (12) of the *VM*. Śālikanātha discards both the alternatives for the definition of a Vākya as stated by the Vaiyākaraṇas one by one. He argues that if it is held that the Ādya pada (i.e., the first word) constitutes the Vākya, then the meanings of all other Padas in a Vākya will be denoted by the meaning of the first Pada. But this does not happen. In support of his argument, our author cites an example from the *Taittirīya-Saṁhitā*, viz., "aruṇayaika-hāyaṇyā piṅgākṣyā somaṁ krīṇāti" which is also stated by Śabara under *MS. 3.1 12.*[132] The meaning of the expression is this 'one purchases Soma with a red-brown-eyed one-year-old' (cow)' which does not mention the object to which these qualifications belong and it is argued that according to this text, these qualifications are auxiliary to the act of purchasing, but only through the object viz., the 'cow' to which they belong. This is what is explained by Śabara under *MS. 3.1.12.*

Śālikanātha says that "in the said expression, the word 'āruṇya' is related to the act of purchasing only. Moreover, there is no hard and fast rule regarding the particular order in using the Padas in a Vākya. If a Pada when used as first will denote the related meaning and when used in the middle or at the end of the Vākya, then also it will perform the same function.

After discarding the first alternative i.e,, the first Pada constitutes the Vākya, Śālikanātha tries to discard the alternative (i.e., Pradhāna pada) as the definition of a Vākya. He argues that all the Padas in the expression have no syntactical relation. Though all the Padas are important for Soma, still they are related to the act of purchasing and the relation between them is that of a Kriyā and Kāraka and the Padas 'āruṇya' etc. become auxiliaries by the act of purchasing.

The Vaiyākaraṇas again trying to make the conception of the Pradhāna Pada more clear by saying that the Pradhāna Pada is that which is bent upon conveying the Vākya. In the expression cited already, the act of purchasing is established as the Karaṇa of all the actions and as such the word 'krīṇāti' becomes the Pradhāna Pada. Again the word 'āruṇya' etc., become related to the act of purchasing. However, this explanation of the Vaiyākaraṇas is not acceptable to Ṣālikanātha. It is said that the purport of a Vākya is the state of being bent upon an Ākhyāta (verbal form). An example of this may be cited with the Vidhi vākya viz., 'Agnihotraṁ juhoti' (one snould perform the Agnihotra sacrifice). It ls a Pradhāna vidhi. Here, the Δkhyāta (the verbal form) 'juhoti' is Pradhāna. But in the case of Guṇa Vidhi or Aṅgavidhi (i.e., subsidiary Injunction), the object with which the sacrifice is to be performen, becomes Pradhāna. In the Vidhi vākya viz., 'dadhnā viz., 'dadhnā juhoti' (one should perform with curd), the word 'dadhi' becomes Pradhāna, while the Ākhyāta viz., 'juhoti' which was Pradhāna in the earlier Vidhi, comes to be secondary here. Thus it may be said that all the Padas may be Pradhana and as a result all the Padas have the Śakti to convey the related meanings. In this way, Śālikanātha by discarding the view of the Vaiyākaraṇas, proceeds to establish his theory of Anvitābhidhāna.

In *V* text viz., 'nanvevam . . . .' etc., of the *VM*, the author refers to some doubts that may arise and then meets the same. It is already stated that according to Śālikanātha all the Padas in a Vākya possess the Śakti to denote the related meanings. Now, an objection may be raised here as to if it is admitted that all the Padas possess the Anvitābhidhāna Śakti, then in the expression like 'gāmānaya' (bring the cow), all the Padas will be mutually synonymous. For instance, in the above expression, the word 'gām' because of being related to 'ānaya' (will convey the meaning 'bring the cow'. Again the word 'ānaya' due to its being related to the word 'gām' will convey the same meaning. Now Śālikanātha comes forward to meet this objection and so he says—both the meanings viz., Gotva (cowhood) syntactically related to Ānayana (act of bringing), denote one meaning each and as such the question of the state of being synonymous in respect of the Padas does not arise. Likewise, the mutual synonymousness among the Padārthas does not take place. There arises, again, doubt—In the expression, 'aruṇayaikahāyaṇyā piṅgākṣyā somaṁ krīṇāti' already cited above, the maaning of the verb 'krīṇāti' (one purchases) denotes many syntactically related meanings of the Padas 'āruṇya' etc., and as such it results in vākyabheda (syntactic split) which is of the nature of repetition. In the said expression which is a vidhi vākya, there are repetitions like 'aruṇayā somaṁ krīṇāti', 'ekahāyaṇyā somaṁ krīṇāti' and 'piṅgākṣyā somaṁ krīṇāti'. Vākyabheda is a demerit that belongs to a vākya, while Lakṣaṇā is a demerit that belongs to a Pada.[133] Iu 'sameṣu vākyabhedaḥ' (MS. 2.1.47), we find Jaimini's reference to vākyabheda. Śabara in his *Bhāsya* explaint vākyabheda clearly. When the vākyas are independent of one another (each vākya having no requirement or expectation of Padas outside itself to complete its meaning), they should be treated as distinct Vākyas (i.e., it splits the syntactical relation with the other).[131]

In K(12) of the *VM*, we have already discussed the Śālikanātha makes the use of the compound word 'nyāyasaṁpāditavykti', Now he explains the significance of the same. The word may be expounded as 'nyāyaiḥ sampāditā vyaktiḥ yasya tat'. The word 'nyāya' refers to the principles of 'Ekavākyatā', 'Bhinnavākyatā' etc., arising out of the Padārthas. Śālikanātha, in brief, says that so long as Vacana and Vyakti are not clearly stated by the principles known from Vṛddhavyavahāra, the Padārthas cannot lead to the knowledge of the Vākyārtha. Rāmānujācārya explains the compound word 'nyāyasaṁpāditavyakti' verb clearly.[135] Unless one understands with certainly the principles in daily life, such as this is to be done, this is to be restated this is principal 'this is subsidiary, this is what is intended and this not etc., one cannot understand the meaning of the vedic sentences. Vacana and the Vyakti are therefore, indispensable for understanding clearly the meaning of the Vedic sentences. Without the knowledge of these two, one's knowledge of the vedic sentences remains doubtful. In support of his view Śālikanātha quotes two verses of Kumārila. Of these two verses, the first one may be traced back to the *Bṛhāṭṭīkā* which is very often quoted by many writers of Mīmāṁsā. But this work is not available in print upto date.[136] The second verse may also, on the strength of its having link in meanings with that of the first one, be said to belong to the same work. These verses state that all sorts of doubt that may arise regarding the meanings of the vedic sentences can be very well. Because of this reason, Mīmāṁsā serves the purpose of Itikartavyatā for acquiring the knowledge of the vedic sentences. The author of the *VM*, in order to receive support, for view, quotes another verse, whieh is from the *Bṛhaṭṭīkā* of Kumārila. The idea of the verse may be explained as—

When a discussion is to be neld on Dharma or the moral duty, then it is the vedas that play the role of a Karaṇa or the instrument and it is Mīmāṁsā that helps in conducting the discussion by taking the part of the Itikartavyatā. The word 'Itikartavyatā' may be expounded as 'iti kartavyaṁ yasyāḥ sā iti-kartavyā tasyāḥ bhāvaḥ itikartavayatā (kartavyaviśeṣa ityarthaḥ).[137] It is Mīmāṁsā that explains the details of procedure of the vedic rites.

In the *V* text viz., 'nanu loke drāgeva . . . .' etc., Sālikanātha rejects an objection that may be raised as to in popular sentences, the Vākyārtha does not depend on all the requisites immediately as it takes in the case of vedic sentences. We have already stated that in order to understand the meaning of the vedic sentence, one must ascertain the Vacana and Vyakti along with all other principles known through Vṛddhavyavahāra. But in case of the popular sentences, it may be argued, all these requisites are not necessary for understanding the Vākyārtha. Śālikanātha, states that all the requisites may not be necessary in respect of those sentences which are repeatediy used but not in the case of the objects in the sentences of the Smṛti works. The arising out of the knowledge of the Vākyārtha without the help of all the requisites does not occur quickly in popular sentences also, because of there being no particular cause. In support of his explanation, Śālikanātha quotes two verses from the *Ślokavārttika* of Kumārila. What is stated there in the verses is this—

Nobody is competent to ascertain the knowledge of the meanings both primary and secondary immediately arising out of many such as Jāti (generic attribute). Guṇa (quality), Dravya (substance) and Karma (action) without any cause. The Mīmāṃsakas who are known as Vākyavādins, divide the meanings into two in order to understand which of them is powerful and which is not.

It may be pointed out here that the two verses viz., 'bahujāti . . . .' etc., are stated to be from the *Tantravāstiika* of Kumārila. But these verses actually belong to the *Ślokavāttika*[138] of Kumārila.

In the *V* text above, again Śālikanātha contends that the state of denoting the related meanings by the Padas is with regard to all the Padas that denote the primary meanings. But, on the other hand, when the Pada is used to convey the secondary meaning, the Pada which denotes the primary meaning, denotes the related meaning and the other Padas are used as being bent upon conveying in contiguity the counter-co-rrelative (meanings).

It is also stated by Śālikanātha in *V* text above that it will be erroneous to conceive that all the Padas in a Vākya are indicative and secondarily significant.

In 'anvitasyābhidhāne' pi . . . . . . , . . etc. of the *K* of the *VM* above, Śālikanātha replies to a question that may be put as to how a Pada denothing related meaning, is capable of recalling its meaning as it is (i.e., in an unrelated state). In his reply to the question Śālikanātha, in the *K* above, asserts that even in respect of Anvitābhidhāna, the meaning of a Pada as it is (i.e., its own nature) remains always unaffected. Therefore, a Śabda or a Pada can produce recollection even in the case of its meaning as it is. According to the prābhāyaras, a Pada conveys an Anvitārtha (related meaning) i.e., an isolated meaning of a Pada). The Prābhākaras contend that the Padas certainly recall their meanings separately, but they do not stop at that. Their respective meanings already recalled, denote again as related to .he meanings of other words and then alone they stop. Thus, in the vıew of the Prābhākaras, Vākyārtha in the form of a relation is denoted by the Padas themslves and not by the Padārthas,[139]

The word 'Svarupa' in the *K* above, means the meanings of a Pada as it is, or the own nature of a Pada, i.e., the isolated or the unrelated meaning of a Pada. The inclusion of the particle 'api' in the word 'Svarupamātre' pi' in the *K*, asserts that even in respect of its meaning as it is, a Pada can Produce recollection. In 'yathārthena . . . .' etc., and 'na hi yatpramāṇam . . . . .' etc., of the *K* and *V* text respectively of the *VM*, the auther states that even the recollection of the meaning of a Pada as it is it, its own nature is from the Pada itself. He also states that as a meaning recalls a Poda without any source of valid knowledges so also a Pada recalls its own meaning. As there is close proximity of the meaning of a word as it is, with the word by way of the meaning included in the related meaning, so, the word produces recollection in respect of the meaning as the meaning produces recollection in respect of the word. Moreover, as the meaning as it is, kdown through Indeterminate cognition and without being denoted recalls the word and thus the word also recalls the meaning. Thus in the view of the Prābhākaras, the knowledge of the meaning of a word as it is, immediately after the utterance of a word is admitted. Śālikanātha nlso states that even, according to the Bhāṭṭas who advocate the theory of Abhihitānvaya, the knowledge of the meaning of a word as it is, is not a Pramāṇa, because of there being no ascertainment of anything more than the recollected meaning. It is again, because of there being the conclusion that 'a Pramāṇa is that which comprehends what is not known.' This definition of a Pramāṇa is accepted by most of the thinkers of the schools of Indian Philosophy. In support of his aseertion, Śālikanātha makes a reference to a verse in half from the *Ślokavārttika* of Kumārila,[140] which states that all Pramāṇas apply with effect, to only such objects as have not bcen perceived by any other pramāṇa. Otherwise it will be a case of recollection.

In the *V* text above, Śālikanātha refers to the four types of knowledge recognised by the thinkers. They are Pramāṇa, Smṛti, Samśaya or Sandheha and Viparyaya.[141] Of them, the first two viz., Pramāṇa and Smṛti are the valid knowledge, while the later two viz., Samśaya and Viparyaya are regarded as invalid knowledge.

Thus Sālikanātha asserts that the followers of the theory of Abhitānvaya who contend that a Paea is the Abhidhāyaka and not not Smāraka,[142] cannot but accept that the Padas recali their meanings i.e., the act of recalling the meanings by respective words.

In 'smṛtisannihitairevam ....' etc. and 'svārthasvarupamātrasmaraṇe ....' etc. of the *K* and *V* text respectively stated above, Śālikanātha discards the objection that the theory of Anvitābhidhāna suffers from the fallacy of mutual interdependence (Itaretarāśraya). For, according to the Prābhākaras, all the Padas convey the meanings related by their own meanings that come to be proximate throught recollection. As they contend, a Pada does not depend on another Pada in the matter of recollecting its own meaning as it is. It is because the meaning brought in contiguity through recollection, comes to be mutnally contiguous.

In the *V* text above, again Śālikanātha replies to a query that as the knowledge of a Vākyārtha arises from observing Vṛddhavyavahāra and as Vṛddhavyavahāra is based on the knowledge of the related meanings, so, from the observation of Vṛddhavyavahāra, one can attain the knowledge of the related meanings by means of inference and not the recollection of the unrelated meanings of words only. But Śālikanātha in order to meet this query, states that the knowledge of the related meaāing inferred from Vṛddhavyavahāra is the source of recollecting the unrelated meanings. Hence, the knowledge of the related meanings canot be acquired without the knowledge of the unrelated meanings.

Thus in the *V* text, the author avoids the fallacy of mutual interdependence in respect of the theory of Anvitābhidhāna.

In the *V* text viz., 'atra kaścidāha. . . . .' etc. as stated above, Śālikanātha presents the objection raised by a follower of the theory of Abhihitānvaya against the theory of Anvitābhidhāna. The objection states that if the Prābhākaras admit Anvitābhidhāna by means of resorting to the meanings which are found to be in proximity through recollection, then because of the recollection which is based on close proximity and as so many meanings have close proximity, in an experssion like 'ukhāyām pacati' (one cooks in the pot), the 'ukhā' (i.e., the pot) will not be denoted as related only with the meaning of 'Pacati'. It is because the 'ukhā' is also understood as related to the potter etc. and because of recollecting the meaning of the potter, the word 'ukhā' is stated as related to the potter. Same is the case with the other factors like earth etc. of making the pots. In this manner, the meaning of 'pacati' which has cake etc. as the auxiliary cause is denoted as related with rice because of its being recollected. Thus Anvitābhidhāna, from all the meanings, the related sentence-meaning should be understood. But this sort of fault does not arise in the case of Abhihitānvaya as in this view only one meaning is denoted from one word only and as such the syntactical relation will take place only from one denoted sense. Thus the Bhāṭṭas prefer the theory of the Abhihitānvaya to the theory of Anvitābhidhāna.

In the *V* text viz., 'atrocyate-padāttāvat. . . . . . .' etc. stated above Śālikanātha refutes the objection raised by the Abhihtānvayavādins that in the Anvitābhidhānavādins accept the theory of Anvitābhidhāna by means of resorting to the meanings found to be proximate through recollection, then because of the recollecttion which is based on close proximity and because of there being close proximity in many meanings in the expression 'ukhāyām pacati', the 'ukhā' is not denoted as related only with the meaning of pacati'. But Śālikanātha states that the knowledge of the Padārthas cannot be said to be different from recollection. It has already been stated that in the view of the Prābhākaras, the Padas recall their meanings. Thus the Padārthas already recalled, they express again as related to the meanings of other Padas. Hence, it should be admitted, say the Prābhākaras, that the Padārthas when recalled convey the syntactical relation. Thus it is better to admit that the syntactial relation is of the meanings of words that are recalled and not of the meanings that are expressed. But the followers of the theory of Abhihtānvaya argue that if it is admitted that the meanings recalled by the Padas convey the syntactical relation as is seen in Vṛddhavyavahāra, then it will be applicable in the case of the theory of Abhihitānvaya also. Moreover, the Abhihitānvayavādhins object to by saying that the words recall many meanings and as such it cannot be ascertained which of them conveys the syntactical relation. Thus it will be difficult on the part of the followers of the Anvitābhidhāna to solve such problem. But on the part of the followers of Abhihitānvaya, it is not a problem due to their admitting the expressed meanings as the conveyor of the syntactical relation. But this argument of the opponents has been considered by Śālikanātha as baseless. For, Abhidhāyakatā or the denotativeness is not different from Smārakatā or the state of recollection. Again, it is admited that Smārakatva or the state of recollection is due to close proximity and as such close proximity which is characterised by the relation of the denoted and the denoter as separate from the state of recollector should be recognised. This is what is argued by the Abhihitāvayavādins. But according to Śālikanātha, this view of Abhihitānvayavādins is incorrect. What is that denotes as being different from that which recalls, which is the basis of the process of syntactical relation. If it is said, the state of that which recalls is that which is the close proximity. Hence, close proximity which is different from the state of that which recalls, should be admitted as characterised by the relation of Vācya and Vācaka. This is not so. It is because the state of that which recalls is obtained by means of the state of that which recalls as is seen from Vṛddhavyavahāra. According to the Prābhākaras, the combination of spearate meanings of words is effected by recollection since the Padas appear in succession and their meanings are recollected by us when we come to the end of the Vākya.[143]

In the *V* text above, Śālikanātha refers to two principles of Mīmāṁsā viz., Ekavākyatā (i.e., the principle of syntactical unity) and Vākyabheda (i e., the principle of syntactical split) and contends that Vākyabheda is not desirable where there is the possibility of Ekavākyatā. In support of his statement, Śālikanātha quotes a verse in half from the *Ślokavārttika*[144] of Kumārilā.

Jaimini state these two principles under *MS. 2.1.46* & *2.1.47* respectively,[145] The meaning of the earlier sūtra is : so long as a single purpose is served by a number of words, which on being separated, are found to be wanting and incapable of effecting the said purpose, they constitute one syntactical unit—one complete yajusmantra.

According to the Bhāṣya of Śabara, the principle is meant to be applicable to vedic wrods only, in the form of yajusmantra. But Prabhākara, in keeping with the Bhāṣya, explains the word 'Arthaikatvāt' as serving the purpose of indicating or reminding of what is to be done; he clearly states that the term 'Artha' in the Sūtra stands for purpose as it is the most important factor and the words of the sentence must be related to that important factor.[175] Pārthasārathi Miśra, a follower of Kumārila favours the Bhāṣya view and takes 'Artha' in the sense of purpose.[176]

The latter Sūtra above lays down the principle of Vākyabheda (Syntactical split). It states thus—'when the sentences are independent of one another (each sentence having no requirement or expectancy of words outside itself to complete its meaning), they should be treated as distinct sentences'.

In connection with such Mantra texts such as 'Āyuryajñena Kalpatām', 'prāṇo yajñena kalpatām', there arises the question as to whether these two can be taken as one sentence i.e., a single syntactical unit or as two distinct sentences ? The conclusion is that such set of words which stand independently by itself and does not stand in syntactical need of another set of words, should be treated as two distinct sentences.

In the *V* text viz., 'ata yathākathañcid. . . . .' etc. stated above Śālikanātha states that where there is the scope of the principle of Ekavākyatā, it is not proper to apply the principle of Vākyabheda. In connection with this, Sālikanātha contends that in common parlance (i.e., in popular sentences), because of there being the possibility of the arising out of Vākyabheda, Lakṣaṇā (implication) and Gauṇī Vṛtti (Secondary denotation) are admitted. Gauṇī vṛtti is accepted even in respect of the Arthavāda vākyas (corroborative statements) in the vedic sentences. It may be mentioned here that the Mīmāṁsakas recognise Gauṇī as a separate vṛtti in stead of recognising it as a type of Lakṣaṇā. This they do, because they think that Lakṣaṇā is competent to bring only that object into light which bears an intimate connection with the thing signified through denotation. Kumārila states that when the acceptance of a primary meaning comes to be impossible being opposed to our ordinary sources of valid knowledge such as pratyakṣa etc., then that function which brings an idea related with the expressed one is regarded as Lakṣaṇā and the other function which conveys the sense of an object connected with its attributes signified through Lakṣaṇā is called Gauṇī vṛtti.[148]

Kumārila finds scope under *MS. 1.4.22* to give his own idea of Laksaṇā and Gauṇī vṛtti. Prabhākara Miśra also deals with Gauṇī vṛtti in his *Bṛhatī.* He illustrates Gauṇī vṛtti with 'Gaurvāhīkaḥ' as the example.[148] Thus in the Arthavāda texts also, Gauṇī vṛtti is admitted. According to the Prābhākaras, the Arthavāda texts cannot be regarded as a trustworthy means of knowledge because they are inexpressive.

In the *V* text above, it is stated that in the Auḍumbarādhikaraṇa, there is the admission of a sacrifice the result which is an animal. In Sammārgādhikaraṇa (MS. 2.1.4), we find the descriptions of the exception of the Vibhakti.[150] In the citrādhikaraṇa (MS. 1.4.2) we find the Vidhi vākya viz., 'citrayā yajeta paśukāmaḥ'. In this case, the term 'citrā' is well known as connoting a female animal of variegated colour and accordingly the text may be easily taken as meaning that one should perform the sacrifice with a female animal of variegated colour'. But this will involve Vākyabheda and so, it is established that the term 'citrā' should be taken as the name of a sacrifice and the text, therefore, should be taken to mean that 'one should perform that sacrifice which is named 'citrā'.[151] Same is the case with the Vājapeyādhikaraṇa (MS. 1.4.5) also. In that Adhikaraṇa, we find the text viz., 'vājapeyena svārājyakāmo yajeta' (i.e., one should perform the sacrifice called vājapeya). Here, the word, 'vājapeyena' is to be taken in the sense of the name of the sacrifice and not its qualities.[152] Again in the Paurṇamāsyādhikarana (MS. 2.3 24), because of there being the possibility of so many performances of many subsidiary rites and as such the Vākyabheda, the sacrifices as a whole are to be understood. In the said Adhikaraṇa, we find the Vidhi vākyas viz., 'ya evaṁ vidvān paurṇamāsīṁ yajate', 'ya evaṁ vidvāṅ amāvāsyāṁ yajate'—or we find these two Vidhi vākyas in one viz., 'darśapaurṇamḥsābhyāṁ svargakamo yajate' (i.e., one desirous of heaven should perform the New and Full-Moon sacrifices). By the use of the word in dual number (viz., darśapaurṇamāsābhyāṁ in the said vidhi), the group of sacrifices is to be taken.[153] In the Prakaraṇāntarādhikarṅa (MS. 2.3.24) again, we find the description of the word 'Agnihotra' in the vidhivākya viz., 'māsamagnihotraṁ juhoti' (one should perform the Agnihotra sacrifice for the whole month) as being used Secondarily. Again in the Grahādhikaraṇa (MS. 1.3.7), we find the vidhi vākya viz., 'sarvāsu tithiṣu amāvasyā kartavyā' (i.e., the New-Moon sacrifice should be performed on days) and thereby the sacrifice on a particular Tithi is not intended to be performed[154] By the Vidhi vākyas viz., 'arddhamantarvedi minoti, ardhaṁ bahirvedi' (one thould measure half within the altar, one should measure half outside the altar) as stated under MS. 3.7.13 & 14.[155] the place is stated by means of Lakṣaṇā and not the altar.[156] In the Kṣaumādhikaraṇa (MS. 6.1.6), by the Sūtra, 'liṅgaviśesanirddeśāt puṁyuktamaitisāyanaḥ'. the performance of a sacrifice by both the persons i.e', the husband and the wife, is avoided. In the Havirārttyadhikaraṇa (MS. 6.4.22) wherein we find Sūtra viz., 'yathā Śrutīti cet', both Haviḥ and Ārti are not intended In the Paryundāsādhikaraṇa (MS. 10.8.7), we find the Sūtra viz., 'pratiṣedhaḥ pradeśe nārabhyavidhyavidhāne ca prāptapratisiddhatvād vikalpaḥ syāt'. Under this Sūtra, the state of indicating the sense of 'nañ' is seen many times. The Mimāṁsakas regard a negative clause as a 'paryudāsa' only when there is either of the two following obstacles standing in the way of regarding the prohibition as a prohibition proper.[157] Where the leading clause in a certain connection is a dirction for the performance of some positive duties and there is a subordinate negative clause regerding the non-performance of some of these acts, the nagative clause is not to be regaraded as a prohibition proper, but as a 'puryudāsa' (exception).[158]

In the *V* text above, the author states thet Ekavākyatā is a principle which we have already elaborately discussed earlier.

In the *V* text viz., 'bhavatu tarhi padārthāntareṇa . . . . .' etc., the author asserts that there cannot be Anvitābhidhāna by means of the meanings of other words recalled by themselves facilitated by Ekavākyatā. It is because, says, the author, Ākāṁkṣā ceases after there being the attainment of Anvitābhidhāna only by two words. Moreover, if it is argued that Ākāṁkṣā does not cease, then who can pervent the theory of Anvitābhidhāna ? That is why in the utterance of one Pada, by the relation of the meaning of that even there being many meanings coming to be in proximity through recollection, only with that meaning the particularity of which ísunderstood, there occurs the Anvitābhidhāna. But in the case of non-acceptance of the particulrrity not being known there arises no knowledge. Hence, in the Vikrti yagas (Ectype sacrifices) because of there being commonness in respect of the procedure between the Vikrti and Prakrti yāga (Achetype sacrifice), the Apūrva which is being recalled, recalls its own upakāraka (helping factor), there is the completion of the Vikṛti yāgas. We have already stated the two yāgas viz., Prakṛti yāga and Vikrti yāga. In the *V* text above, Śālikanātha refers to the speciality in respect of the Darvi Homas (the sacrifices called Darvi). The Darvi Homas are neither the Prakṛti yaga nor the Vikṛti yāga and as such they are called Apūrvas. It may be mentioned here that the vedic sacrifices are classified into four classes—(1) Prakṛti (Archetype), for example, Agnihortra yāga; (2) Vikṛti (Ecytype), for example, Māsāgnihotra yāga; (3) Prakṛti-vikṛti (partaking of the character of both i.e., Prakṛti and Vikṛti) for example, the Agnisomīya yāga and (4) Na prakṛti Na vā vikṛti (Neither Archetype nor Ectype), for example, Darvi Homa. The word 'Darvi-Homa' is explained by Śabara as—'darvau homo darvihomo, darvervā homo darvihoma iti' is the sacrifice performed in daru woods or of the daru woods.[159] We shall find scope to deal with the Darvi Homa at length in our exposition of the 2nd chapter of the *VM* in subsequent pages.

In the *V* text viz., 'api ca yathāvṛddhavyavahārāvagamaṁ

........' etc., the author asserts that the Śakti of conveying the related meaning should be admitted in respect of only the Padas and not in respect of the Padārthas as the followers of the theory of Abhihitānvaya contend. Śālikanātha states that if there will be the admission of two powers of denotation even in the case of admitting the power of denoting the related meaning in respect of the Padas, then also there will be no fault. It is because, says Śālikanātha, first the Padas denote unrelated meanings and thereafter they convey their respective related meanings with the help of meanings denoted by the counter-correlative words. Thus Śālikanātha asserts that in the view of the Prābhākaras, there is the simplicity in assumption in respect of Śakti because of discarding the assuption of Ādhāna Śakti which conveys the relation of the meanings of words. We have already stated that the Bhāṭṭas admit Ādhāna Śakti of the Padas and the Prābhākaras do not. Śālikanātha also contends that even if there is the case of the equal assumption of Śakti, then it is to be admitted in respect of only the Padas and not in respect of the Padārthas. For, the Padas are understood first and the Padas convey the purport of the Vākyārtha. This is the repetition of what has been stated by the author under *K*(11) of the *VM* and as we have discussed the same at length there in the relevant *K* text, we refrain from discussing the issue here again.

In the 'anviteṣu padairevam........' etc. and 'āśaṅkitottaramidam........' etc. of the *K* and *V* text respectively above, Śālikanātha asserts that in order to understand the Anvaya from the Anvita, no other Śakti as the Bhāṭṭas think, should be assumed. We have already come to know that Śabara under *MS. 1.1.25*, states that the Padas perform the task of denoting their own individual meanings and cease functioning when this task is finished; the padārthas thus conveyed later on produce the Vākyārtha. In connection with this Bhāṣya text, it may be argued that this Bhāṣya is the reply in apprehension. What is apprehended ? It is said—if the Padas denote the related meaning, then they will not denote the relation and as such in order to understand the relation, another Śakti is to be assumed in respect of the Padas, This is not in favour of the theory of Anvitābhidhāna. But Śālikanātha rejects this opinion of the followers of Kumārila by stating that the Padas which denotes the related meaning also denotes the syntactical relation i.e., to be a related, a Pada must have the relation. If it is not accepted, then it will only be the related and not denoted and so, the syntactical relation is admitted in the form of a related meaning. As there can be no related meaning wirhout the relation, so no other Śakti of the Padas is to be assumed in respect of that mutual relation. Thus, according to Śālikantha as Anvaya is included in the Anvita so, when it is said that the Padas denote related meaning, it is to be understood that they also denote the syntactical relation. Thereby Śālikanātha rejects the idea of assuming another Śakti in respect of the Padas and thus he advocates the theory of Anvitābhidhāna.

In 'pratīyānnanvayaṁ yasmāt . . .' etc. and 'anvayavāneva hyanvitaḥ . . .' etc. of the *K* and *V* text respectively the author of the *VM* states that a person understands the related meaning by way of understanding the syntactical relation as he understands the Jāti (universal) by way of understanding the Vyakti (individual), Śālikanātha compares the related meaning to the Jāti and the syntactical relation to the Vyakti, Thus Śālikanātha in the *V* text above, discusses the concept of Jāti and Vyakti. Before going to deal with these two, Śālikanātha explains the related meaning and the syntactical relation. A related meaning is that which is qualified by a relation. If the relation is not known, then the related meaning will also not be known, but only the meaning as it is known and the meaning as it is, of a word is not stated as related. It is because one can understand the related meaning after understanding the relation as one can understand the Jāti after knowing the Vyakti. Here lies the difference – a related is that which is qualified by a relation and as such the Anvaya (relation) is also included in Abhidhāna. But yet it cannot be said that relation and related meaning are not different from each other. Only the state of that having Vyakti is not the nature of Jāti, but the Jāti even being in the shape of Ākṛti (confuguration) is different from the Vyakti. It may be pointed out here that the compound word viz., 'Vyakterākāntarābhūtā' in *V* text above, is wrongly printed and so, the correct roading will be 'Vyakterākārabhūta'. If it is said that the Jāti is denoted by the word 'Ākṛti', then the Vyakti will not be included in denotation. But the Jati meaning the Ākṛti though different from the Vyakti by way of its being the attribute of the object cannot be known without the Vyakti.

It may be argued here : how the Vyakti attained through one cognition is not denotable ? It is because the object of cognition presented by the Śabda is the state of being denoted and same is the case in respect of the Vyakti also and so how Vyakti is stated to be undenotable ? In order to avoid this objection, Śālikanātha states the findings of the Prābhākaras in this regard. Although it is true, that both the Jāti and the Vyakti are the object of single Samvitti (subjective cognition), yet it is to be considered as to how the Saṁvitti is with reference to both the Jāti and the Vyakti. Whether there is the function of the Śabda only in respect of the Saṁvitti the object of which is both the Jāti and the Vyakti or the Śabda by its own nature operates only in respect of the Jāti. It is because in the case of the Vyakti being the object of denotation i.e., verbal cognition and the Jāti not being denotable, the Jāti cannot be known otherwise.

In the *V* text above, Śālikanātha states that the Ākṛti does not comprehend the Vyakti, but the Śabda itself along with the Jāti in its own nature as the denoter of the Jāti conveys the Vyakti and as such Vyakti is stated to arise from the Ākṛti. Thus because of the meaning of the relation being understood for the denotation of the correlated meaning, the syntactical relation is not denoted. It may be mentioned here in the present context that the issue of the exact nature of Śakyārtha has drawn the attention of all most all the thinkers of ancient India working in various fields of philosophy, Grammar and Rhetorics. The problem is whether a word through Śakti implies a Jāti (certain generic meaning) or the idea of a Vyakti (a particular object) or an Ākṛti (a configuration) or more than one of these entities. This has become a controversial issue amongst the scholars who can be broadly divided into seven groups in this regard :

(1) Ākṛtivādinaḥ; (2) Jātivādinaḥ; (3) Vyaktivādinaḥ; (4) Jātyākṛtivyaktivādinaḥ; (5) Jātiviśiṣṭavyaktivādinaḥ; and Jātyākṛtiviśiṣṭavādinaḥ; (6) Apohavādinaḥ and (7) Jātyādivādinaḥ.

The Jainas mny be identified as Ākṛtivādins because of their admitting that the words denote an Ākṛti which is nothing but an avayava that every Vyakti must posses. The Mīmāṁsakas, both the Bhāṭṭas and the Prābhākaras as well as the Vedāntins may be identified as the Jātivādins due to their accepting only the Jāti as the import of a word. The Sāṁkhya philosophers may be identified as the Vyaktivādins. For, they think that a word cannot convey a Jāti inasmuch as portrability, growth, colour, sensibility etc. are Superimposed on the Vyakti MM. P.V. Kane refers to a section of Naiyāyikas who can be identified as Vyaktivādins.[160]

Gotama, the fonnder of the Nyāya system of Indian philosophy, may be said to have initiated the Jātyākṛtivyaktivāda. For according to him the three entities viz., Jāti, Ākṛti and Vyakti get themselves combined to be the import of a word.[161]

The Navya thinkers of other group may be identified as Jatyākṛtiviśiṣṭavādins because of their admitting Ākṛti along with Jāti as qualifying the Vyakti. Viśvanātha Nyāyapañcāna also advocates this view.

The Buddhists are called Apohavādins as they believe that the import of all the words is Apoha or Atadvyāvṛti (distinction from other different object).

The Vaiyākaraṇas and the Ālaṁkārkas may be identified as Jātyādivādins iaasmuch as they contend that the import of a word is either a Jāti or a Guṇa or a Dravya or a Kriyā.[163]

The Navya Naiyāyikas can be divided into two groups and as such they may be identified as Jātiviśiṣṭavyaktivādins and Jātiyākṛtiviśiṣṭavyaktivādins. The thinkers of the first group do not give importance to the view that Ākṛti is the import of a word. Regarding Jāti and Vyakti, they accept a balanced view and thus they contend that the Ākṛti as determined by a Jāti is the import of a word.[162]

It may be added here that on the question of the denotation of words, the Mīmāṁsaka's view is that the word denotes the Jāti (i.e., universal) which is also called Ākṛti. Jaimini under *MS. 1.3.33.*[164] states that Ākṛti is what is denoted by the word.[165] Kumārila points out that it is Jāti itself which has been called Ākṛti in the sense that it is what serves to define the Vyakti.

According to Prabhākara, the Jāti is something real distinct from the Vyaktis which are its substrata, receptable and is perceptible by the senses.[166] In the *Jātinirṇayaprakaraṇa* of the *Prakaraṇa-pañcikā*, Śālikanātha has held a detailed discussion on Jāti. Thus the Mīmāṁsakas of the Prābhākara school assert that a word denotes a Jāti only and is not further competent to denote a Vyakti or Vyaktis belonging to that Jāti.[167]

It may be concluded here that of modern scholars, Dr. Gaurinath Sastri has discussed at length the entire issue critically and analytically.[168]

In the *V* text viz., 'bhāṣyākṣarāṇāmayamarthaḥ. . . .' etc., Śālikanātha explains the idea of the text of the *Śābarabhāṣya* viz., 'padāni hi svaṁ svamarthamabhidhāya nivṛttavyāpārāṇi . . . . . vākyārthamavagamayanti' etc., stated under *MS. 1.1.25*. According to Śālikanātha the idea of this Bhāṣya text is that the Padas denote related meanings and then cease functioning and do not denote the relation separately. Thereafter the related word-meanings when understood give rise to the knowledge of Anvaya (relation). In common parlance (i.e., in popular sentence), as the Padārthas are understood at the time of ascertaining the relation and because of understanding other relation in respect of other Vākya, the purport of the Vākya lies in the Anvaya.

In the *V* text above, Śālikanātha states that Śabara, the author of the *Bhāsya*, by the word 'Vākyārtha' in the said Bhāṣya text, means Anvaya (i e., relation). It may be pointed out here that the Prābhākaras explain this Bhāṣya text as supporting their theory of Anvitābhidhāṇa. According to them, what is brought about by the meaning of a word is the notion of a qualified thing—the meaning of words as qualified by one another.[169]

In the 2nd pariccheda of the *VM*, we shall find Śālikanātha's view that in the Vedic sentences, Apūrva (unseen potency) in the form of related meaning is the Vākyārtha. In the said chapter of ihe *VM*, we find that the Prābhākaras admit Apūrva or Niyoga or Kārya as the Vākyārtha and as such they are known as Apūrvavākyārthavādins or the Niyogāvākyārthavādins or Kārya-vākyārthavādins. In course of our exposition of the 2nd pariccheda of the *VM*, we shall take up the issue on the Apūrva and the Apūrvavākyārthavāda for discussion.

In the *V* text viz., 'ye' anvitābhidhānavādina evamāhuḥ . . .' etc., the author of the *VM* presents the view of a section of thinkers who also advocate Anvitābhidhāna. According to these thinkers, the Pada, the relation of which is established through Vṛddhavyavahāra, denotes the meaning and the relation between the Pada and a Padārtha can be ascertained by means of the process of Anvaya and Vyatireka. But both Anvaya and Vyatireka cannot be said to be the object of the particular syntactical relation. It is because, these scholars contend, the Kriyāpada attains both Anvaya and Vyatireka with a Kriyā which is not found to be invariably present with the Kārakas in general. It is again because, there arises the irregularity, in the case of particular relation. In this manner, the Kārakapada also attains both Anvaya and Vyatireka with a Kāraka which is not found to be invariably present with the Kriyā in general.

In the *V* text above. Śālikanātha presents the view of a sectlon of thinkers as a prima facie view and in succedlng *K* and *V* text, he rejects the same.

In 'Sāmānyenā'nvitaṁ vācyam . . .' etc , of the *K* and *V* text respectively Śālikanātha refutes the view of the section of the thinkers who advocate viśeṣānvitābhidhāna. In the *K* above, we find Śālikanātha putting question to those thinkers as to how in their view there can be the syntactical relation regularly with the particular meanings as they admit the denoted meanings of the Padas as being related with the general senses. Śālikanātha contends that even in respect of Viśeṣānaya, the relation can easily be ascertained by means of Upādhi (limiting adjunct) in the form of the three factors viz., Ākāṁkṣā, Sannidhi and Yogyatā. Therefore, it is proper to admit that the Padas denote the particular meanings. If again, it is not accepted that the Padas denote the particular meanings, then there will arise no knowledge of the Vākyārtha. It is because of the fact that the Vākyārtha is taken in the form of Viśeṣānvaya. It has already been stated by Śālikanātha that Śabara takes the word Vākyārtha in the sense of Anvaya.

In 'yadyapyākṣipyate nāma . . . .' etc. and 'yāthā—jātirvyaktim . . . .' etc., of the *K* and *V* text respectively Śālikanātha replies to the objection raised by the followers of the Viśeṣānvaya that the knowledge of the Viśeṣānvaya is consistent. For, the Sāmānyānvaya being denoted will also imply the Viśeṣānvaya and because of the general not being understood without the particular. But according to Śālikanātha the Viśeṣānvaya is inconsistent and as such he states that though a particular is indicated as the Vyakti is indicated by the Jāti, yet the particular is not understood as such. As the Jāti even indicating the Vyakti does not indicate the particular Vyakti regularly i.e., invariably, so also because of the non-attainment of the invariable particular, the Vākyārtha in the form of invariable pārticular is inconsistent. In other words, the invariable particular cannot be obtained.

As the advocates of Jātivāda, the Prābhākaras do not accept Viśeṣānvaya, in stead, they forward Sāmānyānvaya.

In 'yadyapyākāṅkṣito yogyo . . .' etc. of the *K* and *V* text the author of the *VM*, replies to an objection that even in the case of the indication of the particular, the meaning which has Ākāṁkṣā, Sannidhi and Yogyatā is offered by another Pada, is accepted. There is no proof in the acceptance of any other meaning beyond that meaning. But Śālikanātha in order to meet the objection states that although a particular meaning has Ākāṁkṣā and Yogyatā and is uttered in contiguity, yet it is not ascertained due to there being no factor of conveying the relation.

Those who accept the theory of Sāmānyānvitābhidhāna, contend that the Śakti of the Padas ceases in conveying the general meaning and they also do not admit the Śakti of conveying the mutual relation of the Padārthas. Moreover, even in respeet of the indication by the general meaning the act of indicating is not the cause of the particular meaning. Therefore, in the case of the particular meaning having Ākāṁkṣā and Yogyatā and hving been brought in contiguity by another Pada due to there being no valid Pramāṇa conveying the relation, the mutual relation will not be understood. Thus in the view of the followers of the Sāmānyānvitābhidhāna, Ākāṁkṣā, Sannidhi and Yogyatā also do not come to be useful for conveying the Vākyārtha on the other hand, in the view of the followers of the Viśeṣānvayavāda, these three factors viz., Ākāṁkṣā, Sannidhi and Yogyatā emerging as the Upādhis towards ascertaining the relation come to be useful for understanding the Vākyārtha.

Thus in the *V* text, Śālikanātha finds fault in respect of the Sāmānyānvitābhidhāna and thereby rejects the same.

In 'sambandabodhe vyutpattau . . . .' etc., and 'padānāṁ padārthāntarasambaddhaḥ . . . .' etc. of the *K* and *V* text respectively Śālikanātha states that in understanding the ascertainment of the relation among the Padārthas, the three factors as already stated viz., Ākāṁkṣā, Sannidhi and Yogyatā emerging as the Upādhls are admitted as Upakārakas (helping factor) by the followers of the view of the Viśeṣānvitābhidhāna. But on the other hand, in the case of the view of the Sāmānyānvitābhidhāna, these factors are not accepted as the Upakārakas in understanding the ascertainment of the relation of the Padārthas. This has already been stated by the author, under *K*(18) of the *VM* above. That is why he has not elaborated this issue here in *V* text again. Moreover, in the *V* text above, Śālikanātha has simply repeated the *K* text in prose.

In 'Kiñca vastubalenaiva . . . .' etc., and 'kriyā-kārakasvabhāva . . . .' etc. of the *K* and *V* text respectively, the author shows another lacuna in the view of the Sāmānyānvitābhidhānā. Śālikānatha contends that as the knowledge of the general meaning can be obtained by means of the objects, so, the thinkers of the Sāmānyānvitābhidhāna who accept the denotativeness of the general meaning in respect of the word make endeavours in vain.

It is stated in the *V* text again that even by means of discussing the nature of Kriyā and Kāraka because of obtaining the knowledge of the relation by means of only the Kriyā and the Kāraka, the advocates of the theory of Sāmānyānvitābhidhāna, accept, in vain, the word as denoting the general related meaning. It is because, says Śālikanātha, in the matter of admitting Sāmānyānvitābhidhāna, it is not possible to attain the relation of the Padārthas. This is already stated by Śālikanātha under *K*(18) of the *VM* in the preceding pāges. Thus Śālikanātha finally rejects the theory of the Sāmānyānvitābhidhāna.

We have already stated that while the Bhāṭṭa Mīmāṁsakas advocate the theory of Abhihitānvaya the Prābhākara Mimaṁsakas advocate the theory of Anvitābhidhāna. We have already made discussion on these two theories. Latter writers of Indian theories of meaning tried to reconcile the theories of verbal comprehension viz., Anvitābhidhāna and Abhihitānvaya. Mukulabhaṭṭa states that both these theories contain partial advantage. Considering from the point of view of the Padas, the theory of Abhihitānvaya is preferable and from the point of view of the Vākya preference must be given to the theory of Anvitābhidhāna. In this way, Mukulabhaṭṭa accepts a combination of both the theories and names the theory as Samuccayavāda.[170]

Jayanta Bhaṭṭa rejecting both Anvitābhidhāna and Abhihitānvaya theories, presents his theory of Tātparya by way of bringing about modification in the Bhāṭṭas' theory of Abhihitānvaya. According to this Tātparyavāda, the Padas express their isolated meanings through Abhidhā, but so far as the comprehension of the Vākyārtha is concerned, it is accomplished through another Śakti called Tātparyaśakti.[171]

Of the modern scholars Dr, Gaurinath Sastri maintains that the difference between the two theories viz., Anvitābhidhāna and Abhihitānvaya lies in their conception of the medium of syntactical relation. The Prābhākaras as the followers of Anvitābhidhāna, make the Padas and the Bhāṭṭas as the followers of Abhihitānvaya, make the Padārthas as the medium.[172] He also contends that the theory of Anvitābhidhāna has the merit of saṭisfying the law of economy. It asserts that a word denotes a related meaning.[173] Prof. S.C. Chatterjee is of the view that of the different views about the meaning of a sentence, that of the Prābhākaras seems to the best.[174] Dr. K.K. Raja is also of the view that the Anvitābhidhāna theory seems to be an advance on the Abhihitānvaya theory of the Bhāṭṭas.[175] It may be added here that Prof. C.K. Raja in his work viz., '*In dance of Mīmāṁsā*' states that the Anvitābhidhāna is a very ancient theory in Indian thought. Yāska attributes this theory to Auḍumbarāyaṇa.[176]

We may conclude here with the words of Dr. G.N. Jha that the Anvitābhidhāna forms a distinctive feature of the Prābhākara school of thought and it has the tacit support of the Sūtra (1.1.25) and also of Śabara.[177]

In 'vākyamekaṁ na nirbhāgam . . . .' etc. and 'tathā coktam . . . .' etc. of the Saṁgrahaślokas (collected verses) and *V* text respectively Śālikanātha sums up the views of different thinkers as to how the Vākyārtha is understood. The author presents these views and then reject them at the beginning of the *VM* and we have also discussed all this in course of our exposition of the relevant text.

By 'vākyamekaṁ na nirbhāgam', the author rejects the view of Bharṭhari who, in his *Vākyapadīya*, maintains that a Vākya is not a divisible unit. Śālikanātha states that Vākya is one and not indivisible.

By 'vākyāntyo varṇa eva vā', the author of the *VM* rejects the view of Śabara and of the Naiyāyikas who contend that the last letter along with the impressions of each of preceding letters convey the vākyārtha.

In 'padavṛndaṁ smṛtisthaṁ vā', Śālikanātha refers to the view of some ancient Mīmāṁsakas like upavarsā etc. who maintain that group of Padas that are obtainnd by recollection denote the Vākyārtha. But Śālikanātha does not accept this view.

By 'prithak padameva vā', Śālikanātha refers to the view of Bhartṛhari according to whom, the first Pada is one of the eight alternatives that constitute a Vākya. But it is also rejected by Śālikanātha.

In 'ākhyātapadamātraṁ vā', the author refers to the view of Kātyāyama, the author of the Vārttikas who holds that Ākhyāta (verbal form) is the Vakya.[178] This is also not accepted by Śālikanātha.

In 'padārthā vā' pyananvitāḥ', Śālikanātha refers to the view of the Bhāṭṭa Mīmāṁsakas who contend that the unrelated meanings of the words denote the Vākyārtha and he has also rejected this view.

In 'padānyeva samarthāni . . . .' etc., Śālikanātha presents his own view that only the Padas denote the Vākyārtha and this is the view of the Prābhākara Mīmāṁsakas.

"*Now Second Chapter of the Vākyārthamātṛkā along with the Commentary*".

In 'nanu vyutpattyapekṣesu . . . .' etc. and 'apūrvādhikaraṇa . . . .' etc., of the *K* and *V* text respectively, Śālikanātha desirous of establishing the view according to the prābhākaras that Apūrva (unseen potency) or Kārya (performable) as the meaning of the vedic sentences, presents the pūrvapakṣa (i.e., the view that may possibly be held by the opponents). According to the prima facie view how the suffixes Liṅs etc., can denote Apūrva or Kārya which is not known by any other pramāṇa. This Kārya is called Apūrva in the Śābarabhāṣya by virtue of its being something new to all other means of valid knowledge except the vidhi (Injunctive sentence). In the Apūrvādhikaraṇa of the *MS. 2.1.2.* it is stated that the meaning of the Liṅs etc., is Apūrva and because of its not being known by other source of valid knowledge, it is called Apūrva, something new, not known before. In the said Adhikaraṇa, it is also discussed that which is denoted by the Liṅs is the Kārya (something to be effected or performable) which is inherent in the Nlyojyo (Agent, the prompted person) in relation to him, the Kārya is indicated. The connection of this Kārya with the Agent and the action may be stated thus—the Kārya by its very nature is something brought about by kṛti or operation and this operation is nothing but the physical effort of the Agent.

According to the Prābhākaras, this Kārya is not denoted by Ākhyāta (verbal form) nor by the Injunctive Suffix nor by any word in the Injunctive sentence, but it is denoted by a sentence as whole. Therefore, the Prābhākaras are known as the kāryāparavākyārthavādins.[179] According to Kumārila and his followers, Apūrva is a force which mediates between the yāga (sacrifice) and the desired result. This Apūrva is also called Niyoga.[180] This Apūrva exists as the result of the actions till the production of the desired result. It is called Niyoga because persons desiring svarga (heaven) etc., are directed to work it out. This is accepted as the meaning of Liṅ because the yāga, being of short period, cannot be called Kārya for the persons desiring svarga and the rest, which are attained after a long period of time.

This Apūrva in view of the Bhāṭṭᴇs is taken as expressed by the Liṅs through its prineipal indication, It is also accepted as produced by the yāga. But on the other hand it is believed that the functioneries in respect of the non-vedic injunctions understand the meaning of the principal root of the sentence (Dhātvartha) as a duty enjoined on them, because of there being no necessity to assume a Niyaga. But in these cases, the vedic Liṅs express the kriyā as the duty by their indication.[181]

In 'śabdāntarāṇyapi kaṭham ....' etc. and 'tasminnapratīyamāna ....' etc. of the *K* and *V* text, Śālikanātha presents the view of the pūrva-pakṣa, according to which Apūrva is not the vākārtha. According to this view of the pūrpakṣa, there is no Apūrva which is expressed by the suffixes Liṅs etc, which constitute the vākyārtha. In the view of these opponents by means of Apūrva, the śabdas cannot convey their own related meanings which remain outside the domain of vyutpatti (denotativeness). These opponents who may be identified as the Bhāṭṭas accept Bhāvanā (urge) as the vākyārtha and as such they come to be regarded as the Bhāvanāvākyārthavādins. But the Prābhākaras are called Niyogavākyārthavādins because of their admitting Niyoga (prompting) as the vākyārtha. In course of our exposition of the present chapter, we shall find scope to deal with, at length, these two theories.

In 'atrocyate yadā nāma ....' etc. and buddhipūrvā mamevā'sya ....' ett. of the *K* and *V* text respectively of the *VM*, above Śālikanātha contends how a person is inclined to an action subsequent to the hearing of a sentence formed with the sufixes Liṅs etc. In the *V* text, the author also states how a child who is learning things by observing a directed elderly person's inclination to somc action after hearing the sentence of the directing elderly person learns. Thus there aises a couple of inference—(1) the pravrtti or the directed elderly person that lies at his command is the patiñā (assertion); the pravṛtti preceded by the knowledge is the attribute of the Sādhya (probandum): the pravṛtti being at his command is the hetu (cause), like the pravṛtti of the child at his command is the udāharaṇa (example), (2) The knowledge which is the cause of the pravṛtti of the prayojya-vṛddha is the pratijñā; the kaowledge which is lhe pravṛtti of the child is also the pravṛtti of the prayojya-vṛddha is the attribute of the Sādhya; knowledge of the pravṛtti is the hetu like the knowledge which is the cause of the pravṛtti of the child is the udāharaṇa. Here, we find the five members of a Syllogism of inference. These are pratijñā. hetu, udāharaṇa, upanaya (application) and Nigamana (conclusion).[182]

It can be said in favour of the Prābhākara view in this connection with the methods of denotative function, that the usage of the elders is the first and best method. For natural is always superior to the artificial. According to the Prabhākaras, expressions like, 'there is a blue jar on the earth' lead to no verbal comprehension (śābdabodha). Since words such as 'a jar' have been concluded to have the power of denoting a jar etc. as connected with certain acts, and since only Liṅ and other suffixes have the power to convey inclination to action, there will be no verbal comprehension as they are lacking in this case.[183] The followers of Prabhākara are not prepared to recognise directly a 'Śaktigrāhka' other than vṛddhavyarahāra which facilitates only kāryānvitaśaktijñāna and not otherwise.[184]

But this view of the Prābhākaras has been discarded by the Naiyāyikas. For, though one may at first conclude, the denotative function of words such as jar etc. is regard to a jar etc. as connected with certain acts, one should afterwards discard this ides for the sake of simplicity.[185]

Śālikanātha, here, refutes the view of the Bhāṭṭas, according to which, the meaning of the Vidhi or injunction is the pravartanā or preraṇā (inducement) or Śābdī Bhāvanā (verbal urge). Bhāvanā or urge is a stimulating activity for that which is to take place.[176] It constitutes the effort or activity of the Agent- It is of two kinds—Śābdī or verbal and Ārthī or objective.[187] This Bhāvanā is expressed by the Suffix as the part of the verbal form. In the Subsequent pages, we shall find Śālikanātha's presentation of the view of the Bhāṭṭas regarding Śāddī Bhāvanā which is, according to the Bhāṭṭas, the meaning of thc Vidhi. In 'tatra buddhvā . . . .' etc. and 'Śabdanirapekṣasvayamaham . . . . . .' etc., of the *K* and *V* text respectivety, Śālikaṇātha explains how a child in order to ascertain what is that meaning which forms the cause of pravṛtti and what is the denotable by a word, enquires the meaning that forms the cause of pravṛtti admitted by himself. The chiid puts a question to himself as to without depending on Śabda knowing what he was inclined fo an action. By using the word 'anyadā' in the *K* the author means the state prior to one's knowledge of the action.

In the *V* text, Śālikanātha also rejects the view of the Bhāṭṭas that Śabda which is the cause of pravṛtti is the Vidhi or the function of the word is as such. It is because a child desirous of learning thus find these two (i.e., Śabda or the function of a Śabda) as the cause of the pravṛtti of a person. According to Śālikanātha, these two views are worse and as such he has rejected the same without directly presenting them.

It may be stated here that Kumārila and some of his followers admit the meaning of the Vidhi as the pravartanā or preraṇā and is understood as the Śabda Bhāvanā. Thus the Bhāṭṭas contend that the knowledge of the Vidhi is the Śabda Bhāvaṇā.

We shall find seope to deal with Śālikanātha's refutation of the view of the Bhāṭṭas on Śabda Bhāvanā in subsequent pages.

In the *V* text viz., 'keyaṁ śabdabhñvanā . . . . . .' etc. stated above, Śālikanātha presents the view of the Bhāṭṭas on Śabda Bhāvanā (verbal urge). It is also known as Śābda Bhāvanā and Śābdī Bhāvanā. Bhāvanā (urge) as defined by the Bhāṭṭas is the stimulating activity for that which is to take place.[188] According to the Prābhākaras, it is the activity of a person towards a certain course of action. That is to say, the injunctive affix in the word 'yajeta' indicates that the person must put forth his effort towards a definite end. In addition to the Śābdī Bhāvanā both the schools of Mīmāṁsā admit another Bhāvanā called Ārthī Bhāvanā (objective urge).[189] Of these two Bhāvanās, say the Kumārila, the objective nrge is common to all the verbs and the verbal urge is to be expressed by the Liṅ etc.[190] The knowledge of the Vidhi is, accordidg to Kumārilas, the verbal urge. Being an action inherent in words, it is called the Śābdī Bhāvanā and being the cause of an inclination towards matters like sacrifices and homa, it is also called pravartanā or preraṇā.[161] This Śābdī Bhāvanā consists of three factors—(a) what is to be thought of (kim bhāvayet), (b) by what instrumentality it is to be thought of (kena bhāvayet) and (c) how it is to be thougut of (kathaṁ bhāvyet) or modus operadi (Itikaratavyatā). The Ārthī Bhāvanā represented by a person's ịnclinatlon, comes into relation as the thing to be achieved, the optative suffix etc., known through study, comes into relation as the instrumentality and the knowledge of praiseworthiness that is conveyed by the Arthavāda Vākyas comes into relation as the Itikartavyatā. It can be said here that Kumārila names the Śābdī Bhāvanā as Abhidhā Bhāvanā also.[192] In connection with the disɔussion on Bhāvanā by the Bhāṭṭas. we deem it proper to warite a few lines on the Bhāttas' thəory on Bhāvanā entitled Bhāvanāvākyārthavāda. According to this theory of the Bhāṭṭas, Dharma is neither Apūrvakārya as interpreted by the Prābhāras nor it is an imperative command expressed by Codanā as stated under *M.S. 1.1.2.*[193] The vedic Liṅs have a capacity for two-fold expression viz., the capacity to impose an action on the persons and the capacity of the persons which is reactive and internal, The former is called pravartanā or Vidhi resting in vedic Liṅs and the latter is called pravṛtti of a person. Both of them are known by a common term called Bhāvanā becausə of their leading to the same result Pravartanā leads to pravṛtti in a yāga and pravṛtti in yāga leads ɿo the desired result from the yāga. It may be infered from the Vidhi or pravartanā when yāga and pravṛtti for it are connected with Vidhi that such pravṛtti to yāga must come as a result. The knowledge of Vidhi or Bhāvanā and pravṛtti or Bhāvaṇā coupled with a sense of result makes a person to undertake an action. In case of vedic injunctions, the result of sacrifice based on injunction is svarga itself as indicated by the words Svarakāma etc. Sacriflces are therefore only the means to produce such results.[194] Sacrffices being momentary do not continue up to the time of the production of the desired result. It is, therefore, necessary for the Bhāṭṭas to invent an unseen potency called Apūrva as a link between the sacrifibe and its result.[195]

As the pravṛtti or Bhāvanā is connected with three things namely a result, an instrument to the result i.e.. sacrifice and the method of performance of the sacrifices—this Bhāvanā is, according to the Bhaṭṭas, important in all vedic and non-vedic sentences.

The Bhāvanāvākyārthavāda of the Bhāṭṭas is condemned by the Prābhākaras who accept Niyogavākyārthavāda which we will discuss in course of our investigation.

In the *V* text viz., 'tanna liṅādestādṛśo vyāpāro. . . . . etc., as stated above, Śālikanātha refutes the view of the Bhāṭṭas with regard to the Śabda Bhāvanā. We have already stated that the Bhāṭṭas advocate the theory of Bhāvanā:vakyārtha which sttaes that the vedic Liṅs express the Bhāvanā. This Bhāvanā is also known as pravṛtti or pravartanā. The Bhāṭṭas contend that Bhāvanā is in the form of a function of the vedic Liṅs which maks a person incline to an action. It is also stated that being an action inherent in words it is called Śabda Bhāvanā and being the cause of pravṛtti towards matters like yāgas, it is also called prerahṇā.[196]

Śālikanātha refutes the view of the Bhāṭṭas by stating that there is no proof that Liṅs etc. have functions in the form of preraṇā and the pravṛtti of a person towards certain actions subsequent to the hearing of the words Liṅ etc. is not the cause of this Bhāvanā. For, the pravṛtti arising out of such Liṅs etc. is not seen in other places. The Bhāṭṭas on the strength of the injunctive sentence, 'svādhāyo' dhyeṭavyaḥ' (i.e., one should study one's own branch of the veda), as an example of the verbal urge maintains that the injunction of the veda serves the purpose of employeng all other injunctions as also the self (sva) mentioned in the word 'svādhyāya' and this employing or urging is in the form—'should think of accomplishing' this is what is stated by Kumārila in his *Tantravārttika.* According to the Bhāṭṭas Śabda Bhāvanā is comprehended as something to be done only in the sentence, 'one should study one's own branch of the veda'.[197]

This view of the Bhāṭṭas is not accepted by the Prābhākaras and so Śālikanātha says that it is the injunction that inspires a person in respect of the objective urge (Ārtha Bhāvana). And he by whom is inspired is also employed. It cannot be said that the insentient injunctions can serve the puapose of employing. Here it can be mentioned that in the view of the Prābhākaras, the study (adhyayana) of the veda is for teaching (adhyāpana). Prabhākara maintains that the expression 'svādhyāo' dhyetavyaḥ' does not express a complete injunction as no specific Adhikārin is mentioned here for whom the order is intended. It does not indicate whether the person desires to know the meaning of the veda or desires to attain heaven or anything else. He further argues that there is no necessity for the addition of such words to complete the injuction in order to put it into action, since the other injunction 'tamadhyāpayita ācāryaḥ' indirectly requires persons to study. So, Prabhākara observes that the study (anhyayana) is to be done only by the force of that injunction which is complete with the Adhikārin who is desirous of being a preceptor (adhyāpaka). The disciples should learn the vedas in order to comply with the Adhyāpana Niyoga or the command of teaching prescribed for the preceptors.[198]

Pārthasārthi Miśra in his *Nyāyaratnamālā* took great pains to show that the view of Prabhākara in connection with the interpretation of the expression 'svādhyāyo' dhyetavyaḥ' is not favoured by the *Bhāṣya* of Śabara and he denied the existence of Adhyāpanavidhi with Adhikārin or Niyojya (prompted person) and showed that the Svādhyāya vidhi alone with an Adhikārin such as a person desirous of knowing the meaning of the veda, added to it is capable of prescribing the learning of the vedas.

Śālikanātha, in the *V* text obove, discards the injunction of the study (adhyayana vidhi) as viewed by the Bhāṭṭas who contend that the expression 'svādhyāyo' dhyetavyḥ' is for adhyayana. Śālikanātha has refuted the saīd view citing the verse from Kumārila viz,, 'dravyādīnā etc.' above. The verse states that as the injunetion of study may be included in the three injunctions relating to the sacrificial material (dravy) deity (devatā) and modus operandi (itikarṭavyatā), it is better to include it in purification (saṁskāra) and it purifies the letters. Svādhyāya is clearly an object (karma) and as such it is directly purified. The Bhāṭṭas admit the Adhyayana Vidhi as an injunction of purification (Saṁskāra Vidhi) and they take the expression 'svādhyāya' dhyetavyaḥ' as a case of purification.[199] In this regard Śālikanātha states that samskāra Vidhi does not employ that which is to be purified bacause of the principal injuncton having its utility been exhausted by any other source of valid knowledge. But a saṁskāra Vidhi finised in the act of purifying cannot be a cause of producing a Kārya of what is purified. So, because of both the views being incapable of stating as to whether the self is employed or not the Adhyayana Vidhi as interpreted by the Bhāṭṭas from the said expression is improper and what is proper is the Adhyāpana Vidhi as interpreted by the Prābhākaras.

The discussion on the expression viz., 'svādhyāyo' dhyetavyaḥ' as to whether it refers to the Adhyayana Vidhi or the Adhyāpana Vidhi has been discussed in detail by Śālikanātha in the Śāstramukhha Prakaraṇa of the *Prakaraṇa-pañçikā*. In the *V* text again, Śālikanātha presents the view of the Bhāṭṭas who accept the inclination of a person as the function of Śabda Bhāvanā and then rejects the same. It has already been stated that the Bhāṭṭas consider verbal urge (Śabda Bhāvanā) in form of an injunction and they conted that person's inclination (puruṣa-pravṛtti) is the Kārya of an injunction or the inclination of a person to an action is due to the Śabda Bhāvanā. But it cannot be so. For, if it is admitted that person's inclination to action is the Kārya of the injunction then the knowledge of the injunction cannot be the instrumentality. For, an instrumentality is a cause which is peculiar and operative.[200] But this is not the case with the knowledge of the injunction. It is because there is no function of the knowledge of the injunction which can give rise to the inclination of a person to certain actions. Moreover, instrumentality is not necessary for the production of the result of an action. It can be illustrated with an example. Going (gamana) needs no instrumentality for its leaving the first place and uniting with the second place. Going (gamana) is deefind by the Naiyāyikas as the conjunction of a place by leaving the earlier one.[201] Hence, for the act of going, nothing is necessary as its instrument. Thus the person's inclination is not the Kārya of the injunction. The Bhāṭṭas may again argue like this—the words 'Liṅ' etc. produce the knowledge of an injunction and as such with the help of the knowledge of the injunction as an instrument,[202] these can start their own functions in the form of inducement (preraṇā) and so there would be no absence of instrumentality. For, instrumentality is for completing the action. But this view held by the Bhāṭṭas does not, says Śālikanātha, stand to reason. For it is seen nowhere that the production of an object is due to the knowledge of that very object.

In the *V* text viz., 'evamarthavādoditaprāśastyajñānasyāpi ....' ete., Śālikanātha discards the view that the knowledge of the praiseworthiness produced by the Arthavādas is the Itikartavyatā. According to the Mīmāmsakas Arthavādas are authoritative as forming Ekavākyatā (unitary passage or syntactical unity) with a sentence including an injunction leading to the impression that the thing enjoined (vidheya) is praiseworthy. So, the function of the Arthavāda vākyas is to demonastrate the praiseworthiness of what is enjoined.[203]

Arthavāda, according to the Prābhākaras, is as much vedic text as the Vidhi itself as it also, like a Vidhi, expresses the Kāryatā of certain actions. Although it is quite true that according to the view of the Prābhākaras, the Arthavāda by itself cannot be expressive in the correct sense of the term, yet this can be urged against only such Arthavādas as are absolutely incapable of being construed with any injunction. Most of the Arthavādas, however, are actually found capable of being syntactically conected with injunctions and as such helping by the praise, the persuasive power of the injunctive word, they serve a most useful purpose by expressing the fitness of the act to be performed.[204] The Bhāṭṭas say that the knowledge of praiseworthiness arising out of the Arthavāda is the Itikartavyatā of a sacrifice. Now what is Itikartavyatā ? The word 'itikartavyatā' may be expounded as 'iti kartavyaṁ yasyāḥ sā iti itikartavyā; tasyāḥ bhāvaḥ itikartavyatā'. So it means duty. Dr. Genganath Jha in his works "*Prābhākara Mīmāṁsā* and *Pūrvamīmāṁsā in its sources*, has translated the word 'itikartavyata' as details of procedure.

In common parlance, it is seen that the pravṛtti of a person is always towards the most praiseworthy one. But a view may be there that the preraṇā does not, indeed, arise in respect of a person as the pravṛtti of a person is impossible towards an unpraiseworthy action. Hence, due to the absence of the Arthavāda, there can be no preraṇā. But this view does not stand to reason. For, the production of an action does not depend on the possibility of the result. But we see in our daily life that the attainment of the result is the due to accomplishment of an action. Hence, in view of the Bhāṭṭas even at the failure of the person's preraṇā, pravṛtti to some action may take place. If it is argued that like the knowledge of the praiseworthiness, the result may also be taken in the sense of Itikartavyatā and as such due to the absence of the result there can be no preraṇā of a person and thus let the result complete the part played by the Itikartavyatā. What is, then the necessity of accepting the knowledge of the praiseworthiness as the Itikartavyatā ? It is correct. But though the result may be taken to complete the part to be played by the praiseworthiness, yet the knowledge of the praiseworthiness should not be excluded from the range of Itikartavyatā. Here an objection may again be raised as to where the praiseworthiness is not heard meaning thereby the context wherein the Arthavāda is not clearly stated, the Itikartavyatā should not be there. As a result, the Atideśa (transference of details) of the praiseworthy statements cannot be assumed and as such to assume the itikartavyatā of the injunction only will be only an assumption as in the case of Darvi homa.

In this present context, we like to write a few lines on Atideśa (transference of details or extended application). In the seventh chapter of the *MS*, Jaimini discusses the subject of 'Atideṣa' i.e.. transference of details or extended application of certain details from one action to the other. There are many sacrifices with regard to which the veda does not prescribe all the necessary details, but lays down simply that 'such and such a sacrifice is to be performed in a manner similar to such and such another'. This Atideśa or transference is a process by which the details prescribed for one sacrifice are extended and transfered to another sacrifice. For instance, with regard to the sacrifice called Iṣu—sacrifice, after having declared its particular features, the vedic text declares that 'the rest is like that of the śyena-sacrifice'. In these cases, the śyena-sacrifice would be called the 'prakṛti yāga' (Archetype) and the Iṣu-sacrifice is called the 'vikṛtiyāga' (Ectype). Thus the transference of the Archetype (prakṛti) to the Ectype (vikṛti) is what is called Atideśa. Śālikanātha, in the Atideśapārāyaṇa prakaraṇa of his *Prakaraṇa-pañcikā*, has defined 'Atideśa' as 'that through which the Ectype becomes connected with the details of the Archetypical sacrifice' or as 'the extension of the details of one sacifice to another, when there is no incongruity in such extension'. It has also been stated that there is transference not only of Actions or procedure but also of other sacrificial details such as substances and so forth.[205]

In the *V* text above, we have a reference to Darvi homa which is neither a prakṛti yāga nor a vikṛti yāga, but it is simply a sacrifice only. Here we can refer to a context of the homa called 'vāstospati' in the *Tai. S. 3.4.10*. There is vedic sentence like 'yadekayā juhuyāt, Darvi-homaṁ kuryāt, puronuvākyāmanucya, yājyayā juhoti sadevatyayā iti'. The idea of the sentence is—the callection of the mantras beginning with 'āsrāvayet etc.' and ending with 'astu śrauṣat' is applied in the form of yājyā and 'Anuvākyā' and these ,Yājyā' and 'Anuvākyā' are used in principal sacrifices. The homa performed along with the principal sacrifices is the most favourite to the deities. But the homa called Darvi (i.e., homa performed by the sacrificial spoon called darvi) does not enjoy the same. As a result, it is not desired by the deities. For, by simply uttering the mantra 'Agnaye svāhā' without doing 'āsravaṇa etc.' i.e., 'āsrāvayet' and 'astu śrauṣat' the oblation is offered by the sacrificial spoon called Darvi. Again 'one should offer oblation by a Darvi'—according to this Vidhi if the homa is performed without the mantras 'āsrāvayet' and 'astu śrauṣat', then it is called Darvi homa. Hence 'let there be no Darvi homa'—by assuming this and uttering the puronuvākyā mantra viz., 'vāstospataye pratijānīhi' one should offer oblation by the yājyā mantra called 'vāstospataye sagmaye svāhā'. This being done so, because of its being desired by the deities, it belongs to the deities.

Thus the offering of oblation with only one mantra performed by the word 'juhoti' and by uttering the word 'svāha' is called Darvi homa. These Darvi homas are neither prakṛti yāgas nor vikṛti yāgas of any homa or yāga nor both but like the puruṣa of the sāṁkhya system of Indian thought, it is Apūrva. Hence, the Darvi homas are Apūrvas and without having the itikartavyatā.[206]

In this way, one cannot assume itikarṭavayatā in case of the injunctions only. It cannot also be said that the instance of the Darvi homa in the present context of the discussion in the *V* text above, is irrelevant. Thus Śilikanātha refutes the view of the Bhāṭṭas that the Śabda Bhāvanā is the Vidhi.

In the *V* text viz., 'Kiñca śabdo' mbaraguṇa iti . . .' etc., Śālikanātha explains how Śabda can have no function. If Śabda is admitted as a Guṇa or attribute then it cannot possess function, because function always resorts to a Dravya (substance). Even if it is accepted as a Dravya, then also it cannot have function due to its being all-pervading.

In admitting the pravṛtti of the persons as the Kārya of Śabda, one of the causes is that the pravṛtti of the persons may be the Kārya of the Śabda when it has the function. But here a question may arise as to whether there may be function in the Śabda ? Before going to examine it is better to discuss what a Śabda is. Whether it may be recognised as attribute or a substance. The Naiyāyikas who contend that the sense-organs become effective when touched by objects consider Śabda as a attribute (guṇa) of ether and sense-organ of ears as the holes in the form of ether.[207] If Śabda as an attribute and sense-organ of ear in the form of ether are admitted, then there will be no relation of Śabda with sense-organ of ear. For, in this case there may be two types of relation—conjunction (Saṁyoga) and inherence (Samavāya). If again Śabda is admitted as a substance (dravya) then it will have no relation with ether and as such there will be inherent relation between this two. For, inherence cannot take place in two substances without their part and whole. But Śabda and Ākāśa are not admitted as having a relation of part and whole. Function (vyāpāra) due to its being in the form of a Kriyā, resorts to a substance and not to a attribute Śabda being an attribute cannot have function (vyāpāra).[208] In this context doubt may arise if it is admitted that function (vyāpāra) does not resort to nothing but the substance only and Sabda is an attribute and not a substance how then the denotative function (abhidhānavyāpāra) is possible in case of Śabda? Śāilkanātha solves the objection raised by the opponents by stating that the knowledge relating to meaning is attained by the knowledge of the Śabda and that is called as possessing denotation (ābhidhānika) when it is intended to be done by Śabda. So Śabda can be taken as the cause of the meaning, because Śabda comes immediately before the meaning and a cause always preceds the effect.[209] Though the function (vyāpāra) resorts to other still it can have agency. Though the movement rests in the elemental objects, yet the agenthood lies with the self. Hence, there will be no fault if we admit that Śabda to which the function does not take resort, has denotativeness.

A question may again be raised as to how the function of Śabda (Śabda Bhāvanā) is related to the objective urge (Ārtha Bhāvanā). If it is tried to solve this problem by saying that because of their being denoted by the same suffix, the function of Śabda (Śabda Bhāvanā) can be related to the objective urge Ārtha Bhāvahā). The followers of Kumārila come forward to place or quote in support of their solution a verse from the vākyādhikaraṇa of the *Slokavārttika* of Kumārila (SV. 7.79½ & 80½). The idea of the verse in brief is this—Vidhi and Bhāvanā are taken to be understood by one suffix only and the relation between Śabda Bhāvanā and Ārtha Bhāvanā is held prior to the meaning of the verbal root (dhātu). Here it may be noted that we have already stated that in view of the Bhāṭṭas, Vidhi is Śabda Bhāvanā. The suffix that ascertains the relation between the two Bhāvanās is the vedic 'Liṅ'.[210] But Śālikanātha does not accept this view of the Bhāttas. He puts his argument by saying the suffix viz., 'Liṅ' cannot denote Bhāvanā, but Apūrva.

Thus Śālikanātha rejects the view of the Bhāṭṭas that knowledge of the praisearthness is the Itikartaryatā.

In the *V* text viz., 'nanu ca sarvākhyātānāṁ bhāvanāvacanatā . . .' etc., the author presents the view of Maṇḍana Miśra, the staunch follower of Bhāṭṭa School, who contends that all the Ākhyātas (verbal forms) denote Bhāvanā. In the present work we have already discussed Bhāvanā. As is rightly stated by Late Pt. A. Subrahamanya Sastri, Maṇḍana Miśra in verse no. 27 of his *Bhāvanāviveka*, deals with the present issue under discussion.[211] The word 'sāmānādhikaraṇya' means bearing the same meaning. Bhāvanā is the stimulating activity towards a course of action which is to take place. Bhāvanā is the kṛti which means the physical effort of the Agent. The word 'karoti' denotes 'kṛti'. All the Ākhyātas denote the meaning of 'karoti'. To get a reply from a person, one must start a question with 'karoti'. For instance, when one puts a question like 'kiṁ karoti', the reply will be 'pacati' 'jānāti' etc., meaning thereby the question is started by a verbal form with the suffix 'Iiṅ'.

According to Maṇḍana, the meaning of the verbal form 'karoti' cannot be understood when it is formed by the kṛt suffixes 'Ghañ' etc. For instance, when the suffix 'Ghañ' is added to the dhātu 'pac', the form will be 'pākaḥ' and as such the meaning of 'karoti' cannot be attained from it.

It may be mentioned here that the term 'Ākhyāta' in the *V* text above refers to the verb with 'Tiṅ' suffix. For example, karoti, gacchati, pacati etc.

According to the view of the Mīmāṁsakas, the Ākhyāta is the most important part of a sentence.[212]

The followers of Kumārila contend that the Ākhyāta is common to all the ten 'lakāras' i.e., moods and tenses. Ākhyāta is one of the two ways by which a vidhivākya performs its function. The other way by which a vidhivākya performs its function is the optative mood and because of its being a verb it denotes the Ārthī Bhāvanā consisting in pravṛtti of a person.[213]

Rāmānujācārya also takes this issue of Bhāvanāvacanatā of the Ākhyātas as held by Maṇḍana. But his exposition is easier than that of Śālikanātha. Rāmānuja explains the word 'sāmānādhikaraṇya' in the vṛtti text of the *VM* above, as bearing the same meaning.[214] He also discards the view of Maṇḍana and supports the view of Prabhākara.

Mādhavācārya also contends that the Ākhyātas denote Bhāvanā and all the Ākhyātas is connected with the sense of the verbal form 'karoti' and this is what is called Bhāvanā. All the verbal forms are expressed by 'karoti'.[215] In the commentary called '*Vistara*' by him on the *Jaiminīyanyāyamālā*, states more clearly that the sense of 'karoti' applies to any verbal form. For instance, when there is the verbal form 'pacati', we understand the meaning as 'pākaṁ karoti' (he performs the task of cooking). Thus the meaning of 'gacchati' is to be taken as 'gamanaṁ karoti'. The verbal form 'pacati' may be used as 'pākaḥ', 'paktiḥ', 'pacanam'.[216]

In this manner, Śālikanātha presents Maṇḍana's concept of the Ākhyāta—as denoting Bhāvanā.

In the *V* text viz., 'tadasat kim karoti . . .' etc., Śālikanātha refutes the view of Maṇḍana Miśra who contends that all the

Ākhyātas denote Bhāvanā.[218] According to Maṇḍana, in order to get a reply, one must put a question beginning with the verbal from 'karoti' (one does). For instance, in order to get the verbal form 'pacati' in reply, the question should be put in the form of 'kim karoti'? (What does he do?). Thus the state of all the Ākhyātas as denoting the Bhāvanā is ascertained because of their being in apposition with the Ākhyāta viz., 'karoti'. In other words, in the view of Maṇḍana, the meaning of the verbal root viz., 'karoti' is denoted by all the verbal forms. But Śālikanātha argues that the verbal forms do not denote the sense of 'karoti' which is other than the meaning of the Dhātu. The meaning of all the Dhātus again give rise to certain meaning in the form of 'being' and thus they mean certain things to be questioned and directed by means of the verbal form viz., 'karoti'.

In the *V* text again, Śālikanātha contends that there may be questions and replies in the case of the actions performed by the persons with proper effort because of there being the possibility of difference in respect of the functions. But in the case of a question like 'kim karoti' (what he does?), if the reply is 'gacchati', then there will be inconsistency because of there being no additional operation to 'gamana' (going).

Moreover, Śālikanātha states that as the meanings of words are determined by means of vṛddhavyavahāra, there will be no inconsistency in the case of any usage of an elderly person without the denotation of Bhāvanā by the Ākhyātas. It is because, says Śālikanātha, the Ākhyātas denote only the number of the agent and as such they denote nothing more than that viz., the number of the agent. As for instance, in the sentence, 'pākam karoti Devadattaḥ' (Devadatta does cooking), the word 'pāka' denotes the meaning of the Dhātu viz., 'pac' and the Dhātu viz., 'kṛ' denotes the physical effort and the Ākhyāta viz., 'karoti' denotes the number of the agent. Thus according to Śālikanātha, the Ākhyātas denote the number of the agent and not the Bhāvanā as contended by Maṇḍana.

In the *V* text viz., 'yastu—"Devadatta . . .' etc., the author of the *VM* presents the view of Maṇḍana and then the author refutes the same. According to Maṇḍana in the expression like 'Devadatta odanam pacati' (Devadatta cooks rice), the verbal root viz., 'pac' gives rise to the knowledge of the physical effort.

Hence, Ākhyāta denotes, in addition to the meaning of the stem, the Bhāvanā. But Śālikanātha does not accept this view of Maṇḍana and so he reminds Maṇḍana of the principle of Mīmāmsā according to which the meaning of a word is to be attained from no other source other than the word itself. In other words, the power of a word is to be admitted in such a meaning that cannot be attained by means of implication. Thus the physical effort is to be understood from the verbal root 'pac' and not from the Ākhyāta as Maṇḍana asserts. Maṇḍana asserts this because of the fact that in his view, all the Ākhyātas denote Bhāvanā. But Śālika because of his admitting Kārya as the Vākyārtha, cannot accept the view of Maṇḍana.

In 'nanu prābhākarā api . . .' etc. of the *V* text, Śālikanātha presents the view of the Prābhākaras that the suffix Liṅs etc. that denote the performable also denote the physical effort. According to them, the performable related to the physical effort does not come to be denoted in the case of the physical effort being not denoted. It cannot be said that while the kṛti is not denoted, the Kārya is denoted. In other words, it may be said that without the krti being denoted, the Kārya also cannot be denoted.

In the *V* text again, Śālikanātha also discards another view according to which in the case of the word 'Daṇḍī' (i.e., a person with a stick), 'Daṇḍa' is not denoted by the suffix but the person with a stick is denoted. According to Śālikanātha this view is not proper, because if the Daṇḍa (stick) is not known, then there can be no knowledge of the person characterised by the Daṇḍa and also there will be no knowledge of the suffix 'vati' in the sense of having the stick. Again, there is the word 'Daṇḍa' which is being in the stem and at the same time it conveys the meaning of the word 'Daṇḍa'. But in the present context in the case of the use of the verbal forms 'pacati' and 'yajeta' etc., this is not the same. It is, because, there is no rule that the verbal roots viz., 'pac' and 'yaj' etc,, denote the function of the person. The person as a sentient being, understands the Kārya by means of the Liṅs etc.

The example of Daṇḍa and Daṇḍi as stated in *V* text above is found in Śabara's Bhāṣya. There in the Bhāṣya, Śabara states that without the viśeṣaṇa, the viśeṣa cannot be known.[217]

In the *V* text again, Śālikanātha also refutes another view. According to this view, the suffixes Liṅs etc., denote the number of the agent and the agent etc. can be known by the Kriyā and thus in the present context as the Kriyā implies the kṛti, so it should not be denoted by the suffixes Liṅs etc. But Śālikanātha is not prepared to accept this view. He contends that though the kṛti is implied by the Kriyā, yet Apūrva cannot be understood, because the attainment of the Apūrva depends on the kṛti. This issue is discussed at length by Śālikanātha in the *Viṣayakaraṇīya prakaraṇa* of the *prakaraṇa-pañcikā*.

In 'tatra na kriyāmātram tāvadaham . . .' etc., and 'āstām tāvat kriyā loke . . .' etc., of the *V* and *K* texts respectively, Śālikanātha states how a person is inclined to action or in other words, it may be said—knowing what the pravṛtti of a person to an action takes place. Śālikanātha contends that a person is not inclined to action by knowing the kriyā only or only the phala or only the relation of the two (viz., the kriya and phala). The pravṛtti of a person does not occur even in respect of knowing the relation of Sādhya and Sādhana from the action and the result respectively. But on the other hand, the pravṛtti of person to certain acts takes place from the knowledge of the kāryatā. In other words, a person prior to his pravṛtti to some act, must have the knowledge like—'This is my Kārya'. This is clearly explained by Śālikanātha in the *KS* above. It is stated there (viz., in the above two *K* texts) that although there may be actions like 'gamana' and 'āgamana', yet so long as the actions like the sucking of milk from mother's breasts though gives satisfaction to the child are not understood as this performable (i.e , this is my Kārya), the pravṛtti of the child to that act will not take placc.

Thus Śālikanātha asserts that the knowledge of the Kāryatā is the cause of the pravṛtti of a person to action.

In the *V* text viz., 'atrā' para āha . . .' etc., Śālikanātha presents the view of Maṇḍana Miśra and then he refutes the same. The word 'apara' in the *V* text refers to Maṇḍana Miśra. According to him, the kāryatā of the Prābhākaras is nothing but the Iṣṭasādhanatā as held by him. Thus Maṇḍana makes no difference between kāryatā and Iṣṭasādhanatā and Iṣṭasadhanta is the cause of the pravṛtti of a person to an action and not the kāryatā. In support of his assertion, Maṇḍana quotes a verse from his work Brahmasiddhi. The verse viz., 'apekṣitopāyataiva . . .' etc., states that Iṣṭasādhanatā is accepted by the thinkers as the Vidhi which is, according to Maṇḍana, the cause of the pravṛtti of a person to an action. The word 'apekṣitopāyatā' in the said verse is used as a synonym of 'Iṣṭasādhanatā'. The word 'ato' in the said verse is found as 'tato'.[218]

In another verse viz., 'pumso . . .' etc., stated above, Maṇḍana states that Dharma and Pravartaṇā are also the causes of the pravṛtti of a person to an action. There is no other Pravartaka (i.e., that which makes one incline to an action) in respect of the actions.

Again in another verse viz., 'karturiṣṭābhyupāye hi . . .' etc., Maṇḍana contends that the knowledge viz., 'this is to be done' etc. arises only in respect of there being the Iṣṭasādhanatā.

In the portion of the *V* text viz , 'tatra tāvadidameva vaktavyam . . .' etc., above, Śāllkanātha refutes the view of Maṇḍana. Śālikanātha states that although there is the Iṣṭasādhanatā in respect of the actions of the past and the present, yet that Iṣṭasādhanatā is not ascertained as the Kāryatā. Thus Śālikanātha shows the difference between the Kāryatā and the Iṣṭasādhanatā and thereby rejects Maṇḍana's assertion that both these are one and the same. In subsequent pages we shall find Śālikanātha showing the difference between the Kāryatā and the Iṣtasādhanatā.

of the *K* (7) above, the author states that the phalasādhanatā is different from Kāryatā though according to Maṇḍana Miśra they are not so. Kāryatā as stated by Śālikanātha is that which is made out (i.e., brought about) by Kṛti. But phalasādhanatā is, says Śālikanātha, the intrumentality in respect of producing the result (i.e., the desired object) and thus these two differ from each other.

It may be said here that although both phalasādhanatā and Kāryatā aim at a single object, yet they have difference in respect of their own nature. That object because of its being the means of producing the desired object (i.e., the result) comes to be known as the phalasādhana or Iṣṭasādhana or comes to have the phalasādhanatā. But that object because of its attaining the result by means of Kṛti comes to be known as Kārya or comes to have the Kāryatā. Thus Śālikanātha presents the difference between phalasādhanatā and Kāryatā.

In 'kintu svayam kleśarupam . . .' etc. and 'svabhāvena hi

. . .' etc. of the *K* and *V* text respectively, Śālikanātha explains Kāryatā and phalasādhanatā and asserts that the knowledge of the Kāryatā is the basis of phalasādhanatā. We have already discussed that Śālikanātha makes the difference between Kāryatā of the Prābhākaras and the phalasādhanatā which is stated by Maṇḍana Miśra in his well known treatises *Brahmasidhi* and *Vidhiviveka*. According to Maṇḍana Miśra phalasādhanatājñāna or iṣṭasādhanatājñāna (the knowledge of instrumentality of a desired object) from any action can alone induce a person to take up an action. The second half of the *K* (B) and the first half of the *K* (9) of the *VM* above, are found quoted by Citsukha in his *Citsukhī* (p. 162) and the same is explained by Pratyakṣvarupa Bhagavan in his commentary called *Nayanaprasādinī* on the *Citsukhī*. This is the refutation of Maṇḍana's view by Śālikanātha regarding phalasādhanatā as the cause of pravṛtti of the persons to actions. The idea of the passage of the *Nayanaprasādinī* may be explained as : A karma (action) which is called a Kārya (performability) produces pain to persons. How, then karma (action) can be called a Kāryatā (performability) ? It is because that which generates distress is not performed. It is said in Mīmāmsā—'akartavyo duḥkhaphalaḥ' (that act should not be performed which bears a painful result). Hence, the phrase is used in the *K*—'phalasādhanatā tatra' etc. Because of being the phalasādhanatā (instrumentality of the desired object) the karma (action) is admitted to have Kāryatā (performability). Again it may be urged here—how phalasādhanatā is the cause of karma (action) ? For, the phalasādhanatā is the cause of pravṛtti (persons' inclination). So, the Kāryatā (performability) belong to the Karma (action) and not to the pravṛtti (person's inclination). Thus in Prābhākara's view, pravṛtti (person's inclination) arises out of the kāryatājñāna (knowledge of the performability) and not out of Iṣṭasādhanatājñāna (knowledge of the instrumentality of the desired object) as held by Maṇḍana Miśra, a follower of the Bhāṭṭa School.[219]

Prabhākara maintains that the verbal comprehension (Śābdabodhaḥ) is obtained only by observing the 'Liṅ' which denotes always a Kārya that is required to be performed. On hearing a 'Liṅ' one learns certain action as his Kārya which is nothing but the undertaking of that 'I should do the work as directed.' Kārya, therefore, is most important in a sentence, and the imports of all other words are subordinate to that Kārya. Accordingly the word 'svargakāma' in the expressions like 'svargakāmo yajata' etc., indicates only a Niyojya (prompted person) on whom the Kārya is imposed and the verbal root denotes a sacrifice which is to be performed. The kāryatājñāna (the knowledge of the performability) alone, as contended by the Prābhakāras, can impel one to do a sacrifice and not necessarily the desire of svarga or any other desired result. This theory regarding the vedic injunctions (Vidhi) was first advocated by Bādari[220] and later on it was upheld by Prabhākara Miśra. Thus according to Prābhākaras the word 'svargakāma' means only a Niyojya (prompted person) who is subordinate to the Kārya which is denoted by 'Liṅ' and that is stated by Śālikanātha in the *V* text above.

The Prābhākaras contend that verbal comprehension is obtained by juniors only through conversation when one commends another to do something. The juniors who observe the seniors to command others to do something and also thus commanded to act accordingly learn that particular Kārya is the meaning conveyed by the sentence. Thus the meaning of the 'Liñ' in that sentence, is learnt by juniors as Kārya. In this way, the persons are inclined to do the actions after understanding the Kārya. Śalikanātha has shown in the *V* text above, the nature of inference (anumānasvarupa) as to how one infers the pravṛtti (inclination) of another to actions.[221]

At the end of the vṛtti above, the author of the *VM* refutes the view of a section of the followers of Kumārila Bhāṭṭa which states that the Iṣṭasādhanatā (instrumentality of the desired object) is the Kāryatā (performability) and not anything else. Only the Iṣṭasādhanatā is the cause of pravṛtti (person's inclination to actions). Rāmānujācārya in his *Tantrarahasya* also, discards the view that desire (icchā) is the cause of pravṛtti (person's inclination to actions). He discards the same in the manner of Śālikanātha.[222]

Citsukhācārya in his *Citsukhī* has refuted the view of the Prābhākaras, according to which the knowledge of kāryatā (performability) is the cause of pravṛtti (person's inclination to actions). Citsukha contends that the view of the Prābhākaras may be accepted, provided a junior understands his knowledge of kāryatā (performability) as his own pravṛtti (inclination to action). But his state of being inclined to action is ascertained by Iṣṭasādhanatājñāna (knowledge of the instrumentality of the desired object) and not by the kāryatājñāna (knowledge of the performability). It cannot be said here that there will be inconsistency in respect of admitting the Iṣṭasādanatājñàna as the cause of pravṛtti (person's inclination to actions) as in the past actions though there is Iṣṭasādhanatā, yet the pravṛtti (person's inclination to action) is not seen. This objection of the Prābhākaras is met with by Citsukha by arguing that he who admits kāryatābodha (knowledge of performability) as the pravṛtti (person's inclination to actions) admits that the Iṣṭasādhanatājñāna as the cause of kāryatājñāna. It is because, there can be no kāryatājñāna without Iṣṭasādhanatājñāna.[223]

In 'Śabdāntarāṇi svārtheṣu . . .' etc. and 'liṅgādiyuktavākyaśravaṇe . . .' etc. of the *K* and *V* text respectively above, Śālikanātha explains how the suffixes Liṅs etc. denote the Kārya or in other words, how these Liṅs etc. are understood in respect of the Kārya. As we have stated in our exposition of the first section of the *VM*, the Prābhākaras lay emphasis on the natural method of learning the words by a child. It is by way of watching the usage and activity of the elders in day to day life that a child comes to understand the wordmeanings. One person asking another, says 'gāmānaya' (bring the cow), the latter thus asked at once brings the cow. A child who hears the sentence uttered by the former and observes the action that follows, infers vaguely that the meaning of the sentence is a command to carry out the act of bringing the cow. In the present stage, what the child understands is only that the whole of that statement means the whole of what is signified. Later on, the child hears another man asking another 'aśvamānaya' (bring the horse) and observes the latter bringing the horse. From this, the child infers that the meaning of this sentnece is a command to carry out the act of bringing the horse. Now by making a comparison between the two sentences, the child understands that the verb 'ānaya' (bring) common to both the sentences must mean the command to 'anaya' (bring) and that the two terms 'gām' (cow) and 'aśvam' (horse) must mean two different animals. In this way, by making comparison among various sentences and by observing the actions performed, a child becomes capable by the process of inclusion and deletion (Āvāpa and Udvāpa or Anvaya and Vyatireka) of understanding the meaning of individual words. This is also same in case of the 'Liṅs' that give rise to the knowledge of Kārya. The meaning of the 'Liṅ' in the sentence, is learnt by a child as Kārya since people do some action on hearing the 'Liṅ' of the elders, Similarly the other words of that sentence also are understood to denote actions such as bringing the cows etc. required by that Kārya.

The Prābhākaras also contend that verbal comprehension is possible only due to observation of actions and none can have verbal comprehension from the words that denote the accomplished facts as they cannot be understood by others during the conversation.

Prabhākara says that Kārya is the meaning of the 'Liṅ' everywhere by its principal power of expression. But outside the Vedas where there is no necessity of Kāryas, the 'Liṅ', according to him, denotes the actions such as bringing the cow etc. as the Kārya by means of Lakṣaṇā.

The same idea of the above *V* text of the *VM*, can also be gathered from Śālikanātha's *Ṛjuvimalā*, the commentary on the *Bṛhatī* of prabhākara.[234]

In 'kāryameva hi . . .' etc. and 'pravarttyapuruṣāpkṣayā . . .' etc. of the *K* and *V* text respectively, above, Śālikanātha asserts that the sufixes Liṅs etc. are understood as denothing the praiṣa (command) etc. The inclusion of the word 'ādi' refers to Āmantraṇa (invitation) and Adhyeṣṇa (request), That Kārya performed by a senior compared to the person inclined to an action is called praiṣa (command); for, a senior always commands an inferior (i.e., a junior) to do some work. When it occurs in the case of both the persons of equal age, then it is called an Āmantraṇa (invitation). In common parlance, what hapaens is that a person never commands nor requests another of equal age to do some action but invites. Again when the Karya comes form the inferior, is called Adhyeṣaṇa (request). An inferior (i.e., a junior) generally makes a request to a senior in order to do something Otherwise, it will be a dishonour to the senior.

This can be explained here – the praiṣa (command) etc. is understood, in common parlance, as the meaning of the 'Liṅs' etc.

The actions performed by the senior, one of equal age and a junior are respectively known as praiṣa, Āmantraṇa and Adhyeṣaṇa. In all cases, in the use of the senior, one of equal age and junior, as the Kārya is not abandoned and as there is no violation of the actions, so it is proper that Kārya is the meaning of the 'Liṅs' etc. Hence, it is called the denota'ion of the Kārya as a synonym to Niyoga (prompting) But the praiṣa etc are only the upādhis (limiting adjunets). An upādhi (limiting adjunct) is that which not being in denotation, establishes the meanings of words in particular place. For example, the woıd 'drtihari'. Here, paśutva (annimalhood) is the upādhi (limiting adjunct). When the act of stealing is relating to the paśu (animal), then the subject of this act of stealing is called 'drtihari'. Likewise, in the present context, when the 'Liṅs' etc. denote Kārya then praiṣa, Āmantraṇa and Adhyeṣaṇa are termed as upādhis (limiting adjuncts)] This is what is stated by Śālikanātha by the above.[235]

Pārthasārathi Miśra, a follower of the Bhāṭṭa School of Pūrvīmāṁsā, in the vidhinirṇaya section of his *Nyāyartnamālā* says that it is not correct to state that the Kāryas accomplished by the senior, one of equal age and a junior are respectively called preṣaṇa, Adhyeṣaṇa and Abhyanujñāna, for, it is said that the 'Liṅ' is used in case of yāsñā (begging) though it is not admitted as a Kārya. So, the meaning of a word is expressed by pravartanā (inducement).[236] Here it may be noted that the words namely praiṣā, Āmantraṇa and Adhyeṣaṇa used by Śālikanātha. have been used by Rāmānujācārya in his commentry called *Nāyakaratna* respectively as preṣaṇa, Adhyeṣaṇa and Abhyanujñāna i.e., what is called Āmantrana by Śālikanātha is named as Adhyeṣaṇa by Rāmanujācārya.[227] But in his *Tantrahasya* Rāmānuja follows Śālikanātha's exposion in this respect.[238] That the praiṣa etc. are not the meanings of words but limiting adjuncts (upādhi) only are seen in the *Bṛhatī* of Prabhākara and the *Ṛjuvimalā* of Śālikanātha.[239]

In 'kāryameva hi sarvatra . . .' ete. and 'pravṛttirhi bālena. . .' etc. of the *K* and *V* text respectively above, Śālikanātha asserts that Kārya and Kārya alone is the single cause of the pravṛtti in all cases and he also lays emphasis in stating that the meaning of the suffixes Liṅs etc. is only the Kārya. It is also stated at the *K* and *V* text above that even in respect of the praiṣa etc. the meaning of the Liṅs etc. is the Kārya, A child understands that pravṛtti is due to one's knowledge of the Kārya and by observing the persons engaged in actions, the child assumes the knowledge of the Kārya.

In 'kṛtisādhyaṁ prədhānam . . .' etc. of the *K* and 'kṛtau Satyām . . .' etc., of the *V* text, the auther defines kārya and how it is known. With the two adjectives (i.e,, qualifications) viz., 'kṛtisādhyam' and 'pradhānam' as stated in the *K* above, Śālikanātha defines Kārya. Kārya is that which is brought about by kṛti and it is the principal element of the kṛti. It has already been stated earlier that in the view of the Prābhākaras, Kārya is what is expressed by the suffix Liṅ. Again it is kṛti that brings about the Kārya i.e., for the Kārya, the kṛti takes place. Now what is the kṛti ? The author says that kṛti is the prayatna and thus what is brought about by the kṛti is what is called Kārya that becomes principal element for the kṛti. In order to avoid ativyāpti, the word 'pradhānam' is used in the definition of Kārya. Otherwise dhātvartha (meaning of the verbal root) will ajso be meant. Here prominence is desired to be given to Kārya. Again the compound word 'kṛtisādhyam' in the definition is used in order to avoid the result svarga (heaven) etc. The kṛtisādhyatā (bringing about by the kṛti) is understood by the process of Anvaya and Vyatireka of the inference of the kṛti, and the kṛtipradhānatva (prominence of the effort) is known by the mānasa-pratyakṣa (mental perception). As a matter of fact, Kārya is known by both perception and inference and this is what is indicated by the word 'mānāntareṇa' used in the *K* above. Here, doubt may arise as to while the object of perception is one and that of inference is another, how it is possible to get a compressed meaning by these two sources ? But it is not correct to object to. For the knowledge produced by perception and inference inhering in mind gives rise to a knowledge like recognition (pratyabhijña). This has been clearly explained by Śālikanātha with the help of an example— 'odanadākavat' (meaning thereby like the cooking of rice). Odana (rice) is known by perception and pāka (cooking) which is a sādhana (means) is known by Anvaya and Vyatireka inference. That where there is rice, there is cooking (tatsatte tatsttā-anvaya) and where there is no rice, there will be no cooking (tadasatte tadasattā-vyatireka). In the example, one part of the knowledge is attained by perception and the remaining part is by inference. But still, there is no harm in getting the compressed meaning.[230]

According to the Prābhākaras, Kārya is the import of the 'Liṅs' and is also known by terms 'Niyoga', 'Apūrva' and 'Dharma'. This may be noted here that Apūrva of Prābhākaras is different from that of the Bhāṭṭas who accept yāga (sacrifice) as Dharma and Apūrva as a connecting link between the yāga (sascrifice) and the phala (result). The Prābhākaras hold that Apūrva, which is a product of the sacrifice and the meaning of the 'Liṅ' ss the Kārya to svargakāma (person desiring heaven) and this Apūrva is not a temporary act like a sacrifice. svargakāma (person desiring heaven) will, therefore be induced to perform this Kārya as it will continue till the production of svarga (heaven) from yāga.[231]

That a Kārya is kṛtisādhya (to be brought about by effort) and kṛti (effort) is also called prayatna (right effort) is also stated by Śālikanātha in the śāstra-pariccheda pramāṇapārāyaṇa prakaraṇa of his *Prakaraṇa-pañcikā*.[232] Again in the Viṣaya-karaṇīya prakaraṇa of the same work Śālikanātha says that Kārya is that which is desired to be attained by kṛti (effort) kṛti (effort) is the function of Ātman (self) and kṛti is another meaning of puruṣaprayatna (right effort of the person)[233]

According to the Prābhākaras, kriyā is, in common parlance, denoted by the term 'Kārya' and Kārya is the import of the 'Liṅ' etc. and Kārya is denoted generally by these 'Liṅ' etc. and the meaning of the dhātu (root) is denoted particularly in ordinary sentence. For example, pakaḥ (cooking) gamanam (going) etc. Thus the Prābhākararas contend that Kārya is the meaning of sentence. But according to the Bhāṭṭas, the meaning of root is not the kriyā. It is either a karaṇa-kāraka or a karmakāraka, sometimes, the kriyā becomes secondary in case of a-dhātvartha (meaning of the root). But the principal kriyā is what is called Bhāvanā (urge) and this Bhāvanā is the meaning of a sentence.[234]

We have already discussed in our exposition of the kārikā 7 of the *VM* where in Śālikanātha defines kāryatā (performability) as kṛtisādhyatva (brought about by effort) and it has been shown how kāryatā (performability) differs from phalasādhanatā (achievability of the desired object which is, according to Maṇḍana Miśra, the author of the *Vidhiviveka*, the cause of pravṛtti (person's inclination to actions). But Śālikanātha describes it as the cause of producing the desired result.

Ācārya Citsukha, a vedāntin refutes the kāryatā of the Prābhākaras and criticises the definition of Kārya as given by Śālikanātha. According to Citsukha, the definition of Kārya is improper as it involves ativyāpti (wide application). For, even the result like heaven etc., there is kṛtisādhyatā. If it is argued that in case of Kārya, kṛtisādhyatā is directly there. But the result is not directly brought about by kṛti There is Apūrva which is a mediator between the action and the result. So, there can be no question of ativyāpti (wide application). But Citsukha says that it cannot be argued so. For even in case of Niyoga, there is no direct bringing about by effort (kṛtisādhyatā), but it is there in case of the acts like yāga etc. Thus Citsukha criticises Śālikhanātha's definition of Kārya and refutes kāryatājñāna (knowledge of performability) as the cause of pravṛtti (person's inclination to actions).[235]

As a follower of vedānta, Citsukha contends that Iṣṭasādhanatājñāna (knowledge of the achievability of the desired object) is the cause of pravṛtti (person's inclination to action). The significative capacity of the 'Liṅs' is ascertained in the Istasādhanatā (achievability of the desired object) and not in Kārya as held by the Prābhākaras. The vedāntins contend that those who accept kāryatājñāna (knowledge of performability) as the cause of pravṛtti (person's inclination to action also accept Istasādhanatājñāna (knowledge of achievability of the desired object) as the cause of kāryabodha (knowledge of performability). For, there can be no kāryatājñāna (knowledge of performability) without the Istasādhanatājñānā (knowledge of the achievability of the desired object).[236] This view of the vedāntins seems to follow the view of Maṇḍana Miśra and that of Pārthasārthi Miśra.

In 'evam kāryātmake . . .' etc. of the *K* text, Śālikanātha sums up what has been stated by him in the immediately preceding *K* (12 and 13). It is why he uses the the word 'upasaṁharati' just before the *K* above. In the preceding *K* texts, it is stated that the import of the suffixes Liṅs etc. is the Kārya. This is again concluded in the present *K* above with the help of a comparison. The comparison is this—just as the popular words denote related meanings. So also the Liṅs denote the meaning of the Kārya.

We have already stated it in our preceding exposition of the *V* text of the *VM*. Śālikanātha did not write the vṛtti on the aforesaid *K*, possibly because he wanted to avoid repetition. The word 'tathā' in the *K* above should be 'yathā'. It is, perhaps, wrongly printed.

In 'Sampradhāryamidantvatra . . .' etc., of the *K* and 'loke hi liṅādiyuktavākyaśravana . . .' etc., of the *V* text, Śālikanātha asserts that the Liṅs etc., denote the Vākya and also the member of the Kartā etc., as the suffixes Lat etc., do. Śālikanātha says that in the case of ordinary sentences Kārya which is known by other source like inference etc., is Kriyā. We have already stated that in the view of the Prābhākaras, the Kriyā is known by the Kārya i.e., the Kriyā is the Kārya and as such both are not different from each other.[237] It is also stated by the Prābhākaras that the 'Liṅs' denote the Kārya. Śālikanātha explains it as –

When the younger hearing the sentence with the suffixes 'Liṅ' etc., uttered by an elder performs an act and as such the knowledge of the Kārya relating to his act is denoted by the suffixes 'Liṅs' etc. It is because of the fact that the parvṛtti (inclination to action) of the younger and the knowledge of the Kāryatā (performability) by the 'Liṅs' etc., are related to the same object. It is nowhere seen that a child knowing an act, is inclined to another act. What happens is this—a person is inclined to an action when he attains the knowledge of the Kārya.[238] It may be argued here : let the verbal root (dhātu) denote the meaning of the Kārya. It is admitted that the suffixes 'Liṅs' etc., are used in respect of verbal root (dhātu) that denotes the meaning relating to Kārya. When the sentences with 'Liṅs' etc., are heard, one may understand that the verbal root (dhātu) is used as denoting the meaning of the Kārya and thus the meaning of the verbal root (dhātvartha) is understood as belonging to the Kārya. For instance, the suffixes 'Laṭ' etc., ascertain the present tense i.e., in order to mean some act to be performed in the present tense, the suffixes 'Laṭ' etc., are used. Pāṇini, under the sūtra 'vartamāne Laṭ' (3.4.54) of his *Aṣṭādhyāyī*, states the use of the suffix 'Laṭ'. According to this sūtra, in case of the present tense, the sufflx 'Laṭ' is used after the verbal root (dhātu). For example, bhavati, pacati etc. Here, the suffix 'liṅ' indicating singular number, is used after the verbal roots viz., 'bhū' and 'pac'. These suffixes 'Laṭ' etc., denote only the number of the Kartā (subject) and Karma (object) etc. To be clear, these suffixes denote all the three numbers viz., singular, dual and plural. Again these suffixes may be used both in active and passive voice. In active voice, the verb is used in the number according to the corresponding number of the Kārta (subject) and in case of passive voice, the number of the verb is in accordance with the number of the Karma (object). That is why the word 'Ādi' is used in the compound word. 'kartrādisamkhyāmātravācitvameva' in the *V* text above. Like the suffixes 'Laṭ' etc., the suffixes 'Liṅ' etc., are also used in the same sense and as such in case of the vedic sentences also, the kriyā is understood as the Kārya.

In 'tathapi vede . . .' etc., and 'ṣaṣṭhādye hyetaduktam . . .' etc., of the *K* and *V* text, the author of the *VM* states that in accordance with the conclusion at the beginning of the sixth adhyāya of the *MS*, the words svargakāma (one who desires heaven) etc., are called Niyojya (the promoted person) in the sacrifices like 'Agnihotra' etc. The *MS*. 1.1.2, has shown that of the Kārya denoted by the injunctive sentence, the Niyojya (the prompted person) is one who is desirous of acquiring for himself some desirable result in the form of heaven or some such thing which is thus related to the said Kārya. According to Prābhākara and his followers, the second sūtra of the *MS* (i.e., 'codanālakṣaṇorthaḥ dharmaḥ') what the injunctive sentence (Vidhi) denotes is Kārya. In his *Ṛjuvimalā* on the *Bṛhatī* also, Śālikanātha contends that as it is established that Kārya is denoted by the related, in the sentences like Agnihotraṁ juhuyāt svargakāmaḥ' (he who desires heaven should perform Agnihotra sacrifice) according to the contents of the sixth chapter of the *MS*, the word 'svargakāmaḥ' is stated as a Niyojya (prompted person) by the person who is svargakāmaḥ (i.e., he who desires heaven). A Niyojya (prompted person) is one who understands the Kārya as alloted to him.[238] In the *K* = (18) of the *VM*, the author has defined, 'Niyojya' and in that connection we will deal, at length, with Niyojya. Prabhākara calls this Kārya as Niyoga (prompting) because of the fact that it acts as an incentive to the Niyojya (prompted person) and makes him put forth efforts towards the action denoted by the verbal root contained in the

Injunctive word. But Śābara calls Kārya as Apūrva (unseen potency) by virtue of its being something new to all other pramāṇas (sources of valid knowledge) except the Injunctive sentence.[239] The Prābhākaras take Niyog (Prompting) Kārya and Āpūrva (unseen potency) in one sense. Literally, the word 'Niyoga' means a Kārya imposed on a person. It is called Apūrvakārya as it has been imposed by vedic Injunctive sentence and not by other agencies. Niyoga (prompting) is according to the Prābhākaras, the most important factor in an Injunctive sentence. Niyoga or Kārya of the Prābhākaras is expressed neither by the verbal root (dhātu) nor by the Injunctive suffix nor by any other word in the sentence, but it is expressed by the sentence as a whole. That the Niyoga (prompting) is expressed by the sentence is also proved by the fact that the general rule is that—that which is the principal thing made known by the sentence forms the denotation of the sentence. Detailed discussion on Niyoga has been made in the works like *Pūrvamīmāṁsā in its sources* and *Prābhākara Mīmāṁsā* of Dr. Ganganath Jha.

It may be mentioned here that while the Bhāṭṭas advance the theory called Bhāvanāvākyārthavāda, the Prābhākaras forward the theory called Niyogavākhyārthavāda. We have already discussed the Bhāvanāvākyārthavāda and now as we are stating about Niyoga, it will be proper to write some lines on the Niyogavākyārthavāda of the Prābhākaras.

The Niyogavākyārthavāda, it is said, was started by Bādari, an ancient Mīmāmsaka. According to Bādari, the Vedic injunctions, refer directly to sacrifices prescribed for the persons desiring heaven etc. He, therefore, differed from Jaimini who held that vedic injunctions refer to the sacrifices only as an instrument for attaining the heaven desired by persons.

The Niyogavākyārthavāda of Bādari was later on developed and improved by Prabhākara. Prabhākara says that 'Liṅ' indicates Kārya or Niyoga (prompting). The Niyojya (prompted person) is directed to function that Kārya or Niyoga (promting). continues to exist till the attainment of svarga (heaven) from the sacrifice (yāga).

It appears from the above that Bādari accepted sacrifices as Kārya, while Prābhākara held that Apūrva, a product of the sacrifice and the meanings of the 'Liṅs' are the Kārya to a svargakāma (one who desires heaven) and the Apūrva is not a momentary act like sacrifice (yāga). A Svargakāma, will, therefore, be attracted to perform this Kārya or Niyoga (prompting) as it will continue till the production of heaven (svarga) from sacrifice (yāga).[240]

Thus, according to Prabhākara, the vedic 'Lińs' denote, by their first denotative power the Kārya or Niyoga (prompting) which differs from sacrifice (yāga) and other actions merely due to the presence of words viz., svargakāma etc., in the same sentence. Niyoga is accepted as the meaning of 'Liń' because the sacrifice, being of short duration cannot be called Kārya for the persons desiring heaven (svarga) etc., which are obtained after a long period. This is not, however, the case in the non-vedic sentences wherein the suffixes 'Liń' etc., can denote the actions expressed by the principal roots as the Kārya to be performed.

It is agreeable that according to K.S. Ramaswami Sastri Siromoni, the Niyogavākyārthavāda of Prabhākara decidedly goes against the views of śabara and Kumārila.[241] According to the Prābhākaras, Kārya that is imposed by the vedic injunction (Vidhi) is called Dharma and this is nothing but the Niyoga which is imposed as a Kārya on the Niyojya (prompted person) through the vedic 'Liṇs'.[242]

In the *V* text above, we have a reference to the maxim 'Lohitoṣṇiṣanyāya'. Śabara under *MS. 3.8.12*,[243] states this 'Lohitoṣṇīṣanyāya' which is nothing but a Vidhi. It runs thus 'Lohitoṣṇīsāḥ rtvijāḥ pracaranti' (i.e., Here do the red-turbaned priest move). This Vidhi is found in context of the śyena-yāga.[244] Here in the Vidhi-vākya, the word 'Lohitoṣṇīsa' is to be understood as a viśesaṇa of the person and as a duty. The Vidhi authorises the Predication that the priests must wear red turbans in respect of those particular sacrifices.

A known thing or an accomplished fact indicated through the various cases (kāraka-padārtha) is incorporated into the predicative sense, when the two i.e., the subject and the predicate are stated together in a vākya. Whatever is not directly related to the predicate of a sentence, becomes obviously the invariable part of the predicate by the hypothesis, 'adagdhadahananyāya' (i.e., burning of what is unburnt). This is what is stated by the 'Lohitoṣṇīṣanyāya'. Ālamkārikas like Mammaṭa[245] make use of this 'Lohitoṣṇīṣanyāya'.

With the help of this maxim. Śālikanātha, in the *V* text above states that the word 'svargakāma' (a person desiring heaven) is understood as a viśeṣaṇa of the Kartā.

Maṇḍana Miśra, a staunch follower of the Bhāṭṭa system contends that though the words 'svarga' etc., are understood as the viśeṣaṇa of the person, still these are mainly concerned with the 'kāmanā' or the desire of the person doing sacrifice. To illustrate his idea, Maṇḍana cites the Vidhi-vākya, 'Lohitosṇīṣā rtvijaḥ pracaranti'. It is because, says Maṇḍana, in case of Bhāvanā, the bhāvya (i.e., that which is thought of or desired) is always required. Svarga etc., is also understood as a bhāvya because of its being desired by a person.[246]

Srimat Pratyaksvarupa Bhagavan in his *Navanaprasādinī*[247] commentary, very clearly explains the idea of the above *V* text of the *VM*. He states that the vākya 'svargakāmo yajeta' refers to the Niyojya and not to the result and this is what is wanted by Prabhākara.

In the *K* viz., 'niyojyassa ca . . .' etc., as stated, Śālikanātha defines Niyojya (prompted person). In our exposition of the preceding *V* text, we have already discussed Niyojya. One who understands the Kārya to be performed by oneself is called a Niyojya. This definition of Niyojya is also given by Pārthasārathi Miśra which is quite similar to that of Śālikanātha.[248] In some vedic injunctions, a svargakāma (one who desires heaven) is Niyojya as he understands that the Kārya is imposed on him or as he is directed to perform the Kārya. In case of the vedic injunctions, the Svargakāma cannot consider a Kārya as his own unless it has the power to produce the result desired by him.[249] He cannot take, therefore, the vedic sacrifice as his duty, because it does not last till the production of the result. The relation of such a Niyojya as svargakāma etc., in these injunctions makes it necessary to invent Niyoga otherwise known as Apūrva (unseen potency) as his duty.

The above definition of Niyojya is also stated by Śālikanātha almost in the same manner in his commentary called *Ṛjuvimalā*[250] on the *Bṛhatī* of Prabhākara.

Following Śālikanātha, the author of the *Tantrarahasya* also defines Niyojya in a similar manner.[251] For example, in the expressions like 'puṣṭikāmaḥ kṣīraṁ pivet' etc., (one who desires to be fat should drink milk), a puṣṭikāmaḥ (one who desires to be fat) makes the relation by way of his understanding that 'I should drink milk'.

It can be mentioned here that Niyojya is the most important person as without him a Niyoga cannot be a true Niyoga. Dr. Ganganath Jha, in his *Prābhākara-Mīmāṁsā*, has very intelligently discussed Niyoga and Niyojya,[252]

Śālikanātha defines Niyoga in *K* (26) of the *VM* which, we shall discuss in course of our exposition of the corresponding *K* text.

In the second half of the *K* (18) above, the author of the *VM* states that svarga etc., in expressions like 'Agnihotraṁ juhuyāt svargakāmaḥ' is understood as the sādhya (to be brought about) because of its being desired by the kartā (person). In all sacrifices, kāmanā (desire) becomes the object which is to be brought about and svarga etc., which is the sādhya (which is to be brought about) due to its being related to kāmanā (desire) prompts a person to action. Svarga etc., prompts a person to actions because of being desired by him.

The definition of Niyojya given by Śālikanātha has been criticised and refuted by the vedāntins like Citsukhācārya, Citsukha while refuting Niyojya of Śālikanātha puts a question as to whether Niyojya is secondary (gauṇa) to kārya or the primary (i.e., the enjoyer of the result) to it ? If it is said to be secondary, then it will be related to the kriyā by reason of being the agent. For, the relation of the kartā arises only through the kriyā and as such how is it possible that kārya which is other than the kriyā gets it related through the Kartā ? If again it is said that Niyojya is the primary to Niyoga or Kārya. then it can be included in Adhikārī by which also Kārya which is different from kriyā cannot be brought about and no third type other than the guṇa and pradhāna is not possible. The deflnition of Niyojya is not proper as the prompted person must be either gauṇa or pradhāna. Again if it is said that the state of being the secondary is the agent of the Kārya which is nothing but the kriyā and the same is the Niyojya of the Kārya which is different from the kriyā, then it has no justification. For, when the Kārya as different from the kriyā is made out, then the relation of

Niyojya cannot be made out and vice versa. Thus it will involve the fallacy of logical see-saw (anyonyāśraya).[253]

In 'sādhyantaparyanta . . .' etc., of the *K* and 'atra kaścidāha . . .' etc., of the *V* text, Śālikanātha presents the view of Maṇḍana Miśra and then the author rejects the same. According to Maṇḍana, although because of its being desirable, the heaven etc , is to be brought about (i.e., to be made out), yet there is no proof in respect of the kriyā as stated by the Vidhi, as being the Sādhya (i.e., to be brought about). It is because there is no such rule that the object which is desired has necessarily a means. A man whose mind is stolen away by desire, for him there is not a single object which is not desired by him.[254] But all his desires have no means for their attainment. It is for this reason that someone may be desirous of being ommscient, but it is not possible for having a means of obtaining the omniscience. Thus he who desires omniscience has no agenthood in respect of the attaining the state of being the omniscient. It is because of the fact that the persons desirous of going to the village are seen engaged in unanticipated actions. As for instance, 'grāmaṁ gacchan tṛṇaṁ spṛśati' (one going to the village, touches the grass). Here, footing on the grass is an unanticipated action, because the intention of the person is to go to the village and not to touch or to give steps on the grass. Thus in the view of Maṇḍana Miśra, there is proof in respect of the knowledge regarding the bringing about of the Kārya.

But this view of Maṇḍana is not acceptable to Śālikanātha. In 'atrocyate . . .' etc. of the *V* text above, Śālikanātha rejects the view of Maṇḍana Miśra. Śālikanātha opines that a person desirous of heaven etc., is prepared to admit that cbject in the form of Kārya, which (object) is conducive for the accomplishment of the desired object. If it is not admitted then a person desirous of something will not understand that desired object as his Kārya. That which is the Kārya of the person desirous of something is the means of the desired object. Thus Śālikanātha refutes the view of Maṇḍana.

In the *K* text ziz., 'liṅādistatra . . .' etc., Śālikanātha states the result that may arise in respect of admitting the Liṅs etc., as the Kārya. Śālikanātha contends that if the Liṅs etc., are admitted as the Kārya then the Kārya will convey the Kriyā which is, according to the Prābhākaras, different from the Kārya. Śālikanātha in *K* (25) of the *VM II*, states that the Kriyā is different from the Kārya. It is stated in the *K* = above, under discussion that if the Kārya conveys the Kriyā then the unity of the Kārya with the Niyojya will be lost i.e., it will be impossible to maintaln the unity between the Kārya and the Niyojya. We have already discussed the relation between the Kārya and the Niyojya.

In 'kriyā hi . . .' etc., and 'kāryavirodhi . . .' etc., of the *Ks* and the *V* text, Śālikanātha explains how the Kriyā is not capable of producing the desired result and how it cannot make relation with the Niyojya. It is stated in the *K* above that the Kriyā is momentary (i.e., it perishes immediately after being performed) and the phala in the shape of heaven etc., is to take place at a subsequent period and as such the Kriyā cannot bring about the desired object. Thus the Kriyā because of its not being the producer of the desired object cannot be the Kārya and as such it cannot be related to the Nfyojya who is desirous of getting for himself a result in the shape of heaven etc. We have already stated that whichever is a Kārya is, in the view of the Prābhākaras, worthy of being related to the Niyojya.

In the *V* text, the author states that the Karma (i.e., the Kriyā) is opposed to the Kārya. It is because the Kriyā perishes after conncting the later stage and the heaven the desired object is enjoyable in a different place at a different time and as such there can be no relation between the two (i.e., the Kriya and the Phala).

In 'nanu prītimātravacanassvarga . . .' etc., of the *V* text, the author presents the view of Meṇḍana Miśra who in his work *Bhāvanāvīveka*, states that the heaven denotes satisfaction and also asserts that his view seeks support from the Bhāsya of Śabara. Śabara under *MS. 6.1.5.*[255] states that the word heaven stands only for a form of satisfaction and it is only in its secondsry figurative sense that it is applied to the thing or substance that produces satisfaction (prīti). As a matter of fact, people always describe heaven in the sense of satisfaction or happiness. Maṇḍana Miśra in his work *Bhāvanāviveka* has discussed the present issue under discussion at length. According to Maṇḍana, the word 'svarga' is used in the sense of only the prīti (satisfaction) and this is, he says, what is stated in the beginning of the sixth

Adhyāya of *Mīmāṁsā—sūtra*. The word 'svarga' is used, says Maṇḍana, in respect of the substances that can bring satisfaction to a person.

It may be pointed out here that according to Maṇḍana, because of the object thought of being desired, the words svarga-kāma etc., are bent on the word svarga. The state of the viśesaṇa (qualification) being the principal is shown in respect of the words 'Daṇḍī' (one having a stick) etc.[256]

In 'ucyate, na prītimātravaeanatayā . . .' etc., Śālikanātha rejects the view of Maṇḍana Miśra who contends that the words Svarga etc. denote only satisfaction. But Śālikanatha contends that the word 'svarga' is not used in respect of the sacrifice viz., 'Jyotiṣṭoma' as denoting only the satisfaction. According to Śālikanātha, even in the case of Arthavādas (i.e., the corroborative statements), we find that there is the satisfaction attained from the desired object devoid of pain and which is enjoyable forever. It is also stated in the *V* text above that the Kriyā, because of its being perishable immediately after its performance, connot be the means of producing result. Because it is a popular belief that whatever is performed in the presence of which becomes its means. Thus the Kriyā connot make any relation as being the performable with the Niyojya who is desirous of (obtaining) heaven. It is because the Kriyā is not the means of obtaining the heaven.

It may be added that Śabara and Kumārila state that the persons can only be inclined to do any action owing to its beneficial effects and no injunction or the knowledge of Kārya as the Prābhākaras contend, can actuate any person to undertake the action. It is also stated that whatever is the object of satisfaction is that to be brought about.[257] According to Śabara and Kumārila, the words svargakāma, etc. denote only svarga as important and other things are as subordinate to it. But Śālikanātha contends that according to the Prābhākaras the Kārya is the important and svargakāma is subordinate to it.

In 'tasmanniyojyasambandha—samartham . . .' etc. and 'nanu kriyaiva kāryatayocyatām, . . .' etc. of the *K* and *V* text respectively as stated above, Śālikanāthatha asserts that Kārya which is capable of making the relation with the Niyojya and which lasts for long, is different from the Kriyā. Thereby he rejects the objection that the Kriyā may be called as the Kārya. According to the objection, the Kriyā is capable of being the means of bringing about the desired result and as such the Kriyā can be related to the Kārya and the Kriyā is not prrishable within a moment. But Śāḷikanātha does not accept this view and he also discards another objection that the power of the Kriyā or Karma lasts long. According to Śālikanātha it cannot be admitted so. Because it will be contradictory to the source of valid knowledge. Whatever is uncontradictory is capable of being assumed for the bringing about of the known object and as the Kriyā is perishable within a moment, so its power also cannot last long. That the kārya is different from the kriyā is slso stated by Śālikanātha in *K* (25) which we shall find in the subsequent pages. The word 'Vidhi vācibhih' in the *K* above is used by Rāmāriuja as 'Vidhivādibhi' which Seems to be appropriate.[258] in the *V* text Śālilikanātha rejects the view of Kumārila who contends that having a power is lost the power belonging to it is also lost and it is established by the source of valid knowledge. Therefore, the power that belongs to the Kārya, says Kumārila, cannot be imagined as lasting forever. Moreover, he says that without the Āśraya, the Āśrayī cannot exist. According to Śālikanātha this power cannot resort to the self as Kumārila argues. Because, a power belonging to one object cannot exist in another, for, it will be contradictory to the source of valid knowledge. Again, when there is not the object having power, the power without its object, the very substratum, cannot produce result. Otherwise, the result will be obtained without a means. As we know, that which has power or capacity is the means and not the power alone. Same is the case with the Kārya also. The Kārya which is also the substratum of its power, lasts forever. Thus Śālikanātha asserts that without the Kārya, its power cannot bring about the result.

Īn 'nanu yāgādikriyā . . .' etc· of the *V* text Śālikanātha presents a pūrvapakṣa according to which the actions like yāga etc. can be accepted as the Kārya and not as different from it. In support of their view, the advocates of the pūrvapakṣa, contend that the yāgas etc. are the means of worshipping the deities. They also contend that the action viz., yāga etc. can produce the result in future. The deities are worshipped by actions because of their being capable of bringing about the result to the sacrificer. The deities when worshipped become pleased with the sacrificer and in return bring the award in the form of heaven etc. to the sacrificer. Of course, not simultaneously with the performance of the action but at a subsequent period.

It may be added here that from the injunctions viz., 'jyotiṣṭomena svargakāmo yajeta' (i.e., one who desires heaven should perform the Jyotiṣṭoma sacrifice) etc., the bringing about of the heaven of the Jyotiṣṭoma sacrifice is understood. But there is divergent opinion among the philosophers. Maṇḍana Miśra who accepts the iṣṭasādhanatā as the vākyārtha, contends that the relation of that to be brought about and that brings about the heaven and the sacrifice is the primary sense. According to Pārthasārathi Miśra, there is no relation of the sādhya and the sādhana of the heaven and the sacrifice. But according to the Prābhākaras the relation of the sādhya and the sādhana of the heaven and the sacrifice is not understood from the verbal testimony but from the upādāna (i.e., the necessary requirement of an injunctions.[259]

Thus Śālikanātha in the *V* text presents the view of the opponents that yāga etc. can be called the Kārya.

In 'naitadevam, yāgādīnām . . .' etc. of the *V* text Śālikanātha refutes the view that the action like sacrifices because of their being the means of worshipping the deities, can be called the Kārya. According of Śālikanātha, this view of the opponents cannot stand to reason as there is no pramāṇa in respect of the sacrifices as being the means of worshipping the deities. Also there is no pramāṇa in respect of the sacrifice as being the means of worshipping the deities. It is known to us that it is accepted by most of the Mīmāṃsakas that the sacrifices are the means of producing results. It may be urged here that the verbal root 'yaj' is recollected in the sense of worshipping the deities and it is also known that all sorts of sacrifices are meant for the worshipping of one who is worthy of being worshipped. But Śālikanātha argues that whichever is the recollection, is not a pramāṇa because of its being recollected and also because, the recollection describes only the objects of the pramāṇas which the recollection follows. Again by no other pramāṇa it is known that the sacrifices are the means of worshipping the delties. And a sacrifice is nothing but the oflering of the materials to the deities. Thus, according to Śālikanātha, the worshipping of the deities is to be understood as secondary. This is also stated by Śabara in his Bhāṣya'[260]

In the *V* text above, Śālikanātha makes a reference to the Devatādhikaraṇa (Ms. 9.1.4.) and states that in that Adhikaraṇa it is shown that the Kārya which is to be effected cannot be held to lead to result through the worshipping of the deities to whom the sacrifice is offered.

Thus Śālikanātha rejects the view that the Kriyā because of its being the means of worshipping the deities, can be called Kārya.

In 'athā'pi syāt puruṣasaṁskārahetubhūtaiva . . .' etc. of the *V* text Śāiikanātha rejects another view that the Kriyā being the cause of the purification of the person (i.e., the sacrificer) is called the Kārya. According to this view again, the Kriyā is related to the person who is desirous of (obtaining) heaven etc. and as such from the saṁskāra of the person, the Kriyā can produce the result at a susequent period. The word 'puruṣa' in the *V* text refers to yajamāna (i.e., the sacrificer). Śālikanātha as an advocate of the Kāryavākyārthavāda. does not accept this view. It is because he says, there is no proof regarding the purification of the person. In support of his assertion, Śālikanātha quotes a sūtra in half. from the Mīmāṁsā-sūtra, viz., MS. 11.1.20.[261] Under this sūtra, Śabara, in his Bhāṣya, it is said, contends that the sacrifices etc. are not the causes of purifying the sacrificers. From no other pramāṇa or from the śāstra it can be ascertained that the sacrifices etc. have the state of being the means of purification of the persons, Hence, the actions viz., the sacrificcs etc. cannot be called the Kārya. In the view of the Prābhākaras, the Kārya is different from the Kriyā. We have already found in *K*(23) of the *VM*, that the Kārya is different from the Kriyā and again in *K*(25) of the present chapter of the *VM*, we shall find that the Kārya is stated to be different from the Kriyā.

It may be mentioned here that Rāmānujācārya also takes the present issue under discussion in a simpler way.[262]

Thus Śālikanātha refutes the view that the Kriyā purifies the sacrificer and is the Kārya.

In the *V* text viz., 'nanu kriyaiva kāryatayocyatām . . .' of the *VM*, the author presents an objectin according to which, the Kārya shoul not be stated to be dented by the suffixes Liṅs etc. and then the author rejcts the objection. According to the objection the Kriyā is, indeed, the Kārya and the substratnm of the phalasādhanatā (i.e., the achievability of the desired object). And in the case of the non-attainment of the desired object otherwise, somelhing other produced the Kriyā as conducive for the production of the result may be assumed and something ever remains and resorts to the Ātman. Thus according to the objection, the Liṅs etc. do not denote the Kārya. But Śālikanātha as a follower of the Prābhākara school, does not accept this view and as such with the *V* text viz., 'ucyate-taddhi tadanupapttyā kalpyate . . . etc. as stated above, discards the objection. We have already stated in several occasions that Śālikanātha contends that the Liṅs etc. denote Kārya and that Kārya is capable of bringing about the desired result, According to Śālikanātha, by means of something produced by the Kriyā, the Kriyā comes to be capable of producing the phalasādhanatā. It is because, in that case there will be two sādhanas (means)—one is the Kriyā and the other is that which is produced by the Kriyā and which will lead to the final result. But it cannot be said so, because a means of a means cannot be the means. So, the Kriyā, says Śālikanātha, cannot be a means of bringing about the desired object but the Kārya which ever remains. Again that Kārya is denoted by the suffixes Liṅs etc. and thus the Kārya can make a relation with the Niyojya. The last line of the *V* text viz., 'niyojyasambandhasamartham . . .' etc. as stated above, is not a quotation from some other work but is the repetition of the text of the *K*(23) with slight difference.

It may be added here that the present issue under discussion has also been taken up by Rāmānujācārya in an easier way.[263]

In the *V* text viz., 'atraisā prakriyā . . .' etc., the author gives a short account of the meaning of some of the Adhikaraṇas of the *MS* in the light of the explanation of Prabhākara. This better be said a summary of what has been stated by Śālikanātha in the preceding pages· In the Codanāsūtra viz., 'codanā lakṣaṇo'rtha dharmaḥ (MS. 1.1,2), it has been shown that what the Vidhi denotes is the Kārya. According to the Prābhākaras, by this sūtra it is taught that the meaning of the Veda is the Kārya and not something that is already known. The word 'codanālakṣaṇa' in the sūtra means Kārya and the word 'dharma' means vedārtha (vedic import).[264] Thus Prabhākara is of the view that the codanāsūtra is meant to establish the validity of those vedic passages which express only Kārya. The Bhāṣya passage of Śabara. however, explaining the word 'Artha' in the sūtra is not favourable to the view of Prabhākara. The Bhāṣyakāra states that 'artha' means useful and 'anartha' means harmful. This kind of Dharma and Adharma should be learnt only from the vedic codanā.[264] Thus the Bhāṣya goes against the view of Prabhākara who takes the word 'Artha' in the sūtra to mean only the vedārtha (vedic import). But Prabhākara and Śālikanātha changed the meaning of the Bhāṣya passage very skilfully in order to secure support for their views.[266]

According to Kumārila, however, it is the knowledge of Dharma and not vedārthavicāra that is considered to be the supreme goal. He, therefore, tried to establish that each Dharma based on vedic Injunctions confers a result and reforms of this kind were introduced by him.[266].

In the vṛtti text above, Śālikanātha states that in the beginning of the sixth adhyāya of the *MS.* 6.1.1 viz., 'dravyāṇāṁ karmasaṁyoge guṇatvenābhisambandhah', it is shown that of this Kāryā denoted by the Injunctive sentence, the Niyojya (the prompted person) is one who is desirous of acquiring for himself some desired result in the form of svarga (heaven) etc. which is thus related to the said Kārya. etc The beginning of the sixth Adhyāya is called the 'svargādiphalasādhanatādhikraṇa' which consists of three sūtras including the first one stated above. The other two sūtras are—'asādhakaṁ tu tādarthyāt' (6.1.2) and 'prītyarthaṁ cābhisaṁyogāt karmato hyabhisambandhah tasmāt karmopadeśaḥ syāt' (6.1.3). Again in the beginning of the eleventh Adhyāya of the *MS.* 11.1.1. viz., 'prayojanābhisambandhāt pṛthaksatāṁ tataḥ sayādaikakarmyameka śabdābhisamyogāt', the name of the Adhikaraṇa of which is 'tantreṇa svargaphalatvam', it is stated that desire for svarga (heaven) etc. is the attribute of the Niyojya (prompted person). It has already been stated by Śālikanātha in *K*(17).

In the Bādaryādhikaraṇa which consists of four sūtras viz., 'dravyguṇasaṁskāreṣu Bādhariḥ' (3.1.3); 'kārmāṇyapi Jaiminiḥ, phalārthatvāt' (3.1.4); 'phalṁ ca puruṣārthavāt' (3.1.5); and 'puruṣaśca karmārthatvāt' (3.1 6) of the *MS.* it has been concluded that it is the Kārya which is the direct cause of producing the desired object of the Niyojya (prompted person) and which qualifies the Niyojya. That Kārya again cannot be the Kriyā for the Kriyā is not capable of producing the desired result. Bādari is of the opinion that vedic and non-vedic injunctions indicate only Kārya to be performed by mankind and exery one who is a functionary to that Kārya should undertake that without questioning its authority and without any idea of the desired result to be achieved. Bādari contends that vedic injunctions verbally do not indicate yāgas as the means of acquiring svarga etc. Even in non-vedic injunctions, says Bādari, knowledge of Kārya alone induces a man to perform the Kārya but not its desired result. But this view of Bādari was criticised by Kumārila on the lines of Jaimini and Śabara who have stated under *MS* 3.1.4-6[268] and 6.1.2[269] that vedic and non-vedic Indjunctions actuate persons by showing the desired results such as svarga etc.

The Bhāṣya in the Devatādhikaraṇa consisting of five sūtras namely 'Devatā vā prayojyedatithivat' (9.1.6); bhojanasya tadarthatvāt' (9.1.7); 'arthāpatyācca' (9.1.8); 'tataśca tena sambandhaḥ' (9.1.9); 'atithau tatpradhānatvamabāvaḥ karmāṇi syāt' tasya prītipradhānatvāt' (9.1.10) of the *MS*.. has stated that the Kārya is not the Kriyā as it can never be the direct cause of the desired result nor can it be held to produce the result through the favour of the Deity to whom the yāga is performed. In the sūtra viz., 'karmaṇyārambhabhāvyatvāt kṛṣivat pratyārambhaṁ phalāni syuḥ' (MS. 11.1.4), it is stated by Śabara that Kriyā cannot be regarded as leading to the result through the potency of the person.

In the Apūrvādhikaraṇa, the sūtra wherein is 'condanā punarāmbhaḥ' (MS, 2.1.5), it has finally been stated that Kārya is that which is denoted by the Injunctive sentence. It has been also said there that either the Kriyā itself or some potency inhering therein does not continue for a longer period to bring about the desired result. This Kārya is called Apūrva (unseen potency) by virtue of its being not known by any other means of knowledge (pramāṇa). Śālikanātha explains Apūrva in *K*(25) of the *VM*, which we will fiad in course of our exposition of the second pariccheda of the *VM*. The Kārya has been called Apūrva by reason of its being something new to all other means of valid knowledge except the Injunctive sentence.

It may be pointed out here that the Prābhākaras held that Kārya or Niyoga or Apūrva is the meaning of the vedic Liṅs' and this is because of their being concerned with the vedārtha (vedic import)?[270] and not with Dharma which is the concern of the Bhāṭṭas. Kumārila[271] rejects the view of the Prābhākaras as regards Apūrva on the ground that such an Apūrva is not known by anybody as Dharma as no one can see it. That the Kārya is something brought by kṛti (effort) and krti (effort) is the physical effort of the persons, has been stated and explained by Śālikanātha many times in the *VM*.

In the Bhāvārthādhikaraṇa which includes four sūtras viz., 'bhāvārthāḥ karmaśabdāstevyaḥ kriyā pratīyetaiṣā hyartho vidhīyate' (2.1.1); 'sarveṣāṁ bhāvo' rtha iti cet' (2.1.2); 'yeṣāmu-ipattu sve prayoge rupopalabddhistāmi nāmāni, tasmāttebhya parākāṅkṣā bhūtatvāt sve prayoge' (2.1.3); 'yeṣāṃ tūtpattāvarthe sve prayogo na vidyate, tānyākhyātāni. tasmāttebhyaḥ pratīyetāśri-tatvāt prayogasyā' (2:1,4) of the *MS*, it is stated that the prayatna (exertion) is not possible independently of some act denoted by the verbal root. Thus what the Injuctive sentence denotes is the Niyoga (prompting) relating to that act. Śbara under *MS*. 2.1.1 says that Kriyā is understood from the words denoting Karma viz, the meaning of the Kriyā is Karma. For example, yajeta etc. from this Kriyā, one should know that sacrifice is to be performed and Kriyā is the means of attaining the desired result.[272]

Moreover, in the śabdāntarādhikaraṇa the sūtra wherein is 'śabdāntare karmabhedaḥ kṛtānubandhatvāt' (2.2.1) of the *MS*, it is stated that Karma being the object of the prompting (Niyoga) is denoted by the verbal root. Thus the act being the object of the Niyoga (prompting) comes to be known as the Karna (means) by which the Niyoga (prompting) is accomplished. This has been stated in the Bādaryādhikaraṇa of the *MS* and is also stated by Mādhavācārya in his *Nyāyamālāvistara*.[273]

Śabara under sūtra 2.2.1[274] states that the Kriyā padas viz., yajati, juhoti etc in the Injunctive sentences like 'somena yajeta', 'dakṣiṇāni juhoti' etc. denote the joint-performance.

Thus, Śālikanātha has given a summary of some of the Adhikaraṇs of the *MS* as conceived by the Prābhākaras.

'In the *K* text viz , 'taddhi kālāntarasthānācchaktam . . .' etc. Śālikanātha states how the Kārya which remains ever can have the relation with the Niyojya. Here, he repeats what has been stated by him in *K*(23). But here in the *K* text above, the author adds that Kārya is also capable of bringing about the heaven etc.

which is the desired object. It is stated that the Kārya continues to exist till the production of the heaven etc. from the yāga and as such it is called Kālāntarasthāyi. This is stated by Śālikanātha in his *Ṛjuvimalā*.[275] In *V* text under *K*(23), Śālikanātha contends that the Kārya which is different from the Kriyā and which continues to exist till the attainment of the svarga etc. is related to the Niyojya.[276]

The word 'kāminā' in the *K* above is the attribute of the Niyojya. We have already stated that in the beginning of the sixth chapter of the *Mīmāṁsā-sūtra*, it has been shown that the Niyojya is one who is desirous of acquiring for himself some desired result in the form of heaven etc. As we have already discussed the present issue in our exposition of the *V* text under *K*(23), so we refrain form explaining the same at length.

'In 'kriyādibhinnaṁ yatkāryam . . .' etc. of the *K* text Śālikanātha contends that the Kārya is otherwise also known as the Apūrva. We have already stated that Kārya because of its being not known by any other source of knowlegge such as pratykṣa etc., is called Apūrva. In *K*(23) we have found that the author states that the Kārya is different from the Kriyā and as such the word 'kriyādibhinnam' in the *K* above bears the same sense of the words viz , 'kariyāto bhinnam' as stated in *K*(23) of the *VM*. It can, therefore, be said that the present *K* text above, which is our concern, is partly a repetition of the *K*(23) of the *VM*. The text above, is introduced by Śālikanātha in order to discard the objection raised by the Bāṭṭas who want to contend that in view of the Bhāṣyakāra Śabara, Kārya is not different from the Kriyā and the meanings of the 'Liṅs' etc' are kṛti or prayatna. We have already explained that Kārya or Apūrva of the Prābhākara school which identifies it with the meaning of the suffix 'Liṅs' is different from that of the Bhāṭṭas who accept yāga as Dharma and accept Apūrva as the connecting link between the two viz., yāga and svarga. It has also been stated by us that in the Apūrvādhikaraṇa of the *Mīmāṁsā-sūtra*, Śabara calls Kārya as Apūrva by reason of its being something new to all other means of knowledge. Śālikanātha also gives the same name.[278] Of course, he has given one more name to it viz., Niyoga. We have already discussed Kriyā, Kārya or Apūrva in context of our exposition of the corresponding vṛtti text of the *VM*.

Śālikanātha did not write any vṛtti on the *K* above perhaps, in order to avoid repetiting what has been stated in preceding *V* text.

In 'kāryatvena niyojyañca. . .' etc, of the *K*, the author rejects an objection that the Niyoga cannot be the vākyārtha and he also asserts that according to the view of the prābhākaras, the Niyoga is also another synonym of Kārya. We have already mentioned that in the view of the Prābhākaras, Apūrva, Kārya and Niyoga are sononymous. Hence, Niyoga is the vākyārtha.

The *K* above is also quoted in the *Nayanaprasādinī* commentary of the *Citsukhī*, but instead of the word 'Niyojyañca', it is used as 'Niyojyaṁ yaḥ'.[277] Dr. Ganganath Jha says in his work viz., *The Prābhākara School of Pūrvamīmāṁsā* that Kārya is called Niyoga or prompting, by reason of the fact that it acts as an incentive to the Niyojya (promoted person) and makes him put forth an exertion towards the accomplishment of the action denoted by the verbal root. What the sentence as a whole expresses is this Niyoga as related to the Niyoiya expressed by one of the words in the sentence. From this, it can easily be understood that Niyoga is the import of the sentence.

It may be mentioned that Kārya is two-fold. One is Kriyā and the other is Niyoga which is other than Kriyā. The agency of the first belongs to the Kārtā and that of the other belongs to the Niyojya and both are secondary and such is the difference between Kartṛtva and Niyojyatva.[279] Śālikanātha mentions the word 'Niyoga'in the *K* above stating that it is identified as the Kārya. As Śālikanātha has already explained Kārya several times in the *VM*, he finds it unnecessary here to explain the same and as such he did write no sentence in the form of vṛtti under the *K* above.

In 'kāryasyaiva pradhānatvād . . .' etc. and 'uktaṁ hyetat. . .' etc , of the *K* and *V* text respectively, Śālikanātha asserts that it is the kārya and kārya alone that is the Vākyārtha. It is stated in the *K* and *V* text alove text whatever is the Pradhāna is the vākyārtha and the Kārya by virtue of its being the Pradhāna comes to be the Vakyārtha. That the Kārya is the Pradhāna is stated by Śālikanātha in *K*(13) viz., 'kṛtisādhyaṁ pradhānaṁ yat tat kāryamucyate' of the present section of the *Vākyārthamātṛkā*. In several occasions in our exposition, we have stated that the

Prābhākaras, as the adherents of the Kāryavākyārthavāda or the Niyogavākārthavāda, accept the Kārya or the Niyoga as the Vākyārtha.

The insertion of the emphatic particle 'eva' after the word 'Kārya' in the *K* text above, implies that it is only the Kārya and not anything that can be called as denoting the vākyārtha.

As we know Śālikanātha Miśra[280] in his *Ṛjuvimalā* states that the Niyoga is the important thing in every sentence and it is also known as Kārya. All other words in the sentence are understood to convey their meanings as related to the principal element i.e., Kārya. The connecting link in respect of each padārtha constitutes the vakyārtha and each word has the power to express its meaning and its relation with a Kārya. The Prābhākaras, as the Anvitābhidhānavādins, urge that the words alone in a vākya are capable of conveying the vākyārtha which is nothing but the relation of each padārtha with the Kārya.

Kumārila, however, maintains that there is no difference between the sentences of the Vedas and outside them in respect of conveying their meanings. Moreover, there exists no difference between the sentences intended to convey either injunctions for actions or simply accomplished facts. In all these sentences, the words denote only their meanings. There is, he says, no Niyoga or Kārya expressed by the suffixes 'Liṅs' etc. either in the vedic sentences or those outside the vedic sentedces.

In the *K* text the author also contends that the vākya denotes that which is related to the Niyojya and it is the Kārya that is related to the Niyojya and as such Kārya is the vākyārtha.

In the *V* text viz., 'niojyānvitābhidhāñaca prāyikam. . .' etc. Śālikanātha contends that the Anvitābhidhāna from the Niyojya is usual. The word 'prāyikam' in the *V* text is used for this reason. That the Niyojyānvitābhidhāna is usual is because of the fact that the denotation of the Niyogas relating to the production of Ādhāna (leading of fire), Adhyayana (study), Aṅga (subsidiary) and Pradhāna (principal) sacrifices, is admitted as occurring without the Niyojya. The author of the *Vivaraṇa* admits another Niyoga relating to the Ādhāna, because of not recollecting the Niyoga with regard to kratu. It may be mentioned here that Prabhākara Miśra because of his writing the *Vivaraṇa* is known as vivaraṇakāra and the *Vivaraṇa* is another name of the commentary called *Laghvī*,[281] Kratu is a sacrifice relating to Agni so by 'Āgneya' one understands kratu.[282] It is also stated in the *V* text that there can be no recognition of the Niyoga by means of the fire related to the kratu which is inconsistent as in the case of the palāśa branch. It is because there can be no knowledge of the words like Āhavanīya etc., prior to the knowledge of the Ādhāna, because of its relation with the kratu being not known.

By the use of the word 'ādi' after Āhavanīya in the *V* text above, the other two types of Agni viz., 'Gārhapatyāgni' and 'Dākṣināgni' are to be understood. It may be added that in the vedas three types of Agni are admitted.[283] But in the case of the Juhu (vessel) etc. because of its denoting the Ākṛti (configuration), there is the recognition of the Niyoga prior to the knowledge of the Vidhi.

In the *V* text above. we find the mention of the word parṇatā' which is to be taken as the parṇatāvidhi. It is also a maxim that indicates the invariable presence of something. For example, the Juhu or branch of palāśa tree which is used in all sacrifices. Śabara under MS. 3.6.1.[284] deals with the parṇatā Vidhi and the maxim i.e., parṇamayī-nyāya. It can be added here that the Juhu etc. is invariably related to the kratu. Śālikanātha in the first section of the Aṅgapārāyaṇa-prakaraṇa of his *Prakaraṇṇa-pañcikā*, deals with the issue of Parṇatāvidhi.[284]

In the *V* text again, the author rejects an objection that because of the fires being the object to be brought about, how the two can be related in a single Vākya. The 'sādhyadvaya' referred to in the *V* text above, refers to Agni and Niyoga. As the Prabhakaras accept Niyoga as the vākyārtha, how can they accept Agni as being the Sādhya which is also to be taken as the vākyārtha ? In order to meet this objection, Śālikanātha asserts that Niyoga is the principal object to be brought about, for, it is the most desirable object and the fire is the undesirable object. In this way, Śālikanātha contends that the Niyojyānvitābhidhāna is not consistent.

Moreover, in the *V* text above, *Ś*ālikaṇātha asserts that there can be Anvitābhidhāna even without the Niyojya. As for instance, he refers to Ācāryakaraṇavidhi. It may be mentioned here that Prabhākara maintains that the vedic injunction 'svādhyayāyo' dhyetavyaḥ' which literelly means 'ones' own branch of the veda should be studied', does not express a complete injunctions; for, no specific Adhikārin is mentioned here for the injunction intended.[286] It does indicate whether the person is Arthajñānakāma, or svargakāma, or desirous of anything else. Prabhākara observes that Adhyayana is to be done only by means of that Vidhi which is complete with the Adhikārin who is Ācāryakāma. He also maintintains that students should learn the Vedas in order to comply with the Adhyāpana Niyoga prescribed for the Ācāryas, and the compliance with that Niyoga is alone the sole object of Adhyāyanavidhi. Thus, in the *V* text above, Śālikanātha asserts that the denotation of the Niyojya is possible because of attaining the performance by means of applying the injunction regarding the Ācāryakarṇa in respect of the Adhyāyanavidhi viz., 'svādhyāyo' dhyetanyaḥ'.

In the *V* text viz., 'aṅgotpattiniyogā api . . .' etc., Śālikanātha presents someones query that there is other Niyoga in respect of the prayāja Vidhi etc. and then he meets the same. The query is—how the prayāja Vidhi etc. are the objects of being applied ? The inclusion of the word 'ādi' in 'prayājādi' etc. in the *V* text refers to Anuyāja and Ājyabhāga also. It may be said here that the Vidhis viz,, prayāja etc. are Aṅgavidhis. In reply to the query stated in the *V* text, Śālikanātha states that the Vidhis viz., prayāja etc. are used in proximity with the Niyoga along with the right and they do not give rise to the knowledge of other Niyoga relating to their own. It is because like the act of thereṣhing (Avaghāta), the Vidhis have the state of being the Anuvādaka (restatement). We have already explained Anuvāda. Avaghāta (i.e., the act of threshing) is the example of the Niyamavidhi (i.e., the restricted injunction).[287]

In the *V* text above, we find Śālikanātha referring to the issue of Grāhakagrahaṇa. Grāhakagrahaṇa is the considering of one as a Grāhaka. To explain—the principal duty which is denoted by the suffix Liṅ and which is imposed on a functionary in the main sentence is what is called Grāhaka because of its including or considering all to the meanings indicated by that sentence and also by other sentences in the same chapter as subordinated to and connected with itself. In this way, the subsidiaries included by a Grāhaka are of two types. These subsidiaries viz., prayāja etc. are prescribed in the same chapter with the help of separate sentences with separate suffixes viz., Liṅs etc. The Liṅs in these sentences do not indicate a different Niyoga from that of the principal injunctive sentence, but they are taken to express the Grāhaka only. This is what is stated by Śālikanātha in the *V* text above.[288] This Grāhakagrahaṇa is stated at the beginning of the chapter of the *Mīmāṁsā-sūtra*. The theory of Anvitābhibhāna is also known as Grāhakagrahaṇa.[289]

In the *V* text again, Śālikanātha refers to the upādāna of the Mīmāṁsakas. According to the Mīmāṁsakas, upādāna is accepted as the seventh Pramāṇa or the means of knowledge to determine the subsidiaries. The subsidiaries called Sannipattya are not known as subsidiaries to the principal sacrifice by any other means other than Upādāna, because they are performed in order to complete the principal sacyifice.[290] Upādāna[291] is, according to the Prābhākaras, nothing but the necessary requirement of an injunction.

In the *V* text viz., 'nāsti tarhi prayṣjādiṣu . . .' etc., the author presents a doubt that may arise and then meets the same. The doubt is—is there no other Niyoga in respect of the Prayāja etc.? Śālikanātha asserts that in respect of the Prayāja etc., another Niyoga is to be admitted. It is because, says Śālikanātha, all actions viz., Prayāja etc., are momentary and so, without a separate Niyoga, there will be no obtainment of the utility of the means together. The suffixes Liṅs etc., denotes the other Niyoga and as such like the act of threshing (Avaghāta), there will be no denotation of the meaning as related to the Niyoga relating to the Adhikāra known from the words viz., 'yajati' (one performs) in the subsidiary sentences. The act of threshing (i.e., Avaghāta) can be had from the Vidhi vākyas like 'brīhīnavahanti' (one should thresh the paddy-grains). We have already stated in our exposition of the immediately preceding *V* text that it is a case of Niyamavidhi.

In the *V* text again, it is stated that the Niyoga in the Prayāja etc., is denoted by its own meaning in the form of the Niyoga relating to the right (i.e., the Adhikāra). In this way, Śālikanātha asserts that Niyoga is to be accepted in respect of the Prayāja etc. .

In 'ātmasiddhyanukulasya . . .' etc. of the *K* and 'yattadapūrvam . . .' etc., of the *V* text, Śālikanātha asserts that in the view of the Prābhākaras, the Niyoga or the Kārya is, indeed, the principal element and the most important for the attaiment of the Niyogya. We have, in several occasions, stated that the Kārya Niyoga and Apurva are synonymous and hence the Kārya in the *K* above refers to Niyoga. That Kārya is the principal factor and by reason of its being so, it constitutes the meaning of the sentence, has been stated by the author in *K* (27) of the *VM*. By reason of their admitting the Niyoga as the Vākyārtha (meaning of the sentence), the Prābhākaras are called Niyogavākyartha-vādins.

In the *V* text, we find some technical issues, like Kārya, Niyogya, Anuṣṭhāna, Kartā, Adhikāra etc., which are indispensable for one another. To explain – the Kārya or Niyoga cannot be a Kārya in the true sense of the term or Niyoga without a Niyojya i.e., the person to be prompted to effort. As without effort there can be no Niyoga, so without an Agent there can be no effort nor the Agent can be a Niyojya unless he is entitled to Adhikāra (right) arising out of the effort. Moreover. it is only the Kāmī (person desiring the result) issuing from the Adhikāra (right) that is entitled to its performance. Thus the result, indirectly in the Agent becomes a necessary factor in respect of the Niyoga. The relation between the Niyoga and the Niyojya is compared to the relation between a svāmī (master) and a gharbhadāsa (born slave). Without the servant, the master cannot be a master worth the name and yet it is the master who is the more important person of the two. Same is the case with the Niyoga also and because of its helping the Niyojya, is the principal element.

The comparison between the master and the servant in one side and the Niyoga and the Niyojya on the other, is also shown by Sālikanātha in his *Ṛjuvimalā*.[292] A garbhadāsa is a born slave and it is found in the *Kātyāyana Śrauta sūtra* of Aśvalāyana. Though a garbhadāsa renders service to his master, yet he is not the principal person. For, he is helped by the master for his livelihood and as such he is much benefited by the master. That is why the master is the more important of the two. Same is the case with the Niyoga and the Niyojya. Niyoga is expressed by the sentence as a whole; for that which is the principal element made known by the sentence constitutes the meaning of the sentence and of all the factors made known by the sentence, the Niyoga is the most important. Though the desired result has all the condition of being the most important element, yet it is the Niyoga which is the principal. The desired result is regarded as subordinate to the Niyoga. For, the desired result comes to be one of the elements necessary for the making up of the full Niyoga.

In the *V* text above, we find the issues like Kartā, Adhikāra etc. A Kartā is one who actually performs the action indicated by the principal root in a Vidhi. One undertakes the action when one understands that one is meant to be the Adhikārī (righiful person) to discharge the action because of his being a functionary to the action imposed by the Vidhi. The Kartā, Niyojya and Adhikārī are combined in one person who is stated to be the functionary in a Vidhi.[293] Adhikāra is the prosperity of the person in the action.[294] Adhikāra always accrues to him who is stated to be a Niyojya.

The *K* above is found quoted by Citsukha[295] in context of his refuting the view of the Prābhākaras that the knowledge of the Kārya inclines a person to an action. We find there the use of the word 'svātma' instead of 'ātma' in the *VM*.

Vācaspati Miśra, in his commentary called *Nyāyakaṇikā* refutes Sālikanātha's view that Niyoga is the principal element like a master. The maxim 'garbhadāsanyāya' cited by Sālikanātha has not been favoured by Vācaspati Miśra. He says that the maxim 'garbhadāsa' is improper. Both the efforts are inherent in the two sentient beings. The effort of the master operates for the welfare of the servant. But his effort is connected with his self-interest. On the other hand, the servant is also inclined to action for the service of his master and his inclination to action is also connected with his own benefit. So, it is not proper to say that the master is more important of the two and as such in the context also it cannot be said that Niyoga is the principal factor.[296] It can be mentioned here that Vācaspati Miśra and Maṇḍana Miśra refute the Niyogavāda of the Prābhākaras by reason of their supporting the views of Kumārila. Maṇḍana Miśra[297] refutes also Sālikanātha's view that Niyoga is the cause of pravṛtti (inclination) of persons in action. We have already stated that according to Maṇḍana Miśra, the Iṣṭasādhanatājñāna (the knowledge of the achievability of the desired object) is the cause of the pravṛtti (person's inclination to action) and constitutes the vākyārtha (the meaning of the sentence). Śālikanātha, in the *K* and *V* text above, asserts that the Niyoga or the Kārya because of its being the principal element, constitutes the vākyārtha and not any other such as Iṣṭasādhanatā etc.

In 'Viṣayānuṣṭitau satyām . . .' etc., and 'eṣā'tra darśanasthitiḥ . . .' etc., of the *K* and *V* text respectively as stated above, Śālikanātha refers to the two fold division of the Niyoga or Apūrva and states that there is mutual requirements between both the divisions. The two divisions of Niyoga are—Pradhānotpatti Niyoga and Aṅgotpatti Niyoga. The Pradhānotpatti Niyoga is one which is produced by a Pradhāna yāga (principal sacrifice) and the Aṅgotpatti Niyoga is that which is produced by an Aṅga yāga (subsidiary sacrifice). The Aṅga yāgas (auxiliary sacrifices) help the Pradhāna yāgas (principal sacrifices). Aṅga yāgas (auxiliary sacrifices) are two-fold viz., Sannipatyopakāraka (componently helpful) and Ārādupakāraka (directly helpful). Sannipatyopakāraka auxiliaries are those that directly or indirectly constitute the body of the Pradhāna yāga and thereby contribute to the utpatyapūrva (initial unseen potency) springing from that sacrifice.[298] For, instance, materials such as rice, threshing, sprinkling etc., relating to them, deities like the fire and acts like recitation from memory of yājyā (sacrificial hymns) and anuvākyā (preliminary hymns) relating to them. Ārādupakāraka auxiliaries are those that generate Apūrva (unseen potency) inhering in the soul. For instance, sacrifices like the prayāja, Ājyabhāga and Anuyāja. These do not cause any purification either in the materials or in the deities, but produce Apūrva (unseen potency) in the soul. Hence, they are called Āradupakāraka auxilaries.[299] It has been stated in the vṛtti that the Paramāpūrva (final unseen potency) is produced by the principal rite together with its prior and posterior auxiliaries and not by the principal rite alone. If the principal rite alone produces the Paramāpūrva, the result of the rite also would accrue from that and as such the auxiliaries would be redundant.[300] The Paramāpūrva is also otherwise known as Phalāpūrva.

It may be said here that the sannipatya auxilaries form a part of the Pradhānāyāga which is the object of the principal duty.

The Liṅ in the sentence that prescribes the Sannipatya Aṅga, repeats the principal duty which is again connected with the meaning of the root as its own Viṣaya (object). But this Viṣaya cannot be its Kāraṇa (chief cause), because the Pradhāna yāga is already known as the chief cause of the duty in the main sentence. The same duty, therefore, includes the Sannipatya Aṅga as a part of its Kāraṇa (chief cause), because without it the Pradhāna yāga is complete.

The Ārādupakāraka auxiliaries[301] again do not lend support physically to the pradhāna yāga which is the object of the principal duty. These auxiliaries are minor sacrifices complete in themselves and lend support to the Pradhāna yāgas in forming the principal duty. The Ārādupakāraka auxiliaries may be of two kinds viz., one that fulfils only an unseen purpose and the other that fulfils a seen as well as an unseen purpose As an example of the second kind, we can take *Payovrata* (the penance of living on milk alone) observed by the sacrificer and his wife, during the performance of the Jyotiṣṭoma yāga. As examples of the first kind, we can take all the acts that are enjoined by the texts like 'samidho yajeta' etc., which do not mention any effects produced by the act either in any substance or in the performing Agent which would help the main act of sacrifice and it is only the effects produced in the substance or in the Agent that could be seen.[302]

The Prābhākaras classify Sannipattyopakāraka into four viz., (1) Utpatti, (2) Prāpti, (3) Vikṛti and (4) Saṁskṛti. The kneading of the dough which produces the cake, is the example of the Utpatti Sannipattyopakāraka, milking of a cow whereby the milk is obtained is the case of Prāpti type of Sannipattyopakāraka; the threshing of the corn which changes its appearance is the example of the Vikṛti Sannipattyopakāraka and the sprinkling of water on the corn is the case of the Saṁskṛti type of Sannipattyopakāraka.[303]

These four types of Sannipattyopakāraka admitted by the Prābhākaras may be compared to the four types of Guṇa Karma admitted by the followers of Kumārila.[304]

Śālikanātha in the Aṅgapārāyaṇaprakaraṇa of his *Prakaraṇpañcikā* shows their classification of Auxiliaries into four heads—(a) Jāti (universal), (b) Guṇa (quality), (c) Dravya (substance) and (d) Bhāvārtha (action). The Sannipattyopakāraka and Ārādupakāraka are the divisions of the Bhāvārthātmaka type of Aṅga.[305] Prabhākaras' classification of Auxiliaries appears to be exhaustive and more logical than that of the Bhāṭṭas.

In 'Sahakārivyapekṣā ca . . .' etc., of the *K* and in 'tathetyarthaḥ ataḥ puruṣakāraśca . . .' etc., of the *V* text, Śālikanātha refutes an objection that Apūrva cannot be the cause of producing the desired object.

In the *K* above, it is stated that the necessity for the auxiliary cause does not hinder the causality. Along with the chief cause for the production of an effect, some auxiliary causes are also required. For instance, in the expression, 'Devadattaḥ odanaṁ pacati', Devadatta is the Agent for the act of cooking and so, he is the cause i e., the efficient cause. But only by him the cooking cannot be completed. It requires some other auxiliary causes. These are fuel, fire and the pot etc This is what is expressed by the words 'tathetyarthaḥ' in the *V* text above.

The second half of the *K* is found with a variant reading in the first edition of the *VM*[306] which is as follows—

'mā vā bādhīṣta sarvatra kārya pākādike yathā'

Sālikanātha in support of his view, quotes the view of some ancient teachers on smṛti which means that the Puruṣakāra (effort of the Agent) and daiva (fate) are the means of attaining the desired result.

Notwithstanding sincere effort, we could not trace the teachers referred to by the expressions 'Ācāryas' in the *V* text above, similar sentences however, are met with in the *Yājñavalkya-smṛti*.[307]

In the present context, the word 'daiva' refers to Apūrva and the word 'Puruṣakāra' refers to sahakāri kāraṇa (auxiliary cause).

The word 'daiva' also refers to the deeds done in previous birth. It has also been said that without the effort of the Agent. Daiva or fate can produce no result.

Moreover, in the *V* text above, the author refutes the objection which states that let the suffixes 'Liṅs' etc., denote Apūrvakārya in respect of the Kāmya (Prospective) acts and not in respect of the Nitya, Naimittika and Niṣedha acts. The Prābhākaras do not hold that no result can accrue from these acts. They say that the non-performance of the Nitya and

Naimittika rites inevitably leads to demerit but their performance produces no result.[308] The Prābhākaras also declare that by doing the Niṣedha (prohibited) actions no bad results are seen to follow. Sālikanātha has discussed it in his *Ṛjuvimalā* on the *Bṛhati*.[309]

The followers of Kumārila Bhaṭṭa, however, maintain that the performance of Nitya and Naimittika rites produces result viz., the destruction of demrit.[310] Regarding this we find discussion on Kumārila's *Bṛhaṭṭīka*.[311]

In 'evaṁ kāmādhikārārtha . . .' etc., and 'uktamidamanyāyyāñca . . .' etc., of the *K* and *V* text respectively, Sālikanātha meets a query that the admission of the Apūrvakārya in respect of the rites like Nitya etc., is without any ground.

Śālikanātha states that Kārya or Apūrva is the principal object and is the Vākyārtha or the meaning of the sentence. It may be stated here that according to the Prābhākaras, Niyoga or Apūrva or Kārya is the Dharma and it is the principal object and subsidiary to nothing. In case of the Nitya and Naimittika rites, only the attainment of the Vidhi is necessary and if there is no attainment of the Vidhi, it comes to be harmful, because it is the puruṣārtha. Even in the case of the Kāmādhikāras, therefore, to attain the Vidhi is necessary. But the attainment of the desired result 'svarga' etc., is not an observation to it. The result that accrues from the performance of the duty consists in compliance with the injunctions for which one happens to be a Niyojya and an Adhikāri to perform the sacrifices.[312] We have already stated that according to the system of Prabhākara, Kārya is the Pradhāna and constitutes the Vākyārtha.

That the knowledge of the meaning of the word can be had even from a popular relation between the word and meaning and with a view to clearly explaining it, Sālikanātha refers to the pūrvapakṣa and the siddhānta as found in the *Yavavarāhādhikaraṇa* of the *MS*. 1.3.8,[313] the sūtra of which is "teṣvadarśanādvirodhasya samā viprapatipattiḥ syāt".

It has been stated in the *Yavavarāhādhikaraṇa* that some take the word 'yava' to mean 'dirghaśūka (long-awned grain) and others 'priyangu'. Thus some use the word 'varaha' in the sense of śūkara' (i.e., a boar) and others in the sense of 'kṛṣṇśśakuni' (black hawk). Thus there are options due to the knowledge of the meaning of the word.[314]

Rāmānujācārya, in his *Tantrarahasya*, discussses this topic in an easier way.[315]

The Nyāya-vaiśeṣikas also the hold above discussion of the Mīmāṁsakas. One of the factor from which arises the knowledge of Śakti in Vākyaśeṣa. In connection, with the citation of the Vākyaśeṣa, the Nyāya-vaiśeṣikas take the above instance of the Mimāṁsakas. In the expression, 'yavamayaścarubhavati', (i.e., the porridge should be of yava), the word 'yava' is used by the Aryans to signify a particular long-owned grain, while the Mlecchas use it in the sense of panic seed. With regard to this there is a statement, 'when other herbs wither, these remain flourshing'. "In the spring season, all grains lose their leaves, but yava with its awn remains flourishing". From this Vākyaśeṣa, it may be concluded that the denotative capacity of the word is with regard to the grain with long awns (dīrghaśūka) and that its use to signify Kaṅgu is due to a mistaken notion about its denotative capacity.[316]

Śālikanātha in the *V* text above, places the views of both the Pūrvapakṣa and the Siddhānta. According to the Pūrvapakṣa, since both the meanings are found to be signified by the word, the acceptance of the one or the other is a matter of option. And according to the siddhānta, that meaning is to be regarded as more authoritative in which the word is used by persons who take their stand on the scriptures, because it is more reliable than the other. This is what has been stated by Śabara under *MS.* 1.3.8.

In regard to the word 'yava' Śabara finds support for its denoting the Barley-corn in the Vedic text which speaks of the 'yava-plant' as flourshing while other plants wither away—which description is applicable to Barley-corn and not to the long-pepper.

In the *V* text above, Śālikanātha shows the difference between the Kārya of the sentences formed with the suffixes Liṅs etc , and the Kārya which is denoted by the suffixes Liṅs etc. It is stated that meaning of the Kārya of the sentences with the Liṅs etc., is ascertained from the Vṛddhavyavahāra, while that being denoted by the suffixes Liṅs etc., is ascertained from its (of the Kārya) relation with the words of the Vedic sentences and that Kārya is known as the Apūrva.

In 'vyavahārata eva . . .' etc., and 'asyārthaḥ-kecidevamāhuḥ . . .' etc., of the *K* and *V* text respectively as stated, Śālikanātha presents the view of a section of Mimāmsakas. According to these Mīmāmsakas, as the Kārya cannot be known by other source of knowledge and as it is different from the Kriyā in the view of the Prābhākaras, so the Kārya can be known from the usage of the sentences. To explain—these Mīmāmsakas contend that a person is inclined to certain action on hearing a sentence which is formed by the suffix Liṅ etc., and it is also stated that the Pravṛtti of the person is because of his knowledge of the Kārya. Thus it can be stated that the Kārya comes to be the import of the sentences with Liṅs etc., and not the Kriyā and thereby the difference between the Kārya and the Kriyā is asserted That the Kārya is the import of the Liṅs etc. is because of the fact that the Pravṛtti of a word in the Kriyā is not useful. As the *K* above is partially a repetition of the *K* (23) and *K* (25) as we have discussed already, here we refrain from explaining the same further.

In 'vyutpattirapi kārye' rthe . . . .' etc., of the *K* and in 'tasyām śabdasya . . .' etc., of the *V* text, Śālikanātha maintains that the Vedic Liṅs etc., have the denotative power in respect of the Kārya. It is stated in the *K* above, the Kārya takes place after the usage of the people i.e., from the observation of the inclination of a person to certain action, one can acquire the knowledge of the Kārya.

Sālikanātha states that although the knowledge of the denotative power of the words Liṅs etc., arises only in respect of the popular actions (Laukika kārya), yet the Liṅs etc., by means of the word 'svargakāma' etc , that refers to the Niyojya, convey the Vedic performable other than the Kriyā, for the momentary sacrifices cannot bring about the result viz., svarga etc., at a subsequent period.

But this view of the Prābhākaras as stated by Sālikanātha, is refuted by Citsukha. According to Citsukha, this view is improper, because the bringing about of the heaven through Apūrva is a case of Arthapātti and thus the view of the Prābhākaras that Apūrva cannot be known by any other pramāṇa except the Sāstrapramāṇa.[317]

The *K* above is found quoted by Pratyaksvarupa Bhagavān

in his *Nayanaprasādinī* commentary in connection with the refutation of the view of the Prābhākaras by Citsukha.[318]

In 'sitetara iva tveṣa . . .' etc. of the *K* text and in 'idamatrā' kūtam . . .' etc. of the *V* text, Śālikanātha refutes the view of a certain section of the Mīmāṁsakas who contend that one can understand the Kārya from only the popular usage and only the Kārya is the meaning of the suffixes Liṅs etc. and not the Kriyā. But Śālikanātha does not accept this view and with the help of a simile, he refutes the same. In *K*(34) above, we find that he compares this view to the black fortnight which is very dark. Just as the fortnight because of having no pleasant moon-beams cannot attract the minds of the people, so also this view because of lacking in satisfying points cannot attract the minds of the scholars, i.e., this view is not acceptable. Why this view is not acceptable, is stated by the author in *K* (35 & 36) and is elaborated in the relevant *V* text. If it is admitted that the Vidhi gives rise to the knowledge of the Kriyā and not that of the Kārya, then how there will be the knowledge of the Kārya ? In the event of the Kārya being not known by any other source of valid knowledge, a person will not know the usage relating to the Kārya prior to the word and without the knowledge of the usage, one cannot have the knowledge of the word relating to the usage. Thus in that case, one cannot assume the denotative power of the words.

Although only the Kārya is conducive for the Pravṛtti of a person in an action and only the Kārya is the Śabdārtha, yet we observe in common parlance that the knowledge of the Kriyā comes to be the cause of the Pravṛtti. Thus it can be assumed that the Pravṛtti is resorted to the Kriyā and the Vākyārtha is what is the meaning of the suffixes Liṅs etc. Just as only the meaning in the form of Ākṛti being admitted as the meaning of the Śabda, the Akrti is understood as pertaining to the Vyakti, and thus there is no obstruction in respect of the knowledge of the Vyakti in the case of the knowledge of the meaning of the word, so also is the case with the Kriyā. As a result, it cannot be established that the word denotes the meaning in the form of the Kārya as different from the Kriyā. Thus in the *V* text above, Śālikanātha contends that the Kārya is not the basis of the usage, but it is the Kriyā which is the basis of the usage.

In 'kāryapratītimātrañca . . .' etc. and 'lokapratītam . . .' etc. of the *K* and *V* text respectively; Śālikanātha maintains the view that from the popular usage, the Kārya is ascertained as the Kriyā and the knowledge of the Kārya is inferred from the Pravṛtti of a person in certain action. We have alerady stated that in the view of the Prābhākaras, the Kārya is different from the Kriyā and it is stated by Śālikanātha in *K* (23) and *K* (25) which we have already explained. In the *V* text above. the author states that the Kriyā is ascertained as the meaning of the Liṅs etc. and is also ascertained in the form of the Kārya in the meaning of only the Kārya. Thus the meaning of the Liṅs etc. is not ascertained as the Apūrva by means of any other source of valid knowledge. we have earlier discussed the issue of the Kriyā and the Kārya and as such we refrain from explaining them further.

Though the word 'Kārya' in the *K* text above is apparently correct from the grammatical point of view, yet from the point of the view of the purport, it is not correct. The word will, therefore, be 'Kāryam'.

The use of the emphatic particle 'eva' after the word 'Kriyā' in the K text above, asserts that it is the Kriyā alone that it is accertained as the Kārya.

Nitya Karma is that the performance of which produces no result. Same is the case with the Naimittika karma also. According to the Prābhākaras, the non-performance of these two rites inevitably leads to demerit.[319]

In the *V* text, it is thus stated that according to those Mīmāṁsakas, the Kārya additional to the Kriyā is understood from the statements of the preceptors.

In the *V* text viz., 'anye punarvedārthabodhaka. . .' etc. Śālikanātha presents the view of some other Mīmāṁsakas who contend that the Pravṛtti of a person to some action is due to the statements of the preceptors that convey the meanings of the Vedic sentence. These Mīmāṁsaks also contend that the suffixes Liṅs etc. are understood in respect of the suprasensible actions. If again it is said that only the Kriyā is understood as the Kārya from the statements of the preceptors and as the Kriyā is in the form of pain and as there arises no pravṛtti without a puruṣārtha, there will be no pravṛtti of a person seeking happiness in the actions being of the nature of pain. And in the case of the Nitya

Karma (i.e,, the regular rite) such as Sandhyopāsanā etc. there is no Purṣārtha and as such there will be no Pravṛtti in such rites. It may be stated here that the Mīmāṁsakas divide Arthakarma (principal rite) into Nitya (regular), Naimittika (occasional) and Kamya (optional). Sandhyopāsanā etc. are the Nitya Karma.

In 'Vedārthācāryavākyeṣu . . .' etc., and 'ācāryavākya Śravaṇādapi. . .' etc., of the *K* and *V* text respectively, Śālikanātha discards the View of a Section of Māmāṁsakas according to whom the Kārya additional to the Kriyā is understand from the statements of the Acāryas, that convey the meaning of the Vedic sentences. But Śālikanatha asserts that the Kriyā as stated by the section of the Mīmāṁsakas to be understood as the Kārya is not the Apūrvakārya. It is stated in the *V* text above, that the Pravṛtti of the disciples to the sandhyopāsanā etc. that takes place subsequent to the hearing of the sentences of Ācāryas in that (Pravṛtti), a child assumes the knowledge of the Kārya from the Kriyā as the cause. He also thinks of the knowledge of the result as without it, there can be no attainment of the Kārya and thus he should assume the result even in the case of the rites viz., Nitya, Naimittika, Niṣedha and Adhikāra Karma and that, too, is after having understood the meaning of the Vedic sentences in accordance with the knowledge of the popular sentences. That very child having understood in childhood, later on securing the post of a preceptor and coming to understand the Vedārtha (i.e., the meaning of the Vedic sentences). Then the child being the preceptor at a time establishes the Kriyā as being the Kārya not the Apūrva as being the Kārya Earlier on several occasions, we have stated that in the view of the Prābhākaras, Apūrva is the Kārya and not the Kriyā and as such the Kārya is to be understood as the Apūrva. But the Mīmāmsakas who accept that the Kārya additional to the Kriyā is understood from the statements of the Ācāryas, cannot establish that their Kārya is to be understood in the form of Apūrva. Thus their view, says Śālikanātha, is not acceptable.

In the *K* text viz.. 'tasmallokānusāreṇa . , .' etc., Śālikanātha draws the conclusion after rejecting the view of some Mīmāmsakas who maintain that from the statements of the Ācāryas that convey the meanings of the Vedic Sentences, the Kārya is understood as different from the Kriyā. But Śālikanātha does not accept this view and he rejects the same which we have discuseed in the preceding *K*(38) and *V* text. According to Śālikanātha, in common parlance, we understand the meanings of the Vedic injunctive sentences only in respect of the Kārya and that this Kārya is known as Apūrva is understood from the Vedic sentences.

In the *K* text above, Śālikanātha also asserts that the Kārya is also otherwise known as the Apūrva. On several occasions, we have mentioned that in the system of Prabhākara Kārya, Apūrva and Niyoga are synonymous. Earlier also in *K*(25), viz., 'kriyādibhinnam yatkāryam etc., we find Śālikanātha's reference to Kārya as Apūrva and as Apūrva and as such in the present *K* text above also, he repeats the same. But in present context, he states that in Vedic sentences, the Kārya is known as the Apūrva. Haridasa Bhattacharya[320] in his commentary called *Vibhā* on the *Nyāyakusumāñjali*, quotes the *K* text obove which is also cited by Yogīndrāñanda in his translation of the *Citsukhī*[321] Because of the *K* above, pratially being the repetition of the *K*(25). Śālikanātha does not write the Vṛtti on the text under discussion.

In the *K* text viz.. 'nanu lokavirodhitvam . . .' etc., the author refers to a query that may arise that if the Kārya is admitted in form of the Apūrva, then it will be contradictory to the popular usage. In *K*(39) it is stated by Śālikanātha that the Kārya is otherwise known as the Apūrva. Therefore, in the *K* text above it is, maintained in the form of objection that as in common parlance, the Kriyā is understood as the Kārya, so, the view that the Kārya is called the Apūrva will be contradictory to the popular usage. It is because, in common parlance, there is no difference between the Kriyā and the Kārya. In other words, both these are understood in common parlance as one and the same thing. We have found earlier in *K*(37) that the Kārya is ascertained in popular usage as the Kriyā alone and in the *V* text under the same, it is asserted by the author that from the point of view of the popular usage, the Kriyā in the form of the Kārya is the meaning of the suffixes Liṅs eic. Thus it may be mentioned here that the *K* text under examination is nothing but the repetition in part of the *K*(37). Although both the Kriyā and the Kārya are taken to be one and the same in common parlance, yet in the view of the Prābhākaras, the Kārya is diffcerent from the Kriyā and it is stated by the author in *K*(23) and *K*(25) which we have discussed in the preceding pages of the present work.

The twice mention of the emphatic particle 'eva' after the 'sarvathā' and the 'kāryaiva' in the *K* text above, asserts that in common porence, both the Kriyā and the Kārya are same.

In 'bhavedevam virudhyate . . .' etc. and 'yadi kriyākāryatva-gocara . . .' etc. of the *K* and *V* text respectively Śālikanātha meets the objection that there will be contradiction to the popular usage in the event of admitting the Kārya as the Apūrva. As we heve already stated, in common parlance the Kriyā is known as the Kārya. But, according to the view of the Prābhākaras, the Kārya is known as the Apūrva and in the case of admitting the Kārya as the Apūrva, the objection says that it will be contradictory to the popular usage. But Śālikanātha with a view to rejecting the objection contends that the view (i.e., the Lins etc. denote the Apūrva, the Kārya) will be contradictory to the common parlance provided the knowledge and the use of the popular sentences that are understood from the action and the performable are contradictory to each other. But the knowledge and the use of the word understood from the Kārya in the form of Kriyā canot be common.

Thus Śālikanātha meets the objection very intelligently and asserts that Kārya is the Apūrva which is also taken to be the Vākyārtha.

In 'apūrvam hi kriyāsādhyam. . .' etc. and 'pratipattiprayogau hi. . .' etc. of the *K* and *V* text respectively Śālikanātha asserts that the view of the prābhākaras who maintain that the Apūrva is called the Kārya, is not contradictory to the popular usage. Śālikanātha contends that Apūrva is brought about by the Kriyā which after being accomplished serves as the cause of producing the Apūrva. Thus it is proper to state that the Apūrva which is the Kārya comes to be the Kārya of the Kriyā also. In the *K* text above, Śālikanātha also states that which is understood by some other means of valid knowledge is stated (i.e. used) by the popular usage. But we have stated earlier that in view of the Prābhākaras, Apūrva is not known by any other source of valid knowledge and as such the use of the Apūrva as the Kārya of the Kriyās being not understood comes to be the object of Lakṣaṇā i.e., comes to be known through Lakṣaṇā. It is because of the fact that Pratipatti (knowledge) and Prayoga (use) do not occur necssarily by means of Abhidhā (i.e., the primary denotation). We find that the Pratipatti and prayoga occur by means of Lakṣaṇā also. Thus although the Apūrva is denoted by the Liṅs etc. as the Kārya, yet because of the Apūrva being invariably the Kārya of the Kriyā, it is not inconsistent that both Kriyā and Kārya are obtained through Lakṣaṇa. It is also stated in the *V* text above that Apūrva is also that which is brought about by the Kriyā which again being performed becomes the means of bringing about the Apūrva and thus it is established that the Kriyā as the Kārya is permanently related with the Apuūrva. As a result, a relation is made between the Kriyā and the Apūrva and so because of there being the relation, they are known through Lakṣaṇā. In our exposition of the concept of Laksaṇā in the *VM*(1), we have stated that there is Lakṣaṇā by means of relation.

The compound word 'śrautavṛtti' in the *V* text above means Abhidhā vṛtti (i.e., the primary denotation). Śālikanātha uses the word Śrautavṛtti in the sense of Abhidhā vṛtti and Śrauta artha in the sense of Mukhy artha. The viz., 'pramāṇāntaragamyāni hi' etc. above is found quoted in *Nayanaprasādinī* commentary.[322]

In 'lakṣaṇābimānastu . . .' eic. of the *K* and 'mukhyārthamaviditvā . . .' etc of the *V* text Śālikanātha meets the query that if it is known by means of Lakṣaṇā that Apūrva is the Kārya of the Kriyā, then why, in common parlance, it is not known, Śālikanātha contends that in common parlance, the knowledge of the Apūrvakārya cannot be ascertained by means of Lakṣaṇā being no knowledge of the primary meaning. But those who are expert in respect of understanding the primary meaning, can understand the Apūrvakārya through Lakṣaṇā. It can be stated here that in order to understand Lākṣaṇika artha one must have the knowledge of the Mukyārtha of a word. It is because of the fact that one has to take resort to Lakṣaṇā when there is the failure of the primary meaning of a word.

In the *V* text above, the author clearly explains the idea. It is said that just as the Mlecchas not knowing the prlmary meanings of the words like yava and Varāha etc. accept the implied meanings in the place of the primary meanings, so, also is the case with the people in common parlance. Only those scholars can understand the Apūrva by means of Lakṣaṇā, who are capable of discriminating the Mukhyārtha and the Lākṣaṇikārtha, In the yavavarāhādhikaraṇa of the *MS.*[323] Śabara discusses this issue which we have discussed earlier in our exposition. Thus Śālikanātha asserts that Apūrva as the Kārya can be known through Lakṣṇā.

In the *K* text viz., 'tasmānmānāntarāvedyam . . .' etc., Śālikanātha concludes his asertion that the Kārya which is also known as the Apūrva or Niyoga cannot be known by any source of valid knowledge except the Śabdapramāṇa or Śāstrapramāṇa. It is also stated that the author states that it is the Vedic sentence that conveys the Apūrva or Kārya.

We have stated earlier that the Prābhākaras are Apūrvākārya-vākyārthavādins and as such their aim is to establish the Apūrva or the Kārya as the Vākyārtha and so, Śālikanātha uses the word Kārya in the *K* above.

In 'Vākyārthamātṛkeyam . . .' etc. and 'racitā saccaritānāma-nugraham . . .' etc. of the *K* and *V* text (which is also in the form of a Kārikā) respectively, the author clearly mentions the name of the work (i.e., the *Vākyārthamātṛkā*), his name (i.e., Śālikanātha) and the purpose of writing the *Vākyārthamātṛkā* and also he states the purpose of writing the Vṛtti for the easy understanding of the readers who are not mallicious.

In order to avert the confusion that may arise in the minds of the readers in future the author of the Vṛtti Śālikanātha mentions his name as the author of the Vṛtti. That Śālikanātha is a follower of Prabhākara Miśra or the system of Prabhākāra, can be easily understood from Śālikanātha's mention of the name of his teacher Prabhākara.

It may be added here that in the *K* above, the author indicates, as is usually done in the beginning of a work, what are called Anubanthas (Incentives or necessary elements of a literary work). The Anubanthas are four in number viz., (1) Viṣaya (subject matter): (2) Prayojana (purpose); (3) Sambandha (connection) and (4) Adhikārī (person for whom the work is written).[324] Of course, it may be pointed out that in the *K* above, the author states the Viṣaya (i.e., the Vākyārthajñāna or the knowledge of the sentence-meaning) and the Prayojana (i.e. the easy understanding of the readers). Again in the *V* above, Śālikanātha refers to the Adhikārī (i.e., the persons who are good in conduct). In both the *K* and *V*, again, the author explains the Sambandha (i.e., the connection of the work with the method of treatment adopted in the work i.e., the method of the treatment of the Vākyārtha).

It is also to be noted here that generally the Anubandhas are indicated in the begininng of a work. The *Sāhityadarpaṇa* of Viśvanātha and Śālikanātha's *Vākyārthamātṛkā* are the works of the same kind wherein the authors themselves write both the texts and the Vṛtti thereon.

REFERENCES

1. SDK, p. X.
2. EPB, p. 1.
3. BR, p. 8.
4. "For the school generally known as the 'Third path' 'trtīyaḥ panthāḥ' associated with the name of Murāri Miśra, and hence called 'Mishra-mata', material is not yet available for a full account'l— PIS, p. 26.
5. Appendix, *Ibid.*, pp. 45-46.
6. Śāstraikadeśasya prakriyā prakaraṇam iti pañcikāśabdo vistarārthaḥ—'paci vistāre' iti dhātorniṣpannaḥ. Introduction to the PP, pp. 56-27.
7. Uktañca—'anvitasyābidhānārthamuktārthaghaṭanāya vā...........etc.' Sā ceyamākāṅkṣā...........na puruṣeṇānvīyate. Sp, p. 281
   Again,—'jijñāsā jāyate boddhuḥ.........abhidhāyitā
   Sp, p. 282
   Sannidhiśśabdajanmaiva.........sabdairanvitabodhanam
   Sp, p. 283
   Padajātaṃ śrutaṁ śrvam......vākyārthabodhanam.
   Sp, p. 286.
8. 'In his Prakaraṇa-pañcikā, Śālika deals with the more important epistemological and metaphysical views of his teacher'.—KM, p. 9.
9. 'In Śālikanātha's Prakaraṇa-pañcikā, we find a learned and scholarly prakaraṇa epitomising and maintaining the distinctive tenets of the Prābhākara school.'—cf.—'The Prābhākara school of Karmamīmāṃsā, (vide, (The proceedings of the 2nd Oriental Conference, Calcutta, 1922).

10. Vākyārthamātṛkeyaṁ prabhākaragurormatānusāreṇa /
anasūyubodhanārthaṁ Śālikanāthena saṃgrathitā //
PP, p. 450.
11. *Ibid.*
12. mātṛkā-strī (māteva). mātṛ + "ive pratikṛtau" (Pā. 5.3.96). iti kan tāp. mātaiva etc.—SKD, (Vol. 3), p. 694.
13. atra vākyārthamātṛketi śabdaprayogādavagamyate—sarveṣāmapi prābhākara—siddhāntānāṁ mātṛsthānīyami-damiti.—Introduction to PP, p. 42.
14. viśvasyate yat brahmasiddhyuktadūśaṇo' nmūlanena niyogavākyārthavādasya prābhākarīyasyoddhāraṇameva vākyārthamātṛkāyā uddeśyam.—Introduction to PP, p. 43.
15. tathā'nyāṁ Śālikanātho nānāprakranātmikām /
mānameyaviekārtha ṁcokre yatnea pañcikām // TR, p. 1,
16. naivāśrāvi gurormataṃ na viditaṁ tautātilaṁ darśanam /
tattvajñānamaho na śārikagrirāṃ vācaspateḥ kā kathā //
PC, 2/3
17. etat sarvaṁ amṛtakalāyāṁ Śālikanāthena samarthitam.
TR, p. 16
also, Śālikanāthena nayavīthyāṁ samarthitam, *Ibid.*, p. 7.
18. tathā cākathayan nayavīthyāṁ Śālikanāthaḥ. SDS, p. 18.
19. "Śālikanātha was a polemical writer, and it may be said that the system of Prabhākara may not have survived, if there was not the able support of Śālikanātha" Vide Introduction to TR, p. XL.
Also
'Śālikanātha is the main piller of the Prābhākara school'.—Vide, Introduction to PP. p. VIII.
20. etacca pañcikādvaye prapañcitam, p. 133.
21. 'Śālikanāthavanumūḍho na jātaḥ na janiṣyate /
prabhākaraprakāśāya yena dīpaśikhā kṛtā //
22. Śarīrendriyavyatikto viṣaya iti Śālikanāthah praśastapādabhāṣyavyākhyāne nyarūpayat. PK, p. 211.
23. Vide, FN under KM, p. 60.
24. sarvasyaiva hi śāstrasya karmaṇo vā' pi kasyacit /
yāvat prayojanaṁ noktaṁ tāvat tat kena gṛhyate //
SV. 1.12
Also,—
prayojamanudiśya na maṇḍo' pi pravartaṭe. *Ibid.*, 5.55.

25. kālānupāti yadrupaṁ tadastīti pratīyate /
paritastu paricchinnaṁ bhāva ityeva kathyate //
Vā. p. III. 8.12.

Also,—
yāvat siddhamasiddhaṁ vā sādhyatvenābhidhīyate /
āśritakramarupatvāt tat kriyetyabhidhīyate //
Ibid., III. 8.1.

26. bhāvanātvaṁ nāma bhavituḥ prayojakavyāpāravam.
MP, p. 62.

27. niyogo hi pramāṇāntaramapūrvamarthamavabodhayati iti.
PP, p. 235.

28. abhedāpūrvakāḥ bhedāḥ kalpitā vākyavādhiḥ /
bhedāpūrvamabhedāṁstu manyante padadarśinaḥ //
Vā. p. 11.57.

29. pūrvapūrvavarṇajanitasaṁskārasahito' ntyo varṇaḥ pratyāyaakaḥ. SB. under MS. 1.1.5.

30. yattu tārkikāḥ—varṇamanityatve' pi uttarottaravarṇe pūrvapūrvavarṇauttamavyavahitatottarasambandhena saṁskāravaśād gṛhyata iti padasya pratyakṣatvācchābadabodhaḥ. PLM, p. 57;
pratyekapadānubhavajanyasaṁskāraiścaramaṁ tāvatpadaviṣayaka—smaraṇasyāvyavadhānenopatteḥ;......................
tāvatpadasaṁskārasahita-caramavarṇajñānasyodbodhakatvāt.
NSM under BP, p. 468.

31. vākyasyāvācakatvaṁ ca padārthānāṁ ca hetutā /
sambandhānapekṣānāṁ vākyārthe sthāpayiṣyate //
SV. 20 under MS. 1.1.2.

32. pūrvapūrvarṇajanitasaṁskārasahito' ntyo varṇaḥ pratyāyakaḥ. SB under MS. 1.1.5.

33. padairabhihitāḥ svārthāḥ smāritā vā padārthā vākyārthaṁ gamayanti. TR, p. 27.

Also,—
padārthā eva tāvat parasparānvitā vākyārtha ityucyante.
NRM, p. 96.

34. tasmānna vākyaṁ na padāni/ sākṣādvākyārthabuddhiṁ janayanti// kiṁtu padasvarupābhihitaiḥ padārthaiḥ / saṁlakṣyate' sāviti siddhametat// *Ibid.*, p. 125.

35. tasmāt suṣṭhu uktam—yāgo guṇabhūtaḥ svargaḥ pradhānabhūtaḥ iti. SB under MS. 6.1.2.

36. ayambhāvaḥ—padānyeva vākyam, padārthā eva vākyārth iti gurumatasthitiḥ.........
tathā ca yadār thānāṁ saṁsargo na vākyārthaḥ, api tvanvitāḥ padārthā eva vākyūrtha iti bhāvaḥ.
FN under PP, p. 378.
37. that the *BK* is not available in print is stated by K.S. Ramaswami Shastri and A. Sankaranan in their article, 'Kumārila and *Bṛahṭṭīkā*'. They say—
'Its very name and the references to it in the catalogues show that it is very voluminous and probably its enormous size has stood unfortunately in the way of its being preserved to posterity.'—Proceedings of the 3rd oriental conference, Madras, 1927, p. 528.
38. na cātra vṛddhavyavahāraṁ muktva anyat kāraṇamupālabhāmahe, BR, p. 258.
39. śaktigrahaṁ vyākaraṇopamānakośāptavākyād vyavahāratśca/ vākyasya śeṣād vivṛtervadanti sānnidhyataḥ siddhapadasya vṛddhāḥ—As quoted in the *NSM* under BP, p. 418.
40. sā ca śaktissādhuṣvivāpabhraṁsvepi, śaktigrāhakaśiromaṇervyavahārasya tulyatvāt.
PLM, p. 27.
41. vṛddhavyavahārapūrvikaiva sarvā śabdavyutpattiḥ.
VM, p. 379, Vide, PP.
42. vṛddhavyavahārādeva sarveṣāmādyā vyutpattiḥ, TC. p. 463.
43. asmākaṁ tu padānyeva vākyaṁ tadratha eva vākyārtha iti na kiñcidanupannam. TR, p. 55.
44. prāthamyādabhidhātṛtvāt tātparopagamādapi.
padānāmeva sā śaktirvaramabhyupagamyatām.
VM, p. 400, Vide, PP.
45. kalpanālāghavaṁ yatra tat pakṣaṁ rocayāmahe /
kalpanāgauravaṁ yatra tat pakṣaṁ na sahāmahe //
46. Regardlng this, there are three saṁgraha Ślokas (i.e., collected verses) which are as follows—
ḍimbhārbhaka Śiśo bāla gām bādhānā' nayeti yat /
padasaptakametena racite vacanāṣṭake (1) //
śaktyaṣṭakṁ kalpanīyaṁ syādvarṇavalvādinah /
padānāmeva saptānāṁ saptaiva khalu śaktayaḥ // (2)
padavādiṁate kalpyā iti syāttasya lāghavaṁ /
śuklāṁiti padanyāsādvākye ṣauḍaśake kṛte // (3)

śaktyaṣṭakantveva bhavedaṣṭānāṁ padavādinnaḥ (32) /

47. pūrvajanpurvaitasamskārasahito'ntyo varṇaḥ pratyāakaḥ. SB, under MS 1.1.5.

48. vākyastheṣu khalu varṇesūccarativarṇaṁ tāvat śravaṇaṁ bhavati, śrutaṁekaṁanekaṁ vā padabhāvena pratisandhatte, pratisandhāya ca padaṁ vyavasyati, padavyavasayena smṛtyā padārthaṁ pratipadyate, padasamūhapratisandhānācca vākyaṁ vyavasyati. sambandhān ca padārthān gṛhītvā vākyārthaṁ pratipadyate. VB under NS. 3.2.58.

49. tatrottarapada-smaraṇena pūrvapadasmaraṇasya nāśāt avyavadhānena tattatpada-smaraṇāsambhava it cet. na pratyeka-padānubhavajanya-saṁskārai-ścaramam tāvat pada-visayaka—smaraṇasyā' vyavadhānenopatteh; . . . . tāvat padasamskārasahitacarama-varṇajñānasyodbodhakatvāt. NSM under BP, p. 466.

50. Saṁskāraṁātrajanyaṁ jñānaṁ smṛtiḥ. TS, p. 22.

51. padānāṁ tatpadārtheṣu śaktiḥ svābhāvikī sthitā, PP, p. 40.

52. kiñca padaśaktitaḥ padārthaśaktireva laghīyasī, MM, p. 97.

53. śrūyatāmavadhānena gatirnaragirīmapi / anumānātpṛthagbhāvam necchanti sūrayah // PP, p. 33.

54. vākyaṁ hi purusādhīnaracanaṁ laukikaṁ sadā / śaṅkymaānayathārthatvaṁ nārthaniścāyakaṁ svataḥ // *Ibid.*

55. yathā hi—vṛddhavyavahāradarśanena proyojpavṛddhasya' rthapratipattiṁ prakalpya.............................. . . . . vṛddhasyā' rthapratipattisāmarthyam kalpayitvā . . . . nūnamasyāpi vṛddhavyahāradarśanameva. . . . . . . loko vyutpadyate. *Ibid.*, p. 25.

56. tatrārthe niścite paṣcāt so' rth vākyena gamyate / tasyāṁ daśāyāṁ vākyasya tasya syādanuvadatā // *Ibid.* p. 36.

57. padairabhihitāḥ padārthā ākāṅksāyogyatāsattimanto lakṣaṇayā padārthasamsargarupaṁ vākyārthaṁ bodyayantīti bhāṭṭamīmāṁsakā aśerate. FN. 1 under PP, p. 381.

58. Kiñca kiṁabhihitena viśeṣeṇa tadvyatisaktamabhīyate, anabhihiṭena vā? abhihitapakṣa iṭaretarāśrayaṁ dvimīyamapi

padamabhihitārthāntaravyatisaktābhidhāyakatayetarapadābhidhānamāśrayatīti prasaktaṁ durūttramitaretarāśrayam, anabhihitapakṣe padāntarayogavaiyartham. RVL, p. 285.

59. atrākāṁksā ca yogyatvaṁ sannidhiśceti tattrayam / vākyārthāvagame sarvaiḥ kāraṇatveṇa kalpyate //
MM, p. 99.

60. tadbhūtānāṁ kriyārthena samāmnāye' rathasya tannimittatvāt.

61. yato'nviteṣu vyutpatteranvitā arthāḥ padairabhidhīyante' to' nvitārthaparāni padānyeva vākyamiti ṭīkākāramatānuvartinaḥ. NK under NRM, p. 97.

62. tenātra padāvagatāḥ punaḥ padārthā mitho'nvayaṁ yānti ityevamabhihitānvayasiddhānto darśito' smadādīnām.
MM, p. 95.

63. tena tenānvitḥ svārthaḥ padairevavāgamyate, BP, p. 467.

64. atrākāṁksā ca yogyatvaṁ sannidhiśceti tattrayam. vākyārthāvagame sarvaiḥ kāraṇatvena kalpyate.
MM, p. 99

65. yena padena vinā yatpadasyā' nvayanānubhāvakataṁ tena padena saha tasyākāṅkṣetyarthaḥ. kriyāpadaṁ vinā kārakapadaṁ nānvayabodhaṁ janayatīti tena tasyākāṁkṣā. NSM under BP, p. 472.

66. aparipūrṇavākyasthale śabdādhyāhāro' bhihitānvayadibhirbhāṭṭamāmsakairaṅgīkriyate. dvāramityatra pidhehīti śabdamadhyāharanti......................... ata evete śabdādhyāhāravādina iti prathante. Anvitābhidhānavādinaḥ prābhākaramīmāmsakā aparipūrṇavākyasthale pidhānarūpamarthaṁadhyāharanti. ata evete'rthādhyāhāravādina iti gīyante, FN, 4 under PP, p. 280.

67. yatra dvāramityuktam, tatra pidhehīti padasya jñānādeva bodhaḥ, na tu pidhānādirupārthajñanāt, padajanya tattapadārthopasthite-staṭhācchābdabodhe hetutvāt.
NSM under BP, p. 468.

68. ata evaśruta padārthasthale tattatpadādhyāhāro yathā dvāramitvādau pidhehīti. VP, p. 86.

69. PLM, p. 118.

70. prakaraṇaṁ nāma parasparākāṁāsā. MP, p. 32.

71. ato mānātarāpūrvamapūrvaṁiti gīyate. PP, p. 441.

72. adhikāraḥ purṣuayaiścaryaṁ karmaṇi. RVL under BR,

p. 14.

73. niyojyaśca sa ucyate yaḥ mamedaṁ kāryaṁiti budhyate. NRM, p. 63.

74. yaśca kāryamavabudhyate sa niyojyaḥ. svargakāmasya ca tasminneva kārye bodhṛtayā' navayaḥ. RVL under BR, p. 288 niyojyassa ca kāryaṁ yassvakīyatvena budhyate. PP. p. 433.

75. yatra tu niyojyo na śrūyate sa tvaprayojakaḥ, ayaṁ tvadhyayanavidhiḥ niyojyāśravaṇādaprayojakaḥ. NK under NRM, p. 4.

76. 'vidhinā tvekavākyatvāt stutyarthena vidhīnāṁ syuḥ'.

77. gaṭha pato bhavati iti, paṭa utpadyate ityarthaḥ, nirākāṅesañca padadvayam. yadā ca tasminneva raktaḥ—ityaparaṁ śrūyate, tadū rāgasambandho bhavatītyarthaḥ, bhavati ca raktaṁ pratyākāṅksā. SB under MS. 1.2.7.

78. ayameti putro rājñaḥ puruṣo' yamapasāryatādau tu putreṇa saha rājapadasya tātparyagrahasattvāt tenaivā'—nvayabbdhaḥ puruseṇaa saha tātparyagrahe tu sahānvayabodhaḥ syādeva. NSM under BP, p. 473.

79. gurustu āvaraṇadyarthasyaiva kalpyatayā śabdakalpanābhāvāt śrutārthāpattirnāsti ityāha. MM, p. 130.

80. yatra tvaparipūrṇasya vākyasyānvayasiddhaye śabdo' dhyāhriyate tatra śrutārthāpattirisyate. *Ibid.*, p. 129.

81. prakṛtivad vikṛtiḥ kartavyā. SB under MS. 7.1.22.

82. agninā siñcatyādāvayānāmananvayāt. yogyatāpi parigrāhyā. MM, p. 99.

83. navyāstu yogyatāyā jñānaṁ na śābdajñāne kāraṇam vahninā siñcatīyādau seke vahnikaraṇakatvābhāvarupā' yogyataniścayena pratibandhānna śābdabhodhaḥ. NSM under BP, p. 471.

84. yaścobhayoḥ samo dosaḥ parihāro' pi tādṛśaḥ.
naikaḥ paryanuyoktavyaḥ tādṛgartha vicāraṇe.

85. nanu 'paśyataśśetimārūpaṁ hresāśabdaṁ ca śṛṇvataḥ.
khuranikṣepaśabdam ca śveto' śvo dhāvatīti dhīriti nyāyādastyeva padārthānāṁ saṁsargabodhajanakatvam iti. CS, p. 256.

86. Vide, SV, p. 1148.

87. Vide, KTS, p. 281.

88. ....na. anumānādarṭhāpaṭterva ṭatra saṁsargāvagamāt.

tathāhi eṣāṁ padārthānāṁ ekādhikaraṇatayā' vagatānām paratyāyakatvenā' numānānatireko viśakalitāvagatāṁ vāirthāntarābhāva niścite' rthāpattireva parisīsyate, aniścite tvanadhyavasāya eva. CS, p. 256.

89. atrākāṁksā ca yogyatvaṁ sannidhiśceti tattarayam. vākyārthāvagame sarvaiḥ kāraṇatena kalpyate. MM, p. 99.

90. The Sūtra of the *MS* is : 'sakṛttu syātkṛtārthatvādaṅgavat'.

91. (a) prakṛtipratyayau sahārthaṁ brūtaḥ prādhānyanṭu pratyayārthasyaiva. TP, p. 112.
(b) Prakṛtipratyayoḥ pratyārtha prādhānyam. VB, p. 481.

92. The Sūtra is—"sārvadhātuke yak".

93. Vide, Ślokānukramaṇikā under NRM, p. 344.

94. dhātunā krlyocyate, pratyayena kartā. tayoḥ kartā-pradhānabhūtaḥ, upasarjanabhūtā kriyā. SB under MS. 11.1.22.

95. asmanmate hi padārthānām ...... vākyarthasyāpi lakṣaṇāsiddhatvāt Śaktyantarakalpanaiva nāsti. MM, p. 97.

96. Vide, SV, p. 814.

97. Vide, TR, p. 28.

98. tadbhūtānām kriyārthena samāmnāyo' rthasya tannimittatvāt. MS. 1.1.25.

99. padāni hi svaṁ svamarthamabhidhāya nivṛttavyāpāraṇi, thedānīṁ padārthā avagatāssanto vākyārthamavagamayanti iti. SB, under *Ibid.*

100. kumārilabhattamate lakṣaṇā śakyārthasyaiva vyāpāraḥ, na tu Śabdasya. KTS, p. 75.

101. tasmānna vākyaṁ na padāni sākṣādvākyārthabudhiṁ janayanti kintu padasvarupābhihitaiḥ padārthaiḥ samlakṣyate'sāviti siddhametat. NPM, p. 125.

102, tena vede yatra darśaśabdo' māvāsyāśabdo vā śrutastatra yāgasamudāyopasthitiḥ—MP, p. 12.

103. niṣādānāṁ sthapatiḥ iti ṣaṣthisamāso bhaviṣyati, śreṣtho niṣādānāṁ. SB, under MS. 6.1.51.

104. niṣāda eva sthapatirbhavitumarhati. kasmāt? śabdasāmarthyāt, niṣādaṁ hi niṣādaśabdaḥ śaknoti vadituṁ śravaṇenaiva, niṣādānāṁ tu sthapatiṁ lakśaṇayā brūyāt. śrutilakṣaṇāviṣaye ca śrutirnyāyyā na lakṣaṇā—SB, under MS. 6.1.51.

.105 ṣthapaṭirniṣadāssyāt śabdasāmarthyāt, SB, under *Ibid.*

106. tasmāt niṣāda eva sthapatiḥ syāt, *Ibid.*

107. ata eva 'niṣādasthapatiṁ yājayet' ityatra na tatpuruṣo lakṣaṇāpatteḥ, kintu karmadhārayo, lakṣaṇābhāvāt. BP, p. 462.

108. MK, Vol. VII, p. 3348.

109. 'tubhyāmetamagnisomīyame4ādasākapālaṁ purṇamaāeprayacchadi' tyagnisomīyayāgo vihitaḥ. MP, p. 9.

110. Kumārila defines 'Ekavākyatā' as—
svārthabodhe samāptānamaṅgāṅgi tvavyapekṣayā.
vākyānāmekavākyatvaṁ punaḥ samhatya jāyate.
TV. 4 under MS. 1.4.24.

111. Vide, TC, p. 660.

112. parantu yadyanvayānupapattirlakṣaṇābījaṁ syāt, tadā yaṣṭīḥ praveśayetyādau lakṣaṇā na syāt, yaṣṭīṣu praveṣānvayasyā' nupapatterabhāvāt. tena yaṣti-praveśe bhojanatātparyānupapattyā yaṣtidhareṣu lakṣaṇā—SM under BP, pp. 444-45.

113. vastutastu tātparyānupapattisanddhānameva tadbījam. anythā gaṅgāyāṁ ghoṣa ityādau ghoṣādipade eva makarādilaksaṇāpattistāvatā' pyanyathānupapattiparihārāt. PLM, p. 45.

114. laksaṇābījantu tātparyānupapattireva, na tu anvayānupapattiḥ; 'kākebhyo dadhi raksyatām' ityatra anvayānupapattyabhāvāt, VP, p. 105.

115. mukhyārthabhādhe tadyukto yayānyo'rthaḥ pratīyate.
rūḍḍheḥ prayojānādvāsau laksaṇā śaktirarpitā. SD. II.5.

116. ...... 'gaṅgāyām ghoṣā' ityadau ca gaṅgādīnāṁ ghoṣādyādhāratvasambhavānmukhyārthasya bādhe vivecakatvādau sāmīpye ca sambandhe rūḍḍhitaḥ prasiddhestathā ... laksaṇā. KP, p. 45.

117. Vastutastu padalaksaṇayaivopapattau na vākyalkasaṇā. TC, p. 722.

118. tathāhi gabhīranadyoranvayabodhottaraṁ nādīpadaṁ gabhīrapadaṁ vā svajñapyagabhiranadyāstīraṁ lakṣayati na vākyam. *Ibid.*

119. vākye tu śakterabhāvāt śakyasambandharūpā lakṣaṇā' pi nāsti. yatra tu gybhīrāyāṁ nadyāṁ ghoṣa ityuktam, tatra nadīpadasya nadītīre lakṣaṇā. ...... nadīpadasya gabhīranadītīre lakṣaṇā, gabhīrapadaṁ tātparyagrāhakam. NSM under

BP, Pp. 453-54.

120. laksaṇā ca na padamātravṛttiḥ, kintu vākyavṛttirapi. yathā 'gabhīrāyāṁ nadyāṁ ghosaḥ' ityatra 'gabhīrāyāṁ nadyām' iti padadvayasamudāyasya tīre laksaṇā. VP, p. 106.

121. na ca 'odanaṁ pacati caitraḥ piṭhare' ityādau caitrapiṭharādīnamarthānāṁ vâkyārthe sambandhānarhatvam, na ca tallakṣitayā anvitāvasthāyā anvayāntaraśālitā, na caivaṁ laksaṇā .... tadidamucyate—'mṛsyāmahe vācyānupapattitaḥ' it, sambandhavaśaprāptasya' iti ca, na punaḥ 'vākyārthe sambandha' iti ca 'anvayāt' iti ca. TB, p. 89.

122. nanu neyaṁ laksaṇā bhavitumarhati, tathāhi—'vācyasyārthasya ...... laksaṇocyate' iti ...... na ca 'odanaṁ caitraḥ pacati piṭhare' ityādau ...... punaranyāntaraśālitā. CS. pp. 261-62.

123. padārthānāṁ hi vākyārthe ...... padairabhihitāḥ svārthāḥ vākyārthasyāvabodhakāḥ. NRM, p. 120.

124. asmanmate hi padārthānāṁ smṛtisiddhatvāt ...... śaktyantarkalpanaiva nāsti. MM, p. 97.

125. padāni tāvat pṛthak padārthān smārayantyeva. na tu tāvatā viramanti. smāritameva tu svaṁ svamarthaṁ punaritarapadārthānvitatvenābhidhāyaiva virmanti. MM, p. 96.

126. ...... śaktitrayakaipanavitabhidhane'pi tulya. CS, p. 260.

127. nyāyasampāditavyaktiti vṛddhavyavahārapravaatitāyāṁ śabdārthapravṛttau ye nyāyāḥ śabdārthagocarāḥ ekavākyatvabhinnavākyatvādayaḥ pūrvoktassādhāraṇāḥ ye ca dvādaśādhyāyipratipādyā vedārthanirṇaye prātisvikāṇ śabdāntarābhyāsādayaḥ śruti-liṅgavākya-prakaraṇādayaḥ śrutyarthapaṭhanasthānādayo vacanāmadkeyacodanādyaśca tairvimarṣadaśayāṁ sampādite śabdārathānāmanvayārtnatvibhāge sati pati paścātsmṛtyupanītaiḥ padairyogyakramena vākyārthāvagatirityarthaḥ. TR, p. 36.
Vide, NPS under CS, p. 255.

128. autpattikastu śabdayārtnena sambandhastasya jñānamupadeśaḥ. MS. 1.1.5.

129. The 2nd verse of the 2nd Kāṇḍa of the *Vākyapadīya*, in full, is as follows :
"padamādyaṁ pṛthaksarvaṁ padaṁ śakāṅkṣamityapi /
vākyaṁ prati matirbhinnā bahudhā nyāyavādinām" //

130. In the 1st and the 2nd verses of the 2nd Kāṇḍa of the

Vākyapadīya, the eight alternatives are stated. The Ist verse is ;

"ākhyātaśabdaḥ saṁhāto jātiḥ saṁghātavartinī /
eko' navayaśabdaḥ kramo buddhyanupasaṁhṛtiḥ" //

131. anvitābhidhānavādimatena tu—ākhyāṭaśbdaḥ, padamādyam, pṛthaksarvaṁ paraṁ sākāṅkṣam, iti taiṇi lakṣaṇāi iti vivekaḥ. FV. 7 under PP, p. 414.

132. The sūtra is :
"arthaikatve dravyauuṇayoraikarmānniyamaḥ syānt".

133. lakṣaṇā hi padoṣaḥ, vākyabhedastu vākyadoṣaḥ. MNP, p. 11.

134. . . . sameṣu vākyabhedaḥ syāt, sameṣu parasparānāukaṁṣe vākyaṁ bhidyate. SB. under MS. 2.1.47.

135. Vṛddhavyavahārapratiāyāṁ ye nyāaḥ śabdārthagocarāḥ ekavākyatvabhinnavākyatvādayaḥ pūrvoktassādhāraḥ ye ca dvādaśādhyāyipratipādyā vedārthanirṇaye prātisvikāḥ śabdāntarābhyāsādayaḥ śrutiliṅgavākyaprakaranādayaḥ śrutyarthapaṭhana—sthānādayo vacananāmadheyaeodanāśca tairvimarśadaśāyāṁ sampādite śabdārthānāmanvayārhatvavibhāge sati paścṣtsmṛtyupanīthaiḥ padairyogyakrameṇa vākyārthāvagatirityarth—TR, p. 36.

136. That the *Bṛhaṭṭīkā* remains unpublished, can be known from the Article "Kumārila add Bṛhaṭṭikā, in which it is stated as—

'Its very name and the references to it in the catalogues show that it is very voluminous and probably its enormous size had stood unfortunately in the way of its being preserved to posterity'. Proceedings of the the 3rd Oriental Conference, Madras, 1924 (p. 528).

137. FN. 4 under MP, p,54.
Also 'kathaṃbhāvākāṅkṣaparipūrakatvamitikartavyatātvam' *Ibid.*, p. 54.

138. The verses (no. 80 & 81) are to be found in the Vākyādhikaraṇa of the work. SV. p. 605.

139. padāni tāvat pṛthak padārthān smārantyeva.
na tu tāvatā viramanti smāritameva tu
svaṁ svarthaṁ purnaritarapadārthānvitatvenābhidhāyaiva viramantīti rādhāntaḥ. MM, p. 96.

140. the second half of the verse is as follows :

codahā copadeśaśca vidhiśaikārthavādinaḥ, SV. AU. 5Ū. 11.

141. pramāṇaṁ smṛtiḥ sandeho viparyaśceti eaturvidham jñānam. PP. p. 43.

142. tasmādabhidhāyakameva padaṁ na smārakamiti. NRM, p. 107.

143. Vide NTY, p. 344.

144. The first half of the verse is as follows : na hyekaṁ lakṣayedeṣu buddhipūrvaṁ kathañtana.

145. The sūtras are :
(i) 'arthaikatvādekaṁ vākyaṁ sākṅkṣaṁ cedvibhāge syāt'.
(ii) 'sameṣu vākyabheadaḥ syāt'.

146. PIS, p. 190.

147. *Ibid.*, p. 190.

148. abhidheyāvinābhūte pravṛttirlakṣaṇeṣyate /
lakṣamāṇaguṇairyogād vṛtteriṣṭā tu gauṇatā //
TV under MS. 1.4.22.

149. nanu cānyatvopalabdhau satyāṁ gaurvāhīkasya ca gauṇa nirdeśa upapadyate—gaurvāhīka iti.
BR, p. 147.

150. sammārṣti srūca ityatra kiṁ pradhānākhyakarmatā /
guṇakarmatvamathavā dṛṣṭa bhāve' avaghātavat //
guṇatvaṁ nahi . . . syād dvitīyayā /
MNP, p. 12.

151. 'citrayā yajeta paśukāmaḥ' ityāmnāyate. tatra citrāśbdo nodbhidavadyaugikaḥ, kiṅtu ruḍhyā citratvaṁ strītvaṁ cābhidhat.e . . . tasmāt citrrśabdaḥ pūrvavadyajisāmānādhikaraṇyena yāgadāmadheyaṁ bhavati. Tā. B. 20.1.2.

152. tasmād vājapeyaśabdo na guṇavidhāyayakaḥ, kiṅtu yathoktadravyaṁ nimittīkṛtyāgnihotraśabdavat karmanādheyam NMV, p. 54.

153. 'darśapaurṇamāsābhyām svargakamo yajeta' ityasmin phalavākye saṅyavivakṣayā dvivacana nirdeśa upapadyate. Tai. S. 2.6.1.

154. kalpe sarvātithau darśakāryatokteḥ . . . JNM. 1.2.7.25.

155. The Sūtras are :
(a) 'tathā yūpasya vediḥ'
(b) 'deśamātraṁ vā' śiṣyenaikyatvāt'.

156. . . . tasmāt laukikadeśa evātra yūpāṅgatvena vidhīyate, na tu samskṛtavedi-bhāgaḥ. JNM, 3.7.6.

157. aprādhānyaṁ vidheryatra pratiṣedhe pradhānatā /
prasajyapratiṣedo' sau kriyayā saha yatra nañ. //
as quoted in SD, VII, pp. 481-82
158. pradhānatvaṁ vidheryatra pratiṣedhe' pradhānatā /
paryudāsa sa vijñeyo yatrottarapadena nañ //
Ibid., p. 482.
159. Vide, SB under MS. 10.4.8.
160. Vide, SD, pp. 41-43.
161. Vyaktyākṛtijātayastu padārthāḥ. N.S. 2.2.68.
162. Vide, PWM, p. 142.
163. sañketo gṛhyate jāṭu guṇadravyakriyāsu ca. SD. 11.4.
164. ākṛtistu kriyārthatvāt.
165. ākṛtiḥ śabdārthaḥ. SB under *Ibid.*
166. jātirāśayato bhinhą pratyakṣajñānagocara. PP, p. 64.
167. prābhākarāstu jātiśaktijñānādeva jātiprakāreṇa vyakteḥ smaraṇam. SKV. 190.
168. Vide, PWM, pp. 136-71.
169. Vide, BR, p. 292.
170. anyeṣām tu mate padānāṁ tattatsāmānyabhūto vācyo' rathah, vākyasya tu parasparānvitāḥ padāpaksayābhihitānvayaḥ, vākyāpekṣayā tvanvitābhidhānam. evamcaitayoḥ samuccaya iti. AVM, p. 41.
171. abhidhātrī matā śaktiḥ padānāṁ svārthaniṣṭhatā /
teṣām tātparyaśaktistu samsargāvagamavadhīḥ //
NM, p. 372
172. Vide, PWM, p. 235.
173. Vide, *Ibid.*, p. 179.
174. Vide, NTK, p. 344.
175. Vide, ITM, p. 212.
176. Vide, ILM, p. 33.
177 Vide, PIS, p. 137.
178. ākhyātaṁ sāvyayakārakeviśeṣaṇaṁ vākyam.
Var, 9 under Pa. SU, 11.1.1.
179. iti kārye' rathe vedasya prāmāṇyaṁ darśayati tallakṣaṇo dharmaḥ iti vadan kāryarūpa eveti darśayati darśayati, B.R., p. 16.
180. pramāṇāntaragocaro liṅādiṣabdamātrālambanaḥ kāryatmā yāgādibhāvārthagocaro svargakāmādiniyojyamātmani prerayanniyojya vidhiḥ. NRM, p. 63.

181. tasmiṅśca kriyātirikte kārye vācye niścite liṅdīnāṁ loke kriyāyāṁ prayogo lākṣaṇiko bhavati anekārthatvasyānyāyyatvāt. evaṁ ca nainittikaniṣedhādhikārayorasatyapi phalavate' pūrvameva vākyārtho bhaviṣyati. *Ibid.*
182. pratijñāhetūdāharaṇopanayanigamanāni pañcāvayavāḥ. TS, p. 38.
183. ghaṭādipadānāṁ kāryānvita-ghaṭādibodhe sāmarthāraṇād kāryatabodhaṁ prati ca liṅādīnāṁ sāmarthyāt tadahhāvānna śābdaboda ityapi kecit. BP. p. 428.
184. vrddhavyavahārapūrvikaiva sarvā śabdavyutpattiḥ—VM. p. 372.
185. prathamataḥ kāryānvita-ghaṭādau śaktyavadhārane' pi lāghavena paścāt tasya parityāgaucityāt—BP. p. 430.
186. bhāvanātvaṁ namā bhavituḥ prayojakavyāpāratvam, MP. p. 62.
187. iha hi liṅādi-yukteṣu vākyeṣu dve bhāvane gamyete-śabdātmikā ceti.—TB., p. 12.
188. iha hi liṅādiyvkteṣu vākyeṣu dve bhāvane gamyete-śabdātmikā' rthatmikā ceti. TV., p. 114.
189. bhāvanātvaṁ nāma bhavituḥ prayojakavyāpāratvam, MP, p, 62.
190. tatrārtha-bhāvanā sarvākhyāsādhāraṇī anyā tu liṅādyabhidheyā. MM, p. 271.
191. śabdaniṣṭhavyāpāratvācchābdī bhāvanetyucyate, yāgahomādiviṣayakapravṛttiheturvāt pravartanā preraṇeti cocyate. MP., p. 56.
192. abhidhābhāvanāmāhuranyāmeva liṅādayaḥ. TV under MS. 2.1.2.
193. codanālakṣaṇo' rtho dharmaḥ.
194. yathā agnihotraṁ juhuyāt svargakāma' ti. atrāgnihotrahotrahomena svargaṁ bhāvayetityarthaḥ pratīyate. MP., p. 5.
195. . . . āśutaravināśināṁ karmaṇāṁ kālāntrṛbhāvipādhanatvopayattyarthṁ-antarā puṇyapāparūrvaṁ kalpyate. *Ibid.*, p. 8.
196. liṅādayo hi preraṇāṁ kurvanti cābhidadhati ca' iti vārttikārīyāḥ. TR., p. 43.
197. iyañca ṣabdabhāvanā . . . kintu 'svādhyāyo' dhyetavyaḥ' iti vākye eva kartavyātvena pratīyate. MP., p. 58.

198. adhyāpanavidhiprayuktatvādadhyayanaspa tat siddhireva prayojanamityarthaḥ, NRM., p. 3.

199. āptisaṁskāro yathā—'svādhyāyo' dhyetavyaḥ' (Tai. S.) iti adhyayanena svādhyāyo āpyata ityāptisaṁskāro' yam. MP. p. 46.

200. asādhāraṇaṁ kāraṇaṁ karaṇaṁ, TS., p. 25.
also—'sarvameva hi kāraṇam kartṛvyāpāragocaram, NRM., p. 78.

201. pūrvadeśaviyogenottaradeśasamyoga gamanam, TS., p. 12.

202. vidhāyako liṅādiḥ kāraṅam. NMV., p. 72.

203. brāhmaṇaśeṣaścarthavādaḥ. tasya vidheya prāśastya-pratītijananadvārā vidbivākyaikavākyatayā prāmāṇyamiti. MP., p. 2.

204. PSM., pp. 122-23.

205. vyutkrameṇopakāreṇa padārthaiścaiva vaikṛtaiḥ /
prākṛtairvidhiranveti so' tideśaśca sammataḥ ṛtideśaḥ //
prakārasya dharmāṇāñcaiva yujyate /
PP. Verse, 12 & 13½. p. 493.

206. vāṣtospatihomavākyaśeṣe śrūyate—'padekayā juhuyāt, darvihomaṁ kuryāt, puromuvākyāmanucya, yājyayā juhoti sadevatyayā' iti. asyāyamarthaḥ—āsrāvayetyādirastuśrauśat ityantaḥ mantrasamghaḥ . . . evaṁ satyatra yadyekayā darvyā juhuyāt tadānīmāsrāvanādimantrāṇāmavakāśābhāxenat . . . darvihomā ityucyante. te ca kasyā' pi yāgasya, hymasya vā na prakṛtayaḥ, na vikṛtayaḥ na vā prakṛtivikṛtayo bhaeanti. TV., p. 115.

207. ākāśasya tu vijñeyaḥ śabdo vaiśeṣiko guṇaḥ. BP., p. śabodaguṇamākāśam. TS., p. 11.
Also—śrotraṁ punaḥ śravaṇavivarasamjñako nabho deśaḥ PPB., p. 26.

208. śabdo guṇaḥ, athavā dravyamiti dvedhā vikalpya, śabdasya guṇatvapakṣe vyāpāravattaaṁ na ghaṭate. śabdo na vyāpāravān guṇatvāt rūpavadityamahumanaṁ bodhyam. dravyatvapakṣepi śabdo na vyāpāravān vibhūtvādākāśavadityanumānena śabdasya vyāpārvattvam nopapadyata ityāha. FN 3 under VM, p. 423.

209. kāryaniyatapūrvavṛttiḥ kāraṇam. TS., p. 25.

210. vākyādhikaraṇe vārttikakāreṇa dhātvarthātprāgeva śabdabhāvanā' rṭhabhāvanayossambaṅdho bhavaṭi. ekapratyaya-

vācyatvena samānā-bhidhidhānaśrutirityuktamityarthah. FN. 4 under VM., p. 424.

211. maṇḍanamiśrairbhāvanāviveke sarvākhyātānām bhāvanāvācitvamuktam (verse no. 27) FN. 5 under pp., p. 424. The verse is— anekārthatvāmanyayyaṁ tenaikādhikaraṇyataḥ/ karotinā tiṅanteṣu bhāvabhedo' numīyate // BV under MK., p. 3042.

212. karmapradhānaṁ kriyāpradhānamityarthaḥ—PR., p. 69. Also—vākyaṁ tadapi manyante yet padaṁ caritakriyam. Vā. P. 11. 326.

213. tatrākhyātatvaṁ sarvalakārasādhāranaṁ tadavacchedena Liṅpratyayaḥ puruṣapravarttirupamārthabhāvanāṁ pratipādayati. MP., pp. 51-52.

214. sāmānādhikaraṇyañcaiJārthanimittam. TR., p. 45.

215. dhātvarthavyatirekeṇa bhāvanā neti cenna tat. sarvadhātvarthasambandhaḥ karotyartho hi bhāvanā. JNM, p. 2.1.16.

216. 'pacati' ityukte 'pākaṁ karoti' ityetamarthaṁ sarve janāḥ pratiyanti. tatra pākaḥ, paktiḥ pacanamityetaiḥ śabdairvyavahṛiyamāṇo lingakārakasamkhyāyogyo dhātvarthaḥ siddhasvabhavah. 'karoii' ityanena vyavahriyamano sādhyasvabhāvaḥ—Visrara under *Ibid.*, p. 71.

217. satyaṁ daṇḍaśabdena daṇḍo nābhidhīyate, nanvapratīte daṇḍe daṇḍipratyayo' sti, asti tu daṇḍiśabdaikadeśabhūto daṇḍaśbdaḥ, yena daṇḍha pratyāyitaḥ. tasmāt sādhu etat, yat pratie viśeṣaṇe viśiṣṭaé pratiyate iti. SB under MS. 1.3.33.

218. Vide, BS., p. 415.

219. ayamarthaḥ—hitasādhanatākāryatayoḥ pūrvaṁ bheda uktaḥ, anantaraṁ hitasādhanesva kimiti kāryatamatirnanyatreti śaṅkām pariharanta āhuṇś ālikanāthah *kimtviti.* satyamastkāryatām vrajet tat svayaṁ kleśarupameva. katham trahi tasya kāryatvam ? na hi duḥkākarasya kāryatvamupapadyate, yatthā' huh—'akartavyo duūkhaphalaḥ' ityatate āha-*Phalasādhanatā tatreti* tasyaivaraṇantena *kārpateti* athava phalasadhanata tatṛa kāranam ? yāvatā pravṛttiṁ pratyeva kāraṇaṁ taditi kecittatrāha—*teneti.* teṇt kāryatāsya bhavati, na tu pravṛtteriti, ata eva tairuktaṁ 'jñāpakakoṭiniviṣṭā

phalasādhanatā kāryatāmanurudhyate. na tvasau tadātmaiveti'—Nayanaprasādinī under CS, p. 162.

220. dravyaguṇasamskāreśu Bādariḥ, MS. 3.13.

221. pūrvoktamevārthaṁ pakṣasādhyanirdeśenā' bhinīya darsayati—caitrasya pravṛttirdharminīti—FN. I. VM., p. 430.

222. naṇu tarhi icchā pravṛttihetuḥ jānāti icchati iti hi nyāaśāstramaryadā. sā liṇādivācyā syāt maivam icchā hyutpannā pravṛttinimittam. na tu jñātā. TR., p. 57.

223. atracyate—bhavediṣṭamanoratho yadi svātmanyapi kāryabodhasya pravartakatvamadhyavasīyate, samīhitasādhanatāyā eva tu svātmani pravartakatvādhyauasāyāt na ca bhūtādau vyahicāraḥ, pataḥ—
kāryasyāvagaterḥeturyādṛśam hitasādham /
pravṛttestādṛśam heturvyhicārastataḥ kutaḥ // 16 //
yenāpi hi kāryāvabodhaspaiva pravartakatvamabhyupeyate' bhyupeyate eva tenāpīṣṭasādhanatāvabodhasya kāryāvabodham prati hetutā, tadabhāve kāryabodhā—nupapatteḥ—C, p. 166.

224. ucyate—liṅādiśabdastāvat pramāṇāntaravisayaṁ kāryamarthamvabodhayati śabdantarāṇyapi ca kāryasyānyārhatvāt tatparaṇeva svārthānabhidadhati—RVL under BR., p. 35.

225. atredaṁ bodhyam—liṅāderathaḥ praisādirloke'vaca-myate tatra sama-hīna-jyāyobhiḥ prayoktrbhiḥ prayujyamānaḥ praisādivyapadeśaṁ bhajate. sarvatra sama—hīna—jyāyasāmprayoge kāryatvasyāparityāgāt avyavabhicārācca kāryameva liṅādyartho yuktyḥ, ato niyogāparaparyāvakāryābhidhānameva, praisadayastūpādhāya ityeva yuktaṁ upādhirnāma—yo'bhidhānānu-praveśī san śabdārthān viśeṣe 'vasthāpayati yathā—drtihariśabdaḥ atra paśutvamupādhiḥ. yadā haraṇakriyā paśusambandhinī, tadā tasyāḥ kartā drtihariśabdenocyate. tathā prakrte linādināṁ kārya vācye praiṣādaya upādhaya ityāśayenā' ha—kāryameveti—FN. 7, VM., pp. 430-31.

226. na ca kāryameva jyāyaḥ—samakanīyobhiḥ dratipadyamāṇam praiṣādivyapadeśabhāk sarvānugataṁ śabdārtha iti sāmpratam akāryatvābhyupagamenaiva yāsñāyāṁ liṅprayogādityuktam. NRM., p. 83.

227. jyāyasā hīnasya niyogaḥ preṣaṇam. samena samasyādhyeṣaṇam. hīnenottamasyābhyanujñānam, NK., on NRM, p. 85.
228. TR., p. 57.
229. BR., p. 289.
230. ayamāsāyaḥ talhāhi—krtiḥ puruṣaprayatnastatsādhyam, krteḥ pradhānañca yat, tat kāryamiti kāryasvarupamuktam bhavati. krtisādhyam kāryamityuktau dhātvarthasyāpi krtisādhyatvenā' tivyāptistatra syāt, atastavāraṇāya pradhānamiti viśesaṇam, atra prādhānyañca krtyuddeśyatvarūpam vivakṣitam. etāvanmātroktau svargādiphale' tiprasaktissyāt, atastadvyāvrttvartham krtisādhyatvamiti viśeṣaṇadalamupāttam . . . tatra krisādhyatvam krtyanvaya—vyatirekarūpānumānapramāṇenā' vagamyate. krtipradhānatvañca—mānasapratyakṣeṇa pratīyata iti, pratyakṣā—numānapramāṇagamyaṁ kāryamityu-cyate . . tattraivā' nukūladrṣṭāntamāha—odanapākavaditi. odanaḥ pratyakṣenā' vagamyate, pākasya tatsādhana—tvgmanvay0vyatirekābhyāṁavagamyata ityarthaḥ FN. 5 under *VM.*, pp. 431-32.
231. yaśca kāryamavabudhyate sa niyojyaḥ. svargakāmasya ca tasminneva kārye boddhrtayā'nvayaḥ yadeva tasya kāmyamānasādhanatāmanubhavitaṁ kṣamate. na ca kriyā kṣaṇabhaṅginī kālāntarabhāvinī phale heturbhavati. tena sa kāryatayā niyojyena saha nānvīyate. yattu kālāntarasthāyi kāryaṁ tādeva tena sahānvayaṁ gantumarhatīti kriyātireki mānāntarāvedyameva liṅādayaḥ kāryamabhidadhati tacca mānāntarāpūrvatvādapūrvamityucyate. RVL. under BR., p. 288.
232. ucyate—kāryameva vidhyarthaḥ kāryañca kṛtisādhyam. kṛtiśca prayatnaḥ, PP, p. 256.
233. kāryañca kṛtīpṣitamucyate. kṛtiḥ—ātmavyāpāraḥ—puruṣprayatna ityanarthāntaram. *Ibid.*, p. 452.
234. prābhākarāstu—kāryaṁ liṅāderarthaḥ, tacca sāmānyarūpeṇa liṅādīnabhidhiyate. viśeṣatastu—tattachatvāratho loke. yathā—pākaḥ, gamanamiti. ato loke ṭanmate kriyaiva kāryaṣabdeṇā'bhi—dhīyate.

bhāṭṭamīmāṁsakāstu—dhātvartho na kriyā, kintu karaṇakārakam, karmakārakaṁ vā bhavati dhātvarthe kvacitkriyavyapadeśo lākṣaṇikaḥ, mukhyā kriyā ṭu bhāvanā, sā cā' khyātapratpārthaḥ, na prakṛtyarthaḥḥ. saiva vākyārtha mukhyaviśeṣyatapa bhāsata it saṅgīrante. tathā coktam—"bhāvanaiva hi vākyārthassarxatrā" khyātavattayā anekaguṇajātyādikārakārthānurañjite". (TV., p. 445) FN. 2 under PP. p. 376.

235. na ca kṛtisādhyaṁ pradhānamiti kāryalakṣaṇaṁ yuktam, phale'tivyāpteḥ. atha sākṣātkṛtisādhyatvaṁ vivakṣitaṁ na ca tatphale' stīti matam, maivam. niyoge tadavhāvenāvyāpteḥ, bhāvārthasyaiva sākṣāt kṛtisādhyatvāt.—CS., p. 167.

236. atrocyate—bhavediṣṭamanorathọ yadi svātmanyapi kāryabodhasya pravartakatvamadhyavasiyate, samīhitaṣādhanatayā eva tu svātmamī pravartakatvādhyavasāyāt . . . yenāpi hi kāryāvabodhasyaiva pravartakatvamabhyupeyate' bhyupeyate eva tenāpīṣṭasādhanatāvabodhasya kāryāvabodhaṁ prati hetutā, tadabhāve kāryabodhānupapatteḥ—*Ibid.*, AP., 166.

237. tena loke kriyaiva kāryatayā śabdenābhidhīyate—BR., p. 36.

238. . . . vyutpitsamānaścaitraṁ pravartamānaṁ dṛṣṭvā'numinoticaitro'pi kāryabodhāt pravartate—iti—PP., p. 430.

239. tacca kāryamanvitamabhidheyamiti sthite 'agnihotram juhuyāt svargakāmaḥ' ityadiṣu vākyeṣu ṣaṣṭhādya-rāddhāntānusāreṇa svargakāmapadena niyojyatayā svargakāmaḥ samarpaṇīya iti sthitam. yaśca kāryamavabhudhyate, sa niyojyaḥ, RVL under BR. p. 288.

240. tacca mānāntarāpūrvatvādapūrvamtyucyate—*Ibid.*, p. 288.

241. yaśca kāryamavabudhyate sa niyojyaḥ. svargakāmasya ca tasminneva kārye boddhṛtayā' nvayaḥ yadeva tasya kāmyamānasādhanatāmanubhavituṁ kṣamate. na ca kriyā kṣaṇabhaṅgimī kālāntarabhāvinī phale heturbhavati tena sa kāryatayā niyojyena saha nānvīyate. yattu kālāntarasthāyi kāryaṁ tadeva tena sabānvayaṁ gantumarhatiti kriyātireki mānāntarāvedyameva liṅādayaḥ karyamabhidadhati tacca mānāntarāpūrvatvādapūrvamītyucyate. nanu tasyāyi kāryasya kutaḥ siddhiḥ. yāgādeḥ—RVL., p. 288.

242. Vide, Introduction to NRM, p. XXXVIII.

243. ayambhiprāyaḥ—dharmo hi niyogaḥ. sa ca svaniṣṭho na kiñcit prati guṇabhūta iti—RVL, p. 14.

244. guṇatvācna vedena na vyavasthā syāt.

245. *Ibid.*

246. KP. p. 227.

247. yadyapi svargādayaḥ puruṣaviśesanatvena śrūyante, tathāpi kāmaśrvtayastatpradhānaḥ. 'dandī praisānanvāha', 'lohitosṇīsā rtvijah pracaranti' iti derṣanāt. kutaḥ? bhāvanāyām bhāvyasyāpeksitatvāt. svargādīnām ca kāmyatatyā bhāvyatvapratiteḥ.—VB under MK, p. 3055.

248. svargakāmo yajetetyetnniyojyasamarpaṇaparaṁ na tu phalaparamiti gurumatam, tathā ca sasṭhādye rāddhāntitam—atastatsamarpakapadena samabhivyāhārāt sahapāṭhāt kriyātiriktaṁ njyogamavagamayanti liṅādaya ityuttareṇa sambandhaḥ—CS, p. 163.

249. niyojyaśca sa ucyate yaḥ kāyyaṁ mamedaṁ kāryamiti budhyate—NRM, p. 63.
Also,—vidhivākyeṣu mamedaṁ kāryamiti kāryapratyeta niyojyaḥ—NR. under *Ibid.*, p. 4.

250. svargakāmasya ca tasminneva kārye boddhṛtayā'nvayaḥ yadeva tasya kāmyamānasādhanatāmanubhavitum ksamate RVL under BR., p. 288.

251. yaśca kāryamavabudhyate sa niyojyaḥ—*Ibid.*

252. niyojyassa ucyate, yo mamedaṁ kāryamiti svasambandhitayā kāryamavaiti ... tathahi—pustikamah kṣiram pivedityādau puṣṭikāmaḥ kśirapānam mayā kāryamiti boddhṛtayā'nveti—TR, p. 54.

253. "To explain—the Niyoga cannot be a true Niyoga, until there is a Niyojya, the person to be prompted to exertion, as without exertion there can be no Niyoga then again, without the agent there can be no exertion, nor can an agent put forth exeriion—and be a Niyogya—until he is entitled to the undertaking resulting from that exertion." PSP, p. 164.

254. kaścāyaṁ niyojyo nāma yadanvayātkriyātiriktaniyogasiddhiḥ? sa kiṁ kāryaṁ prati guṇabhūtaḥ? pradhādabhūta vā? nādyaḥ guṇative kartṛtvāyāntarbhāvāt. na dvitīyaḥ, pradhānye' dhikṇryanvayapātāt ... kāryamātmīyatvena yo'vabudhyate sa niyojya iti cet ... niyojyatvamiti viṣayabhedādheda iti cet, maivam ... parasparaśrayaprasaṅgāt. CS, pp. 175-76.

255. na jātu kāmaḥ kāmanamupabhogena śāmyati /
haviṣaḥ kṛṣṇavarṭmeva bhūya evābhivardhate //
MT. p. 2/94.

256. dravyāṇāṁ karmasaṁyoge guṇatvenābhi-sambandhaḥ. MS. 6.1.5.; tasmāt anvayavyatirekābhyāṁ etadavagamyate, prītau svargaśabdo vartate iti. SB. under *ibid.*
257. 'apeksitatvāt bhāvyasya svargakāmā hi ttatparāḥ / viseṣaṇapradhānatvaṁ daṇḍītyādiṣu darsitam // BV. 57, vide MK, p. 3053.
258. yadi ca yāgo na prītyartho bhavet asādhakaṁ karma bhavet . . . yo hi prityarthaḥ sa sādhyate. SB., under MS. 6.1.2.
259. Vide, TR, p. 55.
260. Vide, FN. 6, under PP, p. 436.
261. api ca yāgo nāma devatāpūjā, pūjā ca pūjanīyaṁ prati guṇabhūta loke dṛśyate. SB, under MS. 9.1.4.
262. The sūtra in full is as follows :— "karmaṇyārambhabhāvyatvāt kṛṣivat pratyārambhaṁ phalāni syuḥ".
263. tarhi yajamānapuruṣasamskāratayā kriyā kāryotayocyatām. samskṛtśca puruṣah kālāntare phalabhāghaviṣyatīti. maivam —samskārakatva pramāṇābhāvāt. TR, p. 55.
264. nanu kriyaiva kāryatayocyotām. tasyāśca phalasādhanatvāśravaṇāyathānupapattyā . . . maivam –na ca . . . , na hi sādhanasādhanaṁ (tasya sādhanam) syāt. TR, p. 55.
265. tallaksaṇo dharma iti. asyārthaḥ—codanālakṣaṇasutreṇa codanālakṣanaḥ kāryarūpa evārtho na siddha-rupa iti pratijñātam. tadanena bhāṣyena vyākhyāyate dharmaśabdaśca vedārthamātraparaḥ. RVL under BR, p. 16.
266. tasmāccodanālakṣaṇo' rthaḥ śreyaskaraḥ. ya eva sreyaskaraḥ sa eva dharmasabdenocyate. ko' rthaḥ yo niḥśrayasāa, ko' nārthaḥ yaḥ pratyavāy. SB under MS. 1.1.2.
267. kathaṁ kartavyatayā 'nupadiśyamāno' rthaścodanālakṣaṇo bhavati, kāthaṁ codanālakṣaṇasya sato dharmatvanivṛtyarthamarthaśabdānvaya upapādyate. kartavyatayā nopadiśyante codanālakṣaṇaśceti śaṅkatāmivopalakṣyate. BR, p. 28.
268. mokṣārthī na pravarteta tatra kāmyanisiddhayoḥ / nityanaimittike kuryāt pratyavāyajihāsayā // SV. 5.110.
269. jaiministu khalvācāryaḥ karmāṇyapi śeṣabhūtāṇi manyate sma. na bādarivāvadhāraṇamanumene. sa hi dadarśa, na

yāgaḥ kartavyatayā codyate. phalakāmasya tu tatsādhanopāyatveneti evam śruto' rathaḥ pariaṛhito bhaviṣyati. *SB* under MS. 3.1.4.

270. asādhakaṁ tu tu tādartthyāt (MS. 6.1.2). yadi ca yāgo na prityartho bhavedasādhakam karma bhavet sādhayitāram nādhigacchat. yo hi prītyarthaḥ sa sādhyate nānya. yadyapi yāgaḥ kartavyaḥ śruyate tathāpi na kartavayaḥ—
Ibid under Ibid.

271. dharmaśabdaśca vedārthamātraparaḥ. EVL under BR, p. 16.

272. śreyo hi puruṣaprītissā dravyaguṇakarmabhiḥ /
codanālakṣaṇaissādhyā tasmātteṣveva dharmatā //
SV, 2. 191,

273. tata ucyate, bhāvārthāḥ karmaśabdāḥ, tebhyaḥ kriyā pratīyeta, yajeta ityevamādibhyah . . . phalasya kriyā kāraṇam niṣpatiriti. *SB* under *MS* 2.1.1.

274. sarvadhātvarthasambandhah karotyartho' hi bhāvanā.
dhātvarthaḥ karaṇaṁ tasyāṁ samānapadavarṇitaḥ.
NMV, 2.1.6½ & 7½.

275. asti jyotistomastatra śruyate, somena yajeta, daksiṇāni juhoti ... yajati juhotayaste kiṁ samhatya kāryam kurvanti, uta viyutya ? ... kiṁ tāvat prāptam, saṁhatya iti.—SB. uuder MS. 2.2.1.

276. yattu kālāntarasthāyi kāryaṁ tadeva tena sahānvayaṁ gantumaratīti kriyātireki mān 'āntarāvedyameva. RVL. under BR, p. 288.

277. niyojyasambandhasamarthaṁ kālāntarasthāyi kāryam ... iti. VM. under pp, p. 440.

278. yattu kālāntarasthāyi kāryaṁ tadeva tenā niyojpena sahānvayaṁ gantumarhatıti kriyātireki mānāntarāvedyemeva linṅādyaḥ kāryambbhidhati. tacca mānātarāpūrvatvādapūrvamityucyate. RVL under BR, p. 288.

279. Vide, SC, p. 176.

280. dvividhaṁ hi kāryaṁ kriyārūpaṁ tadariktaṁ niyogarūpam ca. tatra prathamaṁ prati guṇabhūtatvaṁ kartṛtvam, dvitiyaṁ prati guṇabhūtatvaṁ niyojyamiti guṇabhāve samāne' pi yatprati guṇabhāvastadvaiṣamyadidaṁ vaiṣamyamityarthah. NPS under CS, pp. 175-76.

281. niyogaśabdenaa kriyāvyatiriktamapūrvaṁ kāryatayā ātmani niyuñjānamucyate. BR, p. 288.

282. Vide, Appendix, p. 30 under PIS.
283. 'ityāneya kratuḥ' iti. SP, p. 2.
284. *Ibid.*, p. 3.
285. sarvārthamaprakaraṇāt. MS. 3.6.1.
286. ucyate—juvādyo' vyabhicāritakratusamandha iti tatsambandhamukhena..................juhvādiṣu parṇatādisambandhāt. pp, p. 461.
287. svādhyāyadhyayanavidhikārāśravanāt, ācāryakaraṇavidhiprayojyatvācca. BR. p. 2.
288. pakṣe' prāptasya prāpako vidhirniyamavidhiḥ. yathā 'brīhīnavahanti' tyadih. AS. p. 121.
289. adhikārāpūrvākāṅkṣāyāśca niraṅkuśaprasaratvāt prayājādiyāgānāṁ ca tadanvayāyogyatvāt ... idameva grāhakagrahanam ...... prayājādīnām tatkaraṇatvāyogāt teṣām grāhakagrahaṇāvagatamapūrvaidamarthyam tatkaraṇopakāradvārā nirvāhatīti NK under NRM.p. 199.
290. saptamādye tīkākṛtā grāhakagrahaṇamanvitābhidhānopādānāyā' bhyupagatam......tadeva anvitābhidhānam, grāhakagrahaṇamiti ca gīyate. Introduction, p. 17 of the pp.
291. sannipātīnamapūruaśesatvam grāhakgrahaṇenā bhavati... kāraṇaśesatvam tu nāñyatḥ siddhamiti upādānameva tesām tacchesatayā viniyojakamāśrayaṇīyamiti. NK. under NRM, p. 208.
292. katham tarhi paśveādīnāmaṅgatvam ? uktam hi paśorupādānaviṣayatvam..................viniyogakṛtameva. BR. p. 3.
293. Vide, BR, p.. 288.
294. tadanu karmanirvartakastu karteti tisro'vasthā ekasyaiva kramabhāvinyaḥ NK under NRM, p. 4.
295. adhikārah puruṣasyaiścaryam karmaṇi. RVL under BR, p. 14.
296. CS, p. 165.
297. yattu garbhadāsavadityuktam, tadayuktam. dvau hi tatra prayatnau cetanadvayasamavāyinau. tatra svāminaḥ prayatnaḥ svārthamuddiṣya garbhadāsopakārāya pravartate. garbhadāso'pi ca svayogaksemasamavahitasvantavṛttireva pravartate svāmyarṭhe ... na ca svamīva 'centanāntaramātrą' sti, yatkrtim prati prādhānyam niyogasya bhavet. —NKK under VV, p. 67.

298. api ca na niyogamātraṁ provṛtthihetuḥ mithyā tarhi niyogajñānam. na ca tadyuktaṁ kāraṇadvyabhāvāt. —VV, p. 76.

299. tānyaṅgāṇi dvividhāni sannipatyopakārakāṇi ārādupakārakāni ceti. yānyaṅgāni sākṣāt poramparayā vā pradhānayāgaśarīram niṣpādya taddvārā tadutpattyapūrvoyogīni tāni sannipattyopakārakāni. MP, pp. 28-29.

300. ātmasamavetāpūrvajanakānyārādupakārāni yathā prayājājyabhāgānuyājādini etāni dravyagataṁ devatāgataṁ vā saṁskāraṁ na janayanti kintvātmagatamadṛṣṭaṁ janayantītyārādupakārakāni—*Ibid.*, pp. 31-22.

301. tadeva phalāpūrvam tatkaraṇatvañca prācyodīcyaṅgoviśiṣṭasya pradhānasya bhavati, na pradhānamātrasya. pradānamātrādeva phalapūrvajanane phalasyāpi tata eva siddheraṅgāmānarthakyāpatteḥ. *Ibid.*, p. 8.

302. avāntarāpūrvakaraṇopakārakatvamevārādupakārakatvam. TR, p. 64.

303. ārādupakārakaṁ dvividham—adṛṣṭaprayojanam, dṛṣṭādṛṣṭaprayojakañca. tatradṛṣṭaprayojanam 'samidho yajotī (S.Ba. 2.6.1.1) tyādi. asya kārakagatam kiñcit prayojanam na dṛśyate, PP, p. 468.

304. tatra sannipattyopakārakam caturvidham, sādhyabhūtotpattiprāpti-vikṛti-samskṛti-bhedāt. yathākramam samyavanadohana-vilapana-proksaṇādirūpam. *Ibid.*, p. 457.

305. punarapi guṇakarma caturvidham—utpattyāptivikrtisamskṛtibhedāt. yathā—'agnīnādadhita' iti . . . ādhāḥasya utpattisamskārakatvam. āptisamskāro yathā—'svādhyāyo' dhyetavyah' (Tai. S.) iti . . . vikṛtiryathā—'brīhīnavahanti' iti . . samskritiryathā—'brīhīn prokṣati', MP, pp. 45-46.

306. iha caturvidhamaṅgajātam — jāti-guṇa-dravya-bhāvārthātmakam. tatra bhāvārthātmakamapi dvividham—sannipattyopakārakam, ārādupakārakañceti. PP. p. 457.

307. Vide, PN. 2 under PP. 444.

308. daiva puruṣakāre ca karmasiddhirAyavasthitā . . . evam puruṣakāreṇa vinā daivam na siddhyati'
PN. 3 under PP, p. 444.

309. nityanaimittikayorakaraṇe pratyavāya eva kṛte phalam nāstīti kecit. MP, p. 48.

310. na hi niṣedhena nānārthasyākāraṇe pratyavāyaparihārthatā

. . . tadā caitadapi siddhyet—pratisiddham pratyavāyayeti na tvevamasti. CVL. on BR, p. 28.

311. nityanaimittikaireva kurvāṇa dūritakṣayam (BK), IPM, p. 160.

312. *Ibid.*, p. 160.

313. nanu kāmādhikāre 'nuṣ ṭhānābhāve phalam na siddhyet. Taccaniṣṭam. nityeṣu tu kim syāt. vidhisiddhirna syāt. tataḥ kimaniṣṭam tadevaniṣṭam, tasyaiva puruṣārthatvāt ata eva kāmādhikāre'pi vidhisiddhiḥ prayojanam, phalasiddhistu nantariyakī . . . tasmät kāryameva pradhānam. tadeva vākyārthaḥ. TR, p. 59.

314. In the vrtti text, the no. of the sūtra of the said Adhikaraṇa is given as *MS. 1.3.5* which is found incorrect.

315. yavamayaścaruḥ, vārāhī upānahau vaitase kaṭe prājāpatyān sañcinoti iti yavavarāhavetasaśabdān samāmananti tatra keciddīrghaśūkeṣu yavaśabdam prayuñjate, kecit priyaṅguṣu. varāhaśabdam kecit śūkare, kecit krṣṇɐśakunau . . . tatrobhayathā padārthāvagamādvikalpaḥ. SB under *MS* 1.3.8.

316. na kevalam vṛddhavyavahārādeva vyutpattiḥ prasiddhapadasamabhivyāhārabapi loke drśyate. vede'pi 'yavamayaścarurbhavati, vārāhi upānahāvupamuñcate ityatra yavavarāhasabdayoḥ priyangou dirghaśūke vayase sūkare ca prayujyamānayorarthavādasambhivyāhārāt dīrghaśūke sukare ca śaktiniyamo drṣṭaḥ. TR, p. 55.

317. evam vākyasesādapi saktigrahaḥ. yathā yavamayaścarurbhavatityatra yavapadasya dīrghaśūka-viseṣg ārtyānām prayogaḥ kaṅgau tu melecchānam tatra hi 'yatrānyā auṣadhayo mlāyante' thaite modamānāstisthanti'. tathā—
"vasante sarvasasyānām jatante patrasātanam.
modamānāsca tisthanti yaxāḥ kaṇisa-sālinaḥ". iti vākyaseṣād dīrghasūke saktirnirnīyate. NSM. Under BP, pp. 433-34.

318. na ca kāryamātre' avasitasaṅgattikā liṅādayaḥ sabdāḥ . . . kriyātiriktameva kāryamavagamayati, . . . iti yuktam vaktum. CS, p. 168.

319. Vide NSP under *ibid.*

320. nityanaimittika yorakaraṇe pratyavāya kṛte tu phalam nāstīti kecit. MP, p. 35.

321. Vide, vibhā under NKM (ii), p. 245.

322. Vide, CS, p. 155.
323. Vide, CS, p. 156.
324. Vide, *MS*, 1.3.8-10.
325. jñātārtham jñātasambandham śrotum śrotā pravarttate / sāstrādau tena vaktavayaḥ sambandhaḥ saprayojanaḥ //
Also—
sambandhaścādhikārī—ca viṣayaśca prayojanam / vinā 'nubandham granthādau mangaiaṁ naiva śasyate //.

Index

वाक्यार्थमातृका-वृत्तिः

प्रथमः परिच्छेदः

गम्भीरविततमर्थं वाचा संक्षिप्तया निबद्धमपि ।
न विदन्ति ये समग्रं कृपया तदनुग्रहः क्रियते ॥

तत्र कार्यवाक्यार्थवादिन एव भावम्, भावनाम्, अपूर्वञ्च वाक्यार्थान्प्रतिजानते । तत्रापूर्वमेव वाक्यार्थ इति साधनीयम् । तस्य मूलं पदानामन्विताभिधायितेति, तामेव तावदादौ परिशोधयति । अत्र ये प्रत्यस्तमितपदविभागं वाक्यमेव वाक्यार्थस्य वाचकमित्याचक्षते । ये च वाक्यान्त्यवर्ण एवेति, ये च पदैरनन्विताः पदार्था अभिहिताः परस्परान्वयमात्मनोऽवगमयन्ति इति । तन्निरासाय प्रतिजानीते—

पदेभ्य एव वाक्यार्थप्रत्ययो जायते यथा ।
तथा वयं निबध्नीमः प्रभाकरगुरोर्मतम् ॥ १ ॥

पदेभ्य एव, न वाक्यात्, नाप्यन्त्यवर्णात् । नापि पदार्थेभ्य इत्यर्थः ।
तं प्रकारं वक्तुमुपक्रमते—

पदैरेवान्वितस्वार्थमात्रोपक्षीणशक्तिभिः ।
स्वार्थाश्चेद बोधिताः बुद्धौवाक्यार्थोऽपि तथा सति ॥२॥

वाक्यार्थप्रतिपत्तौ हि पदानामनुपायत्वे तदन्यथानुपपत्त्या वाक्यमेकं तदुपायभूतं कल्प्यते । यद्यपि व्युत्पत्त्यनपेक्षाच्छब्दादर्थो नावगम्येत । यद्यपि चानन्त्याद्वाक्यानां तदर्थानाञ्च वैदिकस्य चार्थस्यानन्योपायत्वाद् व्युत्पत्तिरशक्या । तथापि काल्पनिकपदपदार्थव्युत्पत्तिसंस्कृताद् वाक्याद् वाक्यार्थमवगच्छतीत्याश्रीयते ।

यदि काल्पनिकत्वे पदपदार्थानां प्रमाणाभावादेकैकवर्णोच्चारणेऽर्थानवबोधात्, क्रमेणोच्चारितानाञ्च युगपच्छ्रवणासम्भवात्, पूर्वपूर्ववर्णानु-

भवजनितसंस्कारसहितोऽन्त्यो वर्णः प्रत्यायकः, तस्य च पारमार्थिकपद-पदार्थव्युत्पत्तिः सहकारिणी इति पक्षः स्वीक्रियते। यदि वा पदैः सुकर-व्युत्पत्तयोऽनन्विता एव स्वार्था अभिहिता वाक्यार्थमवबोधयन्तीत्यङ्गी-क्रियते। यदि तु पदान्येवाऽन्वितान्स्वार्थानभिधदधातीति शक्येत साधयितुम्, तदा वाक्यार्थस्यावबुद्धत्वान्नैताः कल्पना आत्मानं लभन्ते ॥२॥

कथं पुनः पदानामन्वितस्वार्थमात्रबोधकत्वे वाक्यार्थावगतिः सिद्ध-यतीत्यत्राह—

प्रधानगुणभावेन लब्धान्योन्यसमन्वयान्।
पदार्थानेव वाक्यार्थान् सङ्गिरन्ते विपश्चितः ॥३॥

ननु तेषां भूयस्त्वाद् भूयांसो वाक्यार्थाः, वाक्यानि च स्युः, इत्य त्राह—

भूयांसो यद्यपि स्वार्थाः पदानां ते पृथक् पृथक्।
प्रयोजनतया त्वेकवाक्यार्थं सम्प्रचक्षते ॥४॥
तत्प्रतीत्येककार्यत्वाद् वाक्यमप्येकमुच्यते।

कथं पुनरेकप्रयोजनत्वमित्यत्राह—

प्रतिपत्तिर्गुणानां हि प्रधानैकप्रयोजना ॥५॥

यद्धि प्रधानभूतं, तदेव कथन्नाम विशिष्टं प्रतीयतामित्येवमर्थं गुणानां प्रतिपादनम्, तेन तत्रैव तात्पर्यम्, तदेवप्रमेयम्, तात्पर्यविषय एव शब्दस्य प्रामाण्याभ्युपगमात्, तस्य तथाभूतस्य प्रतिपत्तिर्नैकनिबन्धनेति, वाक्यमेव तत्र प्र माणम्। अतएव च "षष्ठाद्ये न पदं नाम किञ्चन वाक्ये, न पदार्था नाम केचन वाक्यार्थे" [बृ० टी० ६. १. १.] इत्युक्तम्। पृथग्भूतं पदं नाम न किञ्चन प्रमाणमस्ति। पृथग्भूताश्च पदार्था न प्रमेयाः इत्यर्थः। एतच्च तत्रैव [बृ० टी० ६. १. १.] स्पष्टमुक्तम्। ॥५॥

सम्प्रति वाक्यमेव बाचकं वाक्यार्थस्येति ये ब्रुवते ये च वाक्यान्त्य-वर्ण एवेति। तन्निराकरणायाह—

व्यवहारेषु वृद्धानां वाक्यश्रवणभाविषु ।
आवापोद्धारभेदेन पदानां शक्तिनिश्चयः ॥६॥

यद्यपि वृद्धव्यवहारपूर्विकैव सर्वाशब्दव्युत्पत्तिः वाक्यैरेव च व्यवहारः । तथापि तत्पदावापे यस्यार्थस्यावापः यदुद्धारे चोद्धारः; तस्मिन्नेवार्थे तस्य पदस्य वाचकशक्तिरवसीयते । न च तथा सति वाक्यार्थप्रतिपत्तिर्नोपपद्यते, वक्ष्यमाणत्वान्न्यायस्य, येन कार्यबलेन वाक्यमेकं प्रत्यक्षपरिदृश्यमानवर्णपदभेदापह्लवेन कल्प्येत ।

किञ्च, शिशो ! गामानय, शिशो ! गां बधान; वत्स ! गामानय, वत्स ! गां बधान; अर्भक ! गामान्य, अर्भक ! गां बधान; डिम्भ ! गामानय, डिम्भ ! गां बधान' इत्यष्टानां वाक्यानामष्टौ वाचकशक्तयः कल्प्याः । पदवादिनस्तु सप्तानां पदानां सप्तैव शक्तय इति कल्पनालाघवम् । अनयैव दिशा शुक्लामिति पदप्रक्षेपे वाक्यवादिनोऽष्टावपराः कल्प्याः, पदवादिनस्त्वेकैव । अपारमार्थिके च पदपदार्थविभागे किमाश्रिता व्युत्पत्तिरभ्युपायतामुपैतीत्यपि चिन्तनीयम् ।

ये पुनः वाक्यान्त्यवर्णस्य वाचकतामाहुः, तन्मतेऽपि तावत् पदार्थविभागस्य पारमार्थिकत्वाद् घटेतैव व्युत्पत्तिः । ननु वाच्यवाचकसम्बन्धग्रहणमेव व्युत्पत्तिरित्युच्यते, न च वाक्यान्त्यवर्णवाचकत्ववादिनां पदं पदार्थस्य वाचकम्, अतस्तन्मते निर्विषयैव व्युत्पत्तिः । उच्यते । न निर्विषया, निमित्तनैमित्तिकभावस्याभ्युपगतत्वात् । केयमवाचकस्य निमित्तता ? नैष दोषः । वाक्याद्धि यत्पदप्रयोगे सति तत्पदान्वितो वाक्यार्थः प्रतीयते, तत्पदं तस्यार्थस्यावाचकमपि भवति निमित्तम् । किन्तु तन्मतेऽपि शक्तिकल्पनागौरवं पूर्वोक्तन्यायेन तुल्यमेव ।

येऽप्याहुः-वाक्यमेव स्मृत्यारूढं वाक्यार्थं प्रतिपादयतीति, तेषामपि प्राच्यमेव शक्तिकल्पनागौरवलक्षणं दूषणमशक्यपरिहारम् । भाष्यकारवचनं च "पूर्ववर्णजनितसंस्कारसहितोऽन्त्योवर्णः प्रत्यायकः"[शा. भा. पृ. ४६] इति निर्विषयम् । अशक्यञ्च महावाक्यस्य सकृत्स्मरणम् । तस्मात्पदानामेव वाचकशक्तिराश्रयणीया ।

अत्र केचिच्चोदयन्ति । ननु वृद्धव्यवहारप्रयुक्ते वाक्ये पदानां वाचकशक्त्यवधारणमेव नोपपद्यते । पुरुषवाक्यानामर्थं प्रति लिङ्गभावेन प्रमाणत्वाभ्युपगमात् । वाक्याद्धि कार्यभूतात्प्रतीतस्य वक्तुः तदर्थविषयं पूर्वविज्ञानं कारणभूतमनुमीयते तस्य च ज्ञानस्य ज्ञेयाव्यभिचारित्वात् ज्ञेयभूतार्थनिश्चय इति न वाचकशक्त्यवगमः । उच्यते । न नूनं भवान् नीतिपथोक्तमर्थं सम्यगाकलयति । परिहृतं हि तत्रेदम्-बालो हि व्युत्पद्यमानः प्रयोज्यवृद्धस्य शब्दश्रवणसमनन्तरभाविनीं विशिष्टचेष्टानुमितामर्थप्रतीतिं शब्दकारणिकामगबगच्छति । स तथा व्युत्पन्नः कदाचित्कस्यचिदनन्वितार्थपदरचनं वाक्यमुपलभते, तथोपलभमानस्य चैष विमर्शो जायते—सम्भाव्यमानानन्वितार्थपदरचनमिदं वाक्यं कथं प्रयोज्यवृद्धस्य अर्थनिश्चयं कृतवत् ? वृद्धस्यापि पुरुषायत्ते वाक्येऽनन्वितार्थपदरचनशङ्का ममेव सम्भवतीति । तस्ययैवं विचिकित्सोदये पुनरेष निश्चयो जायते—नूनमनेनायं प्रयोक्ता इत्थमवधारितो यदन्वितार्थान्येव पदान्ययं प्रयुक्ते इति । तथाविधपदप्रयोगनियमश्चास्यानुपलब्धेऽन्वये नोपपद्यत इत्येवमन्वयोपलम्भमनुमिमानेनान्वयो निश्चीयते, निश्चिते चान्वये वाक्यमेतदनुवादभूतमर्थस्येति । एवञ्चेदनुवादकतया तस्यार्थस्य तद्वाक्यं वाचकमेवेति पूर्ववाचकशक्तिज्ञानं नाऽयथार्थमिति मन्यते । यदि परं मया प्रागनुमानपुरस्सरोऽर्थनिश्चयोस्येति नावगतम्; यापि चेयमर्थस्यानिश्चितेऽस्एये विशिष्टवक्तृज्ञानानुमा, सापि पदानां स्वरूपमात्रावगमादेव नोपपद्यते, किन्तु विशेषावगमात् । न च शक्तेरन्यः पदानां विशेषोवगम्यते । ततो मयेवानेनापि पदानां वाचकशक्तिरवधारिता । तेन विशिष्टान्वयवाचकपदप्रयोगात्तद्विषयं वक्तुः पूर्वज्ञानमनुमितवान्, इति गभीरोऽयं नीतिमहाहृदः ।

अत्र केचिदाचक्षते-भवतु पदानां पदार्थेषु शक्तिज्ञानम्, तथाऽप्यन्विताभिधानं न सिध्यति इति । तथाहि प्रतियोगिनामनन्ततया अन्वयानामानन्त्यात्, तदानन्त्ये चान्वितानामप्यानन्त्यात्सम्बन्धग्रहणं दुष्करम् । अगृहीतसम्बन्धस्य च पदस्य वाचकत्वे एकस्माच्छब्दात्सर्वार्थप्रतीतिप्रसङ्गः । सामान्यान्वयाभिधानञ्च नाशङ्कनीयमेव वाक्येभ्यो विशेषान्वयावगमात् । स्वरूपमात्राभिधानेनाऽपि च वाक्यार्थप्रतिपत्त्युपपत्तावन्विताभिधानाश्रयणे शक्तिकल्पनागौरवम् ।

तथा पदेनान्वितस्वार्थोऽभिधीयमानः किमभिहितेन पदार्थान्तरेणान्वितोऽभिधीयते ? उत अनभिहितेन ? इति विकल्पनीयम् । अनभिहितेन चेत् पदान्तरप्रयोगवैयर्थ्यम् । एकस्माच्च सर्वान्वयप्रतीतिप्रसङ्गः । अभिहितेन चेत्, तदपि तर्हि पदमन्विताभिधायितया पदान्तरोपात्तमर्थमभिधानायापेक्षत इति, इतरेतराश्रयः प्राप्नोति । तस्मात् पदान्तराभिधानानपेक्षस्वरूपमात्राभिधानमेवार्थानां पदैः क्रियते । ते च तथाभूताः पदैरभिहिताः पदार्था आकांक्षासन्निधियोग्यतावन्तो वाक्यार्थमवगमयन्ति । न तेषां सम्बन्धग्रहणापेक्षा शङ्कनीया । यतः पदधर्मोऽयम्, नायमर्थधर्मः । तदाह भाष्यकारः "पदानि हि स्वं स्वमर्थमभिधाय निवृत्तव्यापाराणि, अथेदानीं अवगतास्सन्त वाक्यार्थमवगमयन्तीति" [मीमांसा शबरभाष्य १.१.२५.]

तदेतन्निराकर्त्तुमुपक्रमते—

ओप्यन्ते चोद्ध्रियन्ते च स्वार्था अन्वयशालिनः ।
अन्वितेष्वेव सामर्थ्यं पदानां तेन गम्यते ॥७॥

अत्राह—सत्यमन्वितपदार्थविषयावेवावापोद्धारौ, तथाप्यन्विताभिधानमशक्यम् । पारम्पर्येणापि तदुपपत्तेः तथाहि पदैरनन्वितोऽप्यभिहितोऽर्थोऽन्वितार्थप्रतिपत्तेर्निमित्तम्भवतीति पदानां पारम्पर्येणान्वितेष्वपि हेतुत्वम् । तदाहुः वार्त्तिककारमिश्राः—

'न विमुञ्चन्ति सामर्थ्यं वाक्यार्थेऽपि पदानि नः ।
तन्मात्रावसितेष्वेषु पदार्थेभ्यस्स गम्यते ॥'

पदार्थप्रतिपादनं च वाक्यार्थप्रतिपत्तये प्रयुक्तानां पदानामबान्तरव्यापार इति च तेषामेव व्यवहारः—

वाक्यार्थमितये तेषां प्रवृत्तौ नान्तरीयकम् ।
पाकज्वालेव काष्ठानां पदार्थप्रतिपादनम् ॥'

[श्लो.वा.७.२४३]

एतामाशङ्कामुपेक्ष्यैव तावद्दोषान्तरं परिहरति—

आकांक्षा-सन्निधिप्राप्तयोग्यार्थान्तरसङ्गतान् ।
स्वार्थानाहुः पदानीति व्युत्पत्तिस्संश्रिता यदा ॥८॥
आनन्त्यव्यभिचाराभ्यां तदा दोषो न कश्चन ।

यत्तावदुक्तम् आनन्त्याच्छब्दशक्त्यवधारणानुपत्तिः, अगृहीतशक्तेश्च वाचकत्वे व्यभिचारप्रसङ्गः इति । तदनुपपन्नम् । उपलक्षणाश्रयणेनापि सम्बन्धबोधः, सौकर्यादाकांक्षितेन योग्येन सन्निहितेन चान्वितं स्वार्थं पदं वक्तीति व्युत्पत्तिराश्रीयते । तेन—

यद्यदाकांक्षितं योग्यं सन्निधानं प्रपद्यते ।
तदन्वितः पदेनार्थस्स्वकीयः प्रतिपाद्यते ॥

इति संग्रहश्लोकः ।

का पुनरियमाकांक्षा ? प्रतिपित्तुर्जिज्ञासा । किन्निबन्धना पुनरसौ ? अविनाभावनिबन्धनेति केचित् । क्रिया हि कारकाविनाभाविनीति तां प्रतीत्य कारकं जिज्ञासते, एवं कारकमपि बुद्ध्वा क्रियामिति । तदयुक्तमिति मन्यामहे, जिज्ञासा विरामानुपपत्तेः । तथाहि-यदा तावत् कारकजिज्ञासा, तदा तदीयजनकतद्गुणतत्क्रिया-तत्कारकान्तरादिजिज्ञासाप्यापद्यते । अथ प्रयोजनाभावत् कारकज्ञानेन प्रयोजनं नास्ति, तत्र जिज्ञासा न स्यात् । अनुष्ठेयतया हि क्रियायामवगतायां कारकमन्तरेण तदनुष्ठानानुपपत्तेः; कारकज्ञानं न प्रयोजनवत्, वर्त्तमानापदेशादौ त्वननुष्ठेयतया नास्ति नः कारकज्ञानेनापि प्रयोजनम् । अथ च यत्रापि वाक्यमपरिपूर्णं मन्यन्ते, साकाँक्षाभिधायितया चापरिपूर्णता । अत एव तत्राध्याहारमपि कुर्वन्ति ।

यत्रापि चानुष्ठेयक्रियावगमः, तत्रापि निश्शेषकारकजिज्ञासा स्यात् । यथा 'देवदत्त गामानयेति' कारणानुपदानापरिपूर्णता स्यात् । अथैककारकज्ञानेनाऽपि तावदनुष्ठानोपपत्तेर्न कारकान्तरजिज्ञासा; तर्हि 'देवदत्त गामानय दण्डेने'ति प्रयुक्तेऽपि दण्डशब्दे, तदाकांक्षा न स्यात् । ततश्च अनाकांक्षितत्वात्तस्य तदन्वयो न स्याद् वाक्यार्थे । अथ दण्ड-पदोच्चारणात् तत्राकांक्षा परिकल्प्यते । अन्यथा दण्डपदार्थस्यानन्वये तत्पदो-च्चारणमनर्थकं स्यात् ।

एवम् 'अरुणयैकहायन्या पिङ्गाक्ष्या सोमं क्रीणाति' [तै. सं. ६. १. ६. [इत्यत्राप्यनन्वयप्रसङ्गः। न हि वेदपदोच्चारणेनानर्थकेन न भवितव्यमिति किञ्चन प्रमाणमस्ति, अतो न तत्रांकांक्षोदये कञ्चित्कारणमस्तीति, 'सोमं क्रीणाति' त्योऽधिकस्यानन्वितता स्यात्। अपि च लौकिकत्वात् क्रिया-कारकयोः यत् किञ्चित्क्रियाकारकोपादानेऽपि तत्सिद्धेरविघातान्नातीव विशेषजिज्ञासा घटते। अज्ञाते हि जानेच्छा घटते न पुनर्ज्ञातेऽपि।

अत्रोच्यते-अभिधानापर्यवसानम्, अभिधेयापर्यवसानञ्च जिज्ञासोदये निबन्धनम्। एकपदप्रयोगे हि द्वारमित्यादावभिधानमेव न पर्यवस्यति। सह्यनुच्चारिते प्रतियोगिसन्निधापके पदेऽन्विताभिधानं शक्यते वक्तुम्। वृद्धव्यवहारवशेनान्वितार्थप्रतिपादनपरता पदानामवधारितेति, तदर्थं युक्तैव प्रतियोगिजिज्ञासा। यस्याप्यभिहितान्वय इति राद्धान्तः तन्मतेऽपि पदार्थस्य पदार्थान्तरमन्तरेणान्वयासामर्थ्यात् तदुपपत्तये युक्तैव प्रतियोगि-जिज्ञासा। प्रकरणादिवशेन योग्यप्रतियोग्यध्याधारः क्रियते।

'अमावाश्यायामपराह्णे पिण्डपितृयज्ञेन चरन्ति' [आ. श्रौ १.३.७. सू. १-२] इत्यादिष्वनेकपदप्रयोगादन्विताभिधानेऽपि, अभिहितस्य कार्यस्यापूर्वात्मनोऽनुष्ठानं विना कार्यत्वानुपपत्तेः, कर्त्रा च विना तदसम्भवात्, अधिकारादृते च तदयोगात्, नियोज्यमन्तरेण च तस्यानव-कल्पनात्, तदुपपत्तये युक्तैव तदन्ववयोग्यनियोज्यजिज्ञासा। तस्यां सत्यामपरिपूर्णत्वावगमात्, लोकवदध्याहारे कर्त्तव्ये सत्यपि विधेरनुष्ठा-नाक्षेपो न कल्पेतेति, तत्परित्यागेन काम्ये नियोज्यविशेषणे स्थिते सर्वकामिपुरुषव्यापिस्वर्गस्यैव नियोज्यविशेषणत्वयोग्यत्वात् 'स्वर्गकामो नियोज्यो' ऽध्याह्रियते।

तथाऽध्ययनविधावन्यप्रयुक्तानुष्ठाननिर्वाहितकार्यभावे नियोज्यो नाध्याह्रियते। अलौकित्वाच्चापूर्वे कार्ये नियोज्यस्याध्याहारमन्तरेणाऽऽकांक्षा न निवर्त्तते। अलौकिकत्वादेव च 'सौर्यं चरुं निर्वपेद् घृते शुक्लानां व्रीहीणां ब्रह्मवर्चसकामः'' [मै. सं. २.२.२.] इत्यादौ करणोपकार-मन्तरेण विधेस्सिद्ध्यसम्भवात् तज्जिज्ञासा तज्जनकपदार्थजिज्ञासा च। अतएव तदभावे भाष्यकारो वाक्यानां न्यूनतामाशङ्क्य परिहृतवान्।

नन्वेवं तर्हि तत्र पदत्रयं प्रयुज्जते 'गामानय शुक्लामिति' लोके तत्र हि कारकद्वयस्यासम्भवान्नाकांक्षाऽस्तीति कथमन्विताभिधानम् । 'गामानये'त्येतावतैव परिपूर्णत्वाद् वाक्यसस्य । सत्यम् । पदान्तरानुच्चारण एवम्, उच्चरिते तु तस्मिन् तस्याप्यानयतिसन्निधानादेकवाक्यत्वाव-गमादानयत्यन्वितस्वार्थाभिधायित्वात्, आकांक्षां विना च तदसम्भवात्, आनयतेराकांक्षा परिकल्प्यते । तथा चोक्तं भाष्यकारेण–'भवति च रक्तं प्रत्याकांक्षा' इति । तेनात्राप्यन्विताभिधानसिद्धयथमेवाकांक्षा । यदि परमयं विशेषः 'द्वारमितयादौ' तस्यैव पदस्यान्विताभिधानायाकांक्षा, 'गामानय शुक्लामित्यादौ' तु पदान्तरस्येति ।

अग्वितस्याभिधानार्थमुक्तार्थघटनाय वा ।
प्रतियोगिनि जिज्ञासा या साकांक्षेति गीयते ॥

इति संग्रह श्लोकः ।

सा चेयमाकांक्षा भवन्ती व्युत्पत्तावुपलक्षणमाश्रियते । किमिति पुनस्सन्निधियोग्यत्व एव नाश्रीयते, निराकांक्षाणामन्विताभिधानादर्शनात् । 'अयमेतिपुत्रो राज्ञः, पुरुषोऽयमपनीयतामित्यादौ' पुत्रपदसम्बन्धनिराकांक्षो राजा न पुरुषेणान्वीयते । कस्मात्पुनरनयोः पुत्रपुरुषयोस्सन्निधियोग्यत्वा-विशेषेऽपि पुत्रेणैव राज्ञस्सम्बन्धः, न पुरुषेण । उच्चते—वाक्यात् वाक्यार्थप्रतिपत्तेः न्यायसापेक्षत्वात्, नित्यसापेक्षेण पुत्रेणैव राजा सम्बध्यते, तत्सम्बन्धनिराकांक्षश्च न पुरुषसम्बन्धमनुभवतीन्याकांक्षाऽपि व्युन्पत्त्युपल-क्षणमाश्रीयते ।

परिपूर्णेन योग्यस्य समीपस्याप्यनन्वयः ।
व्युत्पत्तौ तेन शब्दानामाकांक्षाप्युपलक्षणम् ॥

संग्रहश्लोकः ।

सा चेयमाकांक्षा प्रतियोगिषु सर्वेषु न सहसैवोपजायते, किन्तु कारणोपनिपातक्रमेण । तथाहि विषयमन्तरेणापूर्वं कार्यं प्रत्येतुमेव न शक्यते इति प्रतिपत्त्यनुबन्धभूतविषयापेक्षा प्रथमं विधेः । अथ प्रतिपन्ने विषयसम्बन्धिनि विध्यर्थे, नियोज्यमन्तरेण तत्सिद्धयसम्भवान्नियोज्या-

कांक्षा । तथा विषयीभूते भावार्थे करणे लब्धे, वैकृतापूर्वाणां करणोपकाराकांक्षा, लब्धे च तस्मिन् तज्जनकपदार्थाकांक्षेति ।

तथा चाहुः—

प्रतियोगिषु सर्वेषु नाकांक्षोदेति तत्क्षणात् ।
कारणोपनिपातानुपूर्व्येण तु यथायथम् ।। इति ।।

तत्क्रमेणान्विताभिधानमपि क्रमेणैव । श्लोकश्चात्र भवति—

जिज्ञासा जायते बोद्धुस्सम्बन्धिषु यथा यथा ।
तथा तथैव शब्दानामन्वितार्थाभिधायिता ।।

अथ सन्निधिः कः ? यस्यार्थस्य श्रवणानन्तरमाकांक्षा-योग्यताभ्यामर्थान्तरे बुद्धिविपरिवृत्तिः । सा च न शब्दनिबन्धनैव, केवलमन्विताभिधानव्युत्पत्तावुपलक्षणम्, अध्याहृतेनापि लोकेऽन्विता-भिधानदर्शनात् । न च वाच्यं शब्द एवाध्याह्रियते, स चार्थमुपस्थापयति इति, अनुपयोगात्, अप्रमाणकत्वाच्च । यद्यप्यर्थापत्तिप्रमाणकोऽध्याहारः, तथापि शब्दकल्पनमनुपपन्नम् । येन हि विनाऽनुपपत्तिः, तदेवार्थापत्ति-प्रमेयम् । नचार्थानां शब्दमन्तरेणानुपपत्तिः । स्यान्मतम्, अर्थकल्पनयै-वार्थापत्तिः प्रर्त्तमाना तस्यार्थस्य सविकल्पकज्ञानवेद्यत्वात्, सविकल्पकज्ञानानाञ्च शब्दपुरस्सरत्वात् पुरोवर्त्तिनि शब्द एव पर्यवस्यति इति । तदसत् । यथैव शब्दपुरस्सरेऽपि सविकल्पकज्ञाने लिङ्गस्य इन्द्रि-याणाञ्च निर्विकल्पकदशायामर्थ एवावधारितशक्तित्वान्न शब्दमात्रे पर्यवसानम्, तथा दृष्टार्थापत्तौ साक्षादुपपादकेऽर्थ एवार्थापत्तेः प्रामाण्या-भ्युपगमात्, श्रुतार्थापत्तावपि तत्रैव तस्याः प्रामाण्यं युक्तं न शब्दे । तस्य साक्षादनुपपत्तिशमनासमर्थत्वात् ।

किञ्च सर्वत्र सविकल्पकज्ञाने शब्दस्मरणविपरिवर्त्ती न प्रमेयतां प्रतिपत्तुमर्हति । सविकल्पकज्ञानेषु पूर्वप्रतीयमानता च शब्दस्य नातीव प्रमाणवती, किन्वर्थप्रतीतावेव समानकालं शब्दस्मरणमिति प्रतीत्यारूढम् । तेन न श्रुतार्थापत्तिश्शब्दविषया । न च शब्दानुपपत्त्या तु शब्दकल्पनैवो-चिता, तस्य स्वतोऽनुपपत्त्यभावात् । अन्विताभिधनानुपपत्त्या तु कल्पना

प्रसरन्ती योग्यप्रतियोग्यर्थविषयैवावतिष्ठते, तस्यैवाकांक्षितत्वात्, दशमाद्यन्यायेन पदार्थवत् पूर्वप्रतीतस्यापि शब्दस्योपेक्षणीयत्वात् ।

न च 'द्वारमि'ति यत्राध्याहारः तत्राप्याव्रियताम्, संव्रियतामिति वा कल्पयितुमर्थापत्तेः प्रभविष्णुता सामान्यकल्पनामात्रहेतुत्वात् । तस्माद-परिपूर्णपरिपूरकतया लोकत एवाध्याहारस्याप्युपपत्तिः । तत्र योग्यता प्रकरणादिवशेन च विशेषावधारणादर्थ एव च परिपूरक इति अनुपयोगी शब्दस्याध्याहारः । अतो विश्वजिदादौ नियोज्येन सर्वत्र च कारणोपकारेण विकृतिषु च प्राकृतपदार्थैरशब्दोपस्थापितैरपि सिद्धमन्विताभिधानम् । आकांक्षावच्च सन्निधावपि सन्निधापकक्रमेणैव क्रमो वेदितव्यः, तदनुसारेण चान्विताभिधानमपि तथैव इति ।

सन्निधिश्शब्दजन्मैव व्युत्पत्तौ नोपलक्षणम् ।
अध्याहृतेनाप्यर्थेन लोके सम्बन्धदर्शनात् ।।
सहसैव न सर्वेषां सन्निधिः प्रतियोगिनाम् ।
सन्निधापकसामग्रीक्रमेण क्रमवानसौ ।।
यथा यथा सन्निधानं जायते प्रतियोगिनाम् ।
तथा तथा क्रमेणैव शब्दैरन्वितबोधनम् ।।

इति संग्रहश्लोकाः ।

अतो यथोक्ताकांक्षा सन्निधिप्राप्तमाकांक्षितं सन्निहितं योग्यञ्च यत् पदार्थान्तरम् तेन सङ्गतमित्यर्थः ।

किं पुनरिदं योग्यत्वं नाम ? उच्यते—यत्सम्बन्धार्हम् । सम्बन्धार्हमिदमिति कथमवगम्यते, सम्बन्धित्वेन दृष्टत्वात् । नन्वेवं तर्हि कथमपूर्वे कार्येऽन्विताभिधानं वेदे, तेन सह कस्यचित्सम्बन्धस्यादर्शनात् । उच्यते-सामान्यतो योग्यतावधारणं विशेषप्रतिपत्तावुपाय इत्यदोषः । यदपि तदपूर्वम्, तदपि कार्यमेवेति दृष्टचरकार्यसम्बन्धं यत् तद् योग्यमित्यवसीयते ।

सामान्येनैव योग्यत्वं लोके यदवधारितम् ।
तदन्विताभिधानस्य व्युत्पत्तावुपलक्षणम् ॥

इति संग्रहश्लोकः ।

अन्ये तु यदयोग्यतया नावधारितं तद् योग्यम् । तेनालौकिकेनापि विध्यर्थेनाऽन्विताभिधानं सिध्यति इत्याहुः । तदिदमसारम् । यथा प्रमाणान्तररावेद्ये वस्तुनि कस्यचिद् योग्यताऽवधारयितुं न शक्यते, तथैवायोग्यताऽपि, इति सर्वस्याप्रतीतेनापि सर्वप्रकारेण तस्मिन्नन्वयस्स्यात् । भावार्थस्यैव विषयत्वेनान्वयः, अनुपादेयविशेषणविशिष्टस्यैव स्वर्गकामादेः नियोज्यतयाऽन्वय इति नियमो नोपद्यते इत्यलमतिप्रसंगेन ॥८॥

नन्वन्विताभिधानपक्षे व्युत्पत्तावुपलक्षणाश्रयणमेव गौरवमित्यत्राह –

पदार्थेष्वपि चैवेषा सामग्र्यन्वयबोधने ॥९॥

यस्यापि मते पदार्था एवान्योन्यान्वयमवगमयन्ति, तनापि प्रतिनियतान्वयबोधसिद्धयर्थमिदमाश्रयणीयमेव - आकांक्षासन्निधियोग्यतावन्त एव पदार्था वाक्यार्थं बोधयन्ति, नान्ये इति, एतदेव कथमिति पर्यनुयुक्तेन वृद्धव्यवहारे तथा दर्शनादिति परिहारो वाच्यः । तस्मादुभयपक्षसाधारणत्वान्नेदं दूषणम् ॥९॥

नन्वेवमपि केन विषेशेणाऽभिहितान्वयं परित्यज्य, अन्विताभिधानमाश्रितमिति । अत्राह—

किन्तु तेषामदृष्टैषा शक्तिर्मानान्तराद् गतौ ।
कल्प्या विशिष्टार्थपरपदसंस्पर्शभाविता ॥१०॥

पदार्थानां हि शब्दादन्यतः प्रमाणात् प्रतीयमानानामन्योन्यान्वयबोधकत्वं न प्रतीतमिति शब्दाभिधेयानां तदवगमशक्तिः कल्पयितव्या । तस्याश्चोत्पत्तौ शब्दसंस्पर्श एव हेतुरित्याश्रयणीयम् । शब्दो हि विशिष्टार्थप्रतिपत्तिपरतया लोकव्यवहारेषु प्रयुज्यमानो दृष्टः । न चासौ

साक्षाद्वाक्यार्थप्रतिपादने समर्थं इति पदार्थानवान्तरव्यापारीकरोति । त च यद्यन्योन्यान्वयबोधने समर्थाः स्युः, तदा तेषामवान्तरव्यापारता स्यान्नान्यथेति, विशिष्टार्थावबोधपरशब्दसंस्पर्शादेव तेषामेषा शक्तिराविर्भवतीति, शब्दस्यापि पदार्थगतान्वयबोधकत्वशक्त्याधानशक्तिराश्रयणीया । स्यादेवम्, यदि मानान्तरावसेयानां पदार्थानामन्योन्यान्वयावगमे सामर्थ्यं न स्यात् अस्ति तु तत्, श्वैत्यस्यानवधारिताश्रयविशेषस्य प्रत्यक्षदृष्टस्य अश्वस्याप्रतिपन्नगुणविशेषस्य प्रत्यक्षह्लेषाशब्दानुमितस्य पदनिक्षेपशब्दानुमितस्य अज्ञातकर्तृभेदस्य धावनस्य च 'श्वेतोऽश्वो धावति' इत्यन्वयबोधकत्वदर्शनात् । तदाहुर्वार्तिककारमिश्राः—

"पश्यतः श्वेतमारूपं ह्लेषाशब्दञ्च शृण्वतः ।
खुरनिक्षेपशब्ञ्च श्वेतोऽश्वो धावतीति धीः ।
दृष्टा वाक्यविनिर्मुक्ता –" इति ॥

[श्लो. वा. वा. अधि. ३५८] ॥

आरूपम्-अव्यक्तरूपमित्यर्थः । तेन गुणविशेषो न प्रत्यक्षमवसीयते इत्यर्थः ।

अत्रोच्यते । किं येनैव पुरुषेण श्वैत्यसमानाश्रयौ ह्लेषाध्वनिपदनिक्षेपशब्दावसगतौ, तस्यैवेयं श्वेतोऽश्वो धावती'ति धीः ? उत यस्यापादानानध्यवसायः, तस्यापि इति ? किमतः । यदि तावदप्रत्याकलितह्लेषाध्वनिपदविहारनिर्घोषापादानस्येत्युच्यते, तदा प्रतीतिविरोधः । स ह्येवं प्रतिपद्यते-भवितव्यमस्मिन्देशे नूनमश्वेन, भवितव्यञ्च केनचिद्धावतेति । अथाश्वसम्बन्धिनमेव खुरपुटटङ्कारवमभ्यासपाटववशादवैति, तदाऽसावश्ववर्त्तिनीमेव वेगवतीं गतिमनुमिनोति इति न पुनः केवलामेवावगम्य, तस्यान्वयं पदार्थसामर्थ्येनावबुद्ध्यते । योऽपि तस्मिन् देशे नास्त्यन्योऽश्वादिति निश्चित्य पारिशेष्यादपादानानध्यवसायेऽपि ह्लेषाध्वनेः श्वैत्यसमानाधिकमणमश्वत्वमप्यध्यवस्यति, तस्यापि गृहाभावदर्शनमिव बहिर्भावावगतावर्थापत्तिः—'योऽयं श्वेतः, स एषोऽश्वः' इत्यत्र प्रमाणम् । यस्तु श्वैत्यसमानाधिकरणौ ह्लेषाध्वनिखुरपुटटङ्कारासध्यवस्यति, तस्याप्यश्वत्वे वेगवति च गमने श्वेतवर्त्तिन्येवनुमानम् न

स्वतन्त्रयोः । अतः प्रमाणान्तरेणासम्बद्धावभातानां पदार्थानां न क्वचिदन्योन्यसम्बन्धबोधकत्वमनुमानार्थापत्तिव्यतिरेकेण प्रतीतम् ।

अपि च यदि पदार्थावगतिमात्रादेव परस्परान्वयावगमः, तदा कस्मिन् प्रमाणे तस्यान्तर्भाव इति वाच्यम् ? न तावच्छाब्दे, शब्दाभावात् । पदार्थाभिधानावान्तरव्यापारेण हि यच्छब्दादन्वयज्ञानम्, तच्छाब्दमित्येष वो राद्धान्तः । तस्मान्नास्य शाब्देऽन्तर्भावः । प्रमाणान्तराभ्युपगमे तु शाब्दस्योच्छेदः, शब्दावगतपदार्थविषयेऽपि तस्यैव प्रामाण्यप्रसङ्गात् । तस्माच्छब्दाभिहितानां पदार्थानामन्यत्रादृष्टं वाक्यार्थबोधनसामर्थ्यं कल्पयितव्यम् । तदाधानशक्तिश्च शब्दानामपीति कल्पनालाघवाच्छब्दानामेवान्वितमस्वार्थावबोधनशक्तिमात्रं कल्पयितुं न्याय्यम् । तेन पारम्पर्येण पदानामन्वितेषु सामर्थ्यमिति निरस्तम् ।

नन्वनन्तप्रतियोग्यन्वितस्वार्थबोधनविषया अनन्ता एव शब्दस्य शक्तयः कल्पयितव्याः स्युः । अभिहितान्वयवादे त्वेकस्मिन्नर्थे एकस्य शब्दस्यैकैव शक्तिरिति; तन्न, एकयैवाकांक्षित सन्निहितयोग्यार्थान्वितस्वार्थाभिधानशक्त्या प्रतियोगिभेदेन कार्यभेदोपपत्तेश्चक्षुरादीनामिव । चक्षुर्यथैवैकया दर्शनशक्त्या घटादिप्रतियोगिसहायभेदाज्ज्ञानानि भिन्नानि जनयति, तथा शब्दोऽपि प्रतियोगिभेदादिति मन्तव्यम् । किञ्च पदार्थेऽपि तुल्यमेतदिति न किञ्चिदेतत् ।

अन्ये त्वाहुः—आकांक्षासन्निधियोग्यतावन्तः पदार्था वाक्यार्थीभवन्ति, न पुनर्वाक्यार्थमेव बोधवन्तीति । तदिदमतिमन्दम्-वाक्यार्थावगतेः कारणभावप्रसङ्गात् । अनुपायत्वे पदानामन्वयप्रतीतौ पदार्था अपि चेन्न कारणम्, अकारणिकैवापद्येत । स्यान्मतम्, क्रियापदेन कारकपदेन वा साकांक्षेऽर्थेऽभिहितं यदेव पदान्तरेण योग्यप्रतियोगिपदार्थान्तरं सन्निधाप्यते, तदेव तस्व सम्बन्धित्वेनावतिष्ठते इति । सत्यमेवम् । अवगतिस्तु तत्सम्बन्धस्य किन्निबन्धनेति वाच्यम् । अथ पूर्वपदार्थे साकांक्षेऽभिहिते, यत्पदान्तरमुच्चरितम्, तत् तत्संबन्धितयैव स्वार्थमुपनयति प्रत्ययवत् । यथा प्रकृत्यर्थे पूर्वप्रतीते प्रत्यय उच्चार्यमाणस्वार्थं तद्विशिष्टमेवाभिधत्ते, तथा पदान्तरमपि । तदुक्तम्– 'प्रकृतिप्रत्ययौ

द्रत्ययार्थं सह ब्रूतः' [महाभाष्यम्] इति । प्रकृतिः स्वार्थं प्रत्ययार्थ-विशेषणत्वेनोपनयतीति, प्रत्ययेन तदर्थमाहेत्यर्थः । तथा चोक्तम्—

नित्यं विशिष्ट एवार्थे प्रत्ययो यत्प्रयुज्यते ।
तत्पूर्वतरविज्ञातप्रकृत्यर्थविशेषणात् ।। इति ।।

अङ्गीकृतं तर्हि द्वितीयस्य पदस्यान्विताभिधानम्, प्रथमस्य तथापि नास्तीति चेन्न । वाक्ये पदानां प्रयोगक्रमनियमाभावात् । यदेव कदाचित्प्रथमं तदेव कदाचिद् द्वितीयमिति सर्वपदानामेवान्विताभिधान-मापतितम् ।

अभिहितान्वयवादी च प्रकृतिप्रत्यययोरप्यन्वयव्यतिरेकावधारित व्यतिरिक्तशक्तिकयोरभिहितान्वयमेव पदवदिच्छति । तथा च—

'द्रकृतिप्रत्ययौ ब्रूतः प्रत्ययार्थं सहेति यत् ।
भेदेनैवाभिधानेऽपि प्राधान्येन तथोच्यते ।।

पाकं तु पचिरेवाह कर्त्तारं प्रत्ययोऽप्यकः ।
पाकयुक्तः पुनः कर्त्ता वाच्यो नैकस्य कस्यचित् ।।" इत्याह ।

किञ्च प्रययश्चेदन्विताभिधायी, तदा तदविशेषात् पदानाम-प्यन्विताभिधायिता किमिति नाभ्युपेयते, किमर्धवैशसेन । यदि प्रकृतिप्रत्यययोरप्यन्विताभिधानमति, न तर्हि द्वारमित्यत्रान्विताभिधा-नानुपपत्तिनिबन्धयाऽऽकांक्षया विव्रियतां संव्रियतां वेत्यध्याहारः । उच्यते । द्वारमिति प्रथमेयं प्रातिपदिकार्थव्यतिरिक्तार्थाभिधायिनी । तेनात्र केन सहान्वितस्याभिधानम् । व्यतिरिक्तार्थे प्रत्यये प्रविशेत्यादौ योऽध्याहारः, सोऽभिहितार्थानुपपत्त्यैव विश्वजिदादिवदिति न दोषः ।

वार्त्तिककारमिश्रास्तु लाक्षणिकान् सर्ववाक्यार्थानिच्छन्तः पदार्थानामन्वयावबोधशक्तिकल्पनां निराकुर्वन्ति । अनन्वितावस्थो हि पदार्थोऽभिहितोऽन्वितावस्थां स्वसम्बन्धिनीं लक्षयति । अवस्थाऽवस्थावतो हि सम्बन्धात्, अवस्थावत्यभिहिते भवत्येवावस्थापि बुद्धिस्था । सर्वत्र च

सबन्धिनि दृष्टे सम्बन्ध्यन्तरे बुद्धिर्भवतीति क्लृप्तमेव । तेन नास्ति पदानामन्वितबोधने शक्तिकल्पनेति । तदाहुः—

वाक्यार्थो लक्ष्यमाणो हि सर्वत्रैवेति नः स्थितिः ।"

अत्रापरे ब्रुवते—नेयं लक्षणा स्वार्थापरित्यागात् । स्वार्थपरित्यागेन हि गङ्गादिषु लक्षणा दृष्टा इति । ते तु मीमांसातन्त्रान्तःपातवैकल्येनैव-माहुः । लक्षणीयवशेन हि क्वचित्स्वार्थस्य त्यागः संग्रहो वा । 'सृष्टीरुपदधाति' इति लक्षणायास्स्वीकारः, गुणिनां तद्गणपठितानां सृष्टिशब्दरहितानामपि लक्ष्यमाणत्वात्, तदन्तर्गतत्वाच्च सृष्ट्यर्थस्य ।

तथा 'पौर्णमासीं यजते' इत्येकवचनानुपपत्त्या पौर्णमासीशब्दो यागवचनो यागसमुदायलक्षणार्थः । न च समुदायपरिग्रहे समुदायित्यागः; तदाश्रयत्वात्तस्य । तथेतरेतरयोगद्वन्द्वे द्विवचनबहुवचनानुपपत्तेरर्थान्तर-सहितावस्था लक्षणयाऽऽश्रीयते, न चावस्थावत्परित्यागः । तथा निषादस्थपति-अधिकरण [मी. द. ६ १-१०] पूर्वपक्षे षष्ठ्यर्थलक्षणा स्यादित्युच्यते, न तत्र प्रकृत्यर्थस्य त्यागोऽप्यापद्यते । तथा 'रथघोषेण' इत्यत्र रथस्यापरित्यागः । तथा 'मेघपतये मेघमि'त्येकवचनान्तस्य मन्त्रस्य लक्षणया प्रकृतौ निवेशः । न च गुणिनोरग्नीषोमयोस्तत्र हानमिति, स्वार्थापरित्यागेऽपि युक्तैव लक्षणा ।

अत्रोच्यते, कथं पुनरियं लक्षणा ?
वाच्यस्यार्थस्य वाक्यार्थे सम्बन्धानुपपत्तितः ।
तत्सम्बन्धवशप्राप्तस्यान्वयाल्लक्षणोच्यते ॥

॥ संग्रहश्लोकः ॥

'गंगायां घोष' इत्यादिषु श्रौतस्य गङ्गापदार्थस्य वाक्यार्थेऽन्वया-सम्भवात् तं परित्यज्य तत्सम्बन्धाल्लब्धबुद्धिसन्निधेः कूलाद्यर्थस्य वाक्यार्थान्वयिताऽध्यवसीयते । अतएवाहुः 'अनुपपत्त्या सम्बन्धेन च लक्षणा भवती'ति । इह च 'गामानाय' इत्यादौ न श्रौतस्यार्थस्यान्वया-योग्यत्वम्, नाप्यन्वितावस्थयाऽऽनयनसम्बन्धार्हता, अन्वितार्थस्या-ऽन्वयान्तरासम्भवात् । अथ मा भूदेषा लक्षणा, किन्तु क्रियावगता

कारकान्वयिनीमात्मानो दशामवगमयति, अविनाभावादिति । उच्यते, शाब्दत्वं तावदित्थमपन्हुतमन्वयावगमस्य, किन्तु सामान्यतोदृष्टानुमानगोचरताऽभ्युपगता भवति । तथा विशिष्टान्वयावगतिरनुपपद्यमाना निर्मूलाऽऽपद्यते । अथ विशेषान्वयं विना व्यवहारानवकल्पनादनर्थकं शब्दोच्चारेणमिति तदाश्रयणम्, एवमपि प्रेक्षापूर्वकारिणां सार्थकवाक्यमात्रप्रयोगिणां वचनाद्विशेषान्वयावगमः । वेदे त्वानर्थक्यं न न भवतिव्यमिति, प्रमाणाभावान्न शक्यते विशेषान्वयोऽवगन्तुम् । न च लोकेऽप्यानर्थक्यमापद्यते इत्येतावता कारणेनापायाद्विनाऽपि विशेषान्वयाध्यवसानं युक्तम् । न हि दग्धुकामस्योदकोपादानमनर्थकमिति जलस्य दाहशक्तिराविर्भवति । काममानर्थक्यम् । न पुनस्सामान्योदृष्टष्य विशेषान्वयावसायिता । अथाकांक्षितसन्निहितयोग्यान्वयपरता वृद्धव्यवहारे पदानामवगतेति, व्युत्पत्त्यनुसारेण विशेषान्वयावगमः । तन्न, तत्र वृद्धव्यवहार एव तत्परता पदानाम्, पदार्थानां वा उपायाभावेन कथं नाम निर्वहति ? चिन्ता हि सा पदानाम्, पदार्थानां वा शक्तिकल्पनां विनाऽनुपपन्नेति मन्यामहे ॥१०॥

सा च पदानामेवोचितेत्याह—

प्राथम्यादभिधातृत्वात् तात्पर्योपगमादपि ।
पदानामेव सा शक्तिर्वरमभ्युपगम्यताम् ॥ ११ ॥

प्रथमभावीनि पदान्यतिलंघ्य, नार्थेषु वाक्यार्थबोधन शक्तिराश्रयितुं युक्ता । किञ्च पदानि तावदभिधायिकानीति निर्विवादम् । तेन तेषामभिधानशक्तिः सम्प्रतिपन्नैवेति, तस्या एवान्वयपर्यन्तता कल्पयितुं सुकरा । पदार्थानां तु बोधनशक्तिरेव कल्प्या । तेन 'धर्मिकल्पनातो वरं धर्मकल्पना लघीयसी' इत्यन्विताभिधानशक्तिः पदानामेव कल्पयितुमुचिता ।

किञ्च पदान्यभिधायकानीष्यन्ते, तत्र यदि स्वरूपमात्रविषयामेव पदार्थबुद्धिमादध्युः, तदाभिधायकता हीयेत, तस्य बुद्धेस्सम्बन्धग्रहणसमयजातपदार्थबोधकसंस्कारोन्मेषप्रभवत्वात् । अवश्यं हि सम्बन्धस्मरणसिद्ध्यर्थं सम्बन्धिभूतार्थस्मरणसंस्कारोद्बोधोऽङ्गीकरणीयः । तस्मात्

सम्बन्धग्रहणसमयानधिगतान्वितार्थप्रतिपादनाभ्युपगम एव शब्दानामभिधायकतेति, तामङ्गीकुर्वता पदानामन्विताभिधायकताऽऽश्रयणीया ।

यस्तु—'पदमभ्यधिकाभावात्स्मारकान्न विशिष्यते ॥

[श्लो. वा. ६. १०७]

तथा—'भावनावचनस्तावत्तां स्मारयति लोकवत् ॥

[तदेव ७. २४८]

इति चाचार्यवचनदर्शनात् स्मारकतामेव पदानामभिधायकत्वमाह तं प्रत्याह—'तात्पर्योपगमादपी'ति ॥

येनापि वादिना पदानां स्मारकत्वमेव पदार्थेष्वङ्गीकृतम्, तेनाऽपि वाक्यार्थप्रतिपत्तिपतां पदानामभ्युपेत्यैव, अन्यथा वाक्यार्थस्याशाब्दत्वप्रसङ्गः । एवञ्चेत् पदानामेव साक्षाद्बोधनशक्तिरस्तु किम्परम्पराश्रयेण ।

तेन पदार्थेषु पदानां स्मारकत्वातिरिक्तं येऽभिधायकत्वमाहुः, तेषां शक्तित्रयकल्पना । एका तावत्पदानामभिधायकत्वशक्तिः, अपरा च पदार्थगतान्वयबोधनशक्त्याधानशक्तिः, पदार्थानाञ्चान्वयज्ञापनशक्तिरिति । स्मारकत्ववादिनस्त्वभिधानशक्तिं हित्वा शक्तिद्वयकल्पनालाघवात्, उक्तेनैव न्यायेन पदानामेव शक्तिकल्पनाया उचितत्वात्, अन्विताभिधायीनि पदानीति स्थापितम् ॥ ११ ॥

सम्प्रति पूर्वोक्तमितरेतराश्रयदोषं परिहर्तुं यथा पदेभ्यो वाक्यार्थप्रतिपत्तिः तथा दर्शयति—

पदजातं श्रुतं सर्वं स्मारितानन्वितार्थकम् ।
न्यायसम्पादितव्यक्ति पश्चाद् वाक्यार्थबोधकम् ॥१२॥

यस्तावदगृहीतसम्बधः, यस्य च सम्बन्धग्रहणसंस्कारो नोत्पन्नः, प्रध्वस्तो वा स वाक्यर्थप्रतिपत्तौ नाधिक्रियते । यस्त्वनभ्रष्टसम्बन्धग्रहणसंस्कारः, स पदं श्रुत्वा नूनं तावदिदं स्मरति—'इदमस्याकांक्षितसन्निहितयोग्यप्रतियोग्यन्वितस्य वाचकमि'ति । एवं च स्मरता स्मृतमेव

अनन्वितमपि स्वरूपमन्वयभाजाम्। न चैकपदश्रवणे वाक्यार्थावगतिरिति कश्चिन्मन्यते। अभिहितान्वयवादिनोऽपि हि यावत्पदान्तरमर्थान्तरं नोपस्थापयति, तावदन्वयावगमो नास्ति, पदार्थस्यान्वयावबोधिनः पदार्थान्तरापेक्षत्वात् प्रतियोगिसापेक्षत्वादन्वयस्य। अतस्तन्मतेऽपि सर्वपदैरनन्विवस्वार्था अभिधानीयाः। पश्चात्तेभ्यः सर्वेभ्यस्स्मृत्यारूढेभ्यो वाक्यार्थप्रतिपत्तिरङ्गीकरणीया। तदाहुर्वार्त्तिककारमिश्राः—

'तेऽपि नैवास्मृता यस्माद् वाक्यार्थं गमयन्ति नः।
तस्मात्तत्स्मरणेष्वेव संहतेषु प्रमाणता॥'

अतएव तत्रभवत आचार्यस्य वाक्यलक्षणं "संहत्यार्थमभिदधति पदानि वाक्यम्"। इति। [शा. भा. ब. अ. पृ० २२२] नन्वन्विताभिधानवादिनां कथं वाक्यार्थप्रतिपतिः। श्रूयमाणेन हि पदेन योऽर्थो नावबोधितः, स कथमन्तर्हिते तस्मिन्नवभासेत। उच्यते—अभिहितान्वयवादिनोऽपि नायं नियमः—श्रूयमाण एव पूर्वपूर्ववर्णजनितसंस्कारसहितो वर्णः पदार्थप्रतिपादक इति, बाल्यदशाधीतात् प्रागनवधृतार्थादङ्गपरिज्ञानसंस्कारात् पश्चात् स्मृतादपि वेदादर्थावगमदर्शनात्। तेन स्मृत्यारूढस्यावगमकत्वमदोषः। श्रूयमाणेन हि पदेन प्रतियोगिसापेक्षत्वादन्विताभिधानस्य प्राक् सहकारिविरहादर्थो नाभिहितः, पश्चादभिधीयते इति किमनुपपन्नम्।

येऽपि वादिन एवमाहुः—एकमेव पदमन्विताभिधायकमस्तु, इतराणि च पदानि प्रतियोगिसन्निधापनमात्र एव व्याप्रियन्ताम्। न चागृह्यमाणविशेषता, प्राथम्येन प्रधानपदेन वा विशेषग्रहणात्। अत एव चाहुः—'पदमाद्यं वा वाक्यम्', 'प्रधानं पदं वा वाक्यम्' [वाक्यपदीय २.२] इति। तान्प्रत्याह—'सर्वमि'ति। प्रथमस्यैव स्याद् वाक्यता यदि, सर्वपदार्थानां प्रथमपदार्थान्वितता स्यात्। न चायं नियमः। 'अरुणयैकहायन्या पिङ्गाक्ष्या सोमं क्रीणाति' [तै. स. ६. १. ६] इति क्रयमात्रान्वयित्वादारुण्यस्य। किञ्च वाक्ये पदानामानुपूर्व्यनियमाभावात्, कदाचित्तदेव प्रथमं सदन्विताभिधायकम्, अन्यदा नेति न युक्तम्। तथा प्रधानपदस्यापि वाक्यत्वमयुक्तम्, सोमपदार्थेन सह सर्वेषामनन्वयात्। यद्यप्यारुण्यादीनां सर्वेषां सोमं प्रति ऐतदर्थ्यमस्ति, तथाप्यस्मिन् वाक्ये क्रय एवारुण्यादीनामैदमर्थ्येन, क्रियाकारकभावेन चान्वयः। क्रयद्वारेण तु सोमं प्रत्यैदमर्थ्यमात्रम्।

अथ यत्प्रतिपादनपरं वाक्यं तत्प्रधानमित्युच्यते। इह तु क्रय एव सर्वकर्मकरणावच्छिन्नः प्रतिपाद्यते। तेन क्रीणातीत्येतदेव प्रधानं पदम्, तदन्वयिता च सर्वेषामारुण्यादीनामिति। अत्रोच्यते—वाक्यस्य यत् तावत् तात्पर्यं तन्न व्यवस्थितम्। क्वचिदाख्यातपरत्वमेव अग्निहोत्रं जुहोति' इति। क्वचिद् गुणविधिपरत्वं 'दध्ना जुहोति। तेन प्रधानपदत्वस्यापि सर्वेषां पदानां सम्भवात्, सर्वेषामेव पदानामन्विताभिधानशक्तिरा-श्रयणीया। तथा सति यत्रापि गुणपरत्वम्, तत्रापि क्लृप्तशक्तिकतया तदन्विताभिधायकत्वमविरुद्धम्। पदार्थेष्वपि चैतत् तुल्यमेव।

नन्वेवं 'गामानय' इत्यादौ परस्परपर्यायिता सर्वशब्दानां स्यात्। 'गाम्' इत्यनेन आनयतान्विताभिधानम्, तथा 'आनयन' इत्यनेनापि गवान्विताभिधानम् इति। उच्यते—द्वावेतावर्थौ यदानयनान्वितं गोत्वम्, गवान्वितञ्चानयनमिति। तेनैकैकेनैकैकस्यार्थस्याभिधानात् कुतः पर्यायत्वप्रसङ्गः। पदार्थेष्वपि चैतत्समानम्। ननु क्रीणात्यर्थस्या-रुण्याद्यनेकार्थान्विताभिधानावृत्तिलक्षणो वाक्यभेदः स्यात्। न। तन्त्रो-च्चारणात्। वैरूप्ये च तन्त्रानुपपत्तेर्वाक्यभेदः स्यात्।

'न्यायसम्पादितव्यक्ती' ति किमिदम्, यावन्न्यायेन वचनव्यक्तिर्न सम्पाद्यते, तावत् पदजातं वाक्यार्थस्यावबोधककं न भवति। लोकव्यवहार-वर्त्तिभिर्न्यायैर्यावत्—'इदं विधेयम्, इदमनुवाद्यम्; इदं प्रधानम्, इदं गुणभूतम्ः इदं विवक्षितम्, ईदम्विवक्षितमि'त्यादि न सम्प्रधार्यते तावन्न क्वचिद् वेदवाक्यार्थोऽवबुद्धचते। तदुक्तं वार्त्तिककारमिश्रैः :

> तावदेव हि सन्देहो वेदवाक्ये श्रुते भवेत्।
> यावन्न वचनव्यक्तिस्तस्य स्पष्टावधार्यते॥
> ज्ञात्वा तु वचनव्यक्तिं मीमांसान्यायकातराः।
> प्रलीयन्ते समस्ताश्च वेदवाक्यार्थसंशयाः॥

(बृहट्टीका) इति।

अतएव मीमांसाया वेदवाक्यार्थप्रतिपत्ताविति कर्त्तव्यतात्वम्। यदुक्तं तैरेव—

'धर्मे प्रमीयमाणे हि वेदेन करणात्मना।
इतिकर्त्तव्यताभागं मीमांसा पूरयिष्यति ।।

(बृहट्टीका)

ननु लोके द्रागेव वाक्यार्थावगतिर्नैयतीं सामग्रीमपेक्षते। उच्यते—अत्यन्ताभ्यस्तेषु वाक्येषु स्यादेवम्, अदृष्टार्थेषु स्मृत्यादिवाक्येषु लोकेऽपि नानाविधविवादोत्थानात् कुतो द्रागेवार्थनिश्चयः। अपि च कारणाभावेनापि लोकस्यायं विवेको नास्ति। तदुक्तम्—

बहुजातिगुणद्रव्यकर्मभेदावलम्बिनः।
प्रत्ययान् सहसा जातान् श्रौतलाक्षणिकात्मकान् ।।

न लोकः कारणाभावान्निर्धारयितुमर्हति।
बलाबलादि सिद्ध्यर्थं वाक्यज्ञास्तु विचिन्वते।

(श्लोकवार्त्तिकम् (०, १) इति।

यच्चेदं सर्वपदानामन्विताभिधायित्मुच्यये, तत्सर्वेषु श्रौतार्थेषु। पदेषु। लाक्षणिकगौणार्थपदप्रयोगे तु यदेव तत्र श्रौतार्थ पदम्, तदेवान्विताभिधायकम्, इतस्तु पदं प्रतियोगिसन्निधापनपरमेव। तत्र वाचकत्वशक्त्यनवधारणात् स्वार्थस्यापि तत्तदानीमवाचकम्, अन्वयायोग्यत्वात्। किन्तु 'तदर्थेन स्मृतेन यत् स्वसम्बन्धि स्वसदृशं वा स्वयमन्वययोग्यमुपस्थाप्यते, तेनान्वितं श्रौतार्थमेव पदं स्वार्थमभिधत्ते' इति दर्शनरहस्यमिदम्। च सर्वपदान्येव लाक्षणिकानि, गौणानि वा वाक्ये सम्भवन्तीति निरवद्यम्। क्वचिदभिधानं निमित्तम्, क्वचिदभिहितोऽर्थः, इति च यदुक्तम् तच्छब्दोपस्थापितता दर्शयितु गौणमभिहितत्वग्रहणम् ।।१२।।

कथं पुनरन्विताभिधायिना पदेन स्वरूपमात्रं स्मारयितु शक्यमित्याह—

अन्वितस्याभिधानेऽपि स्वरूपं विद्यते सदा।
तेन स्वरूपमात्रेऽपि शब्दो जनयति स्मृतिम् ।।१३।।

एवं तावत् सम्बन्धग्रहणान्तर्गतं स्वरूपस्मरणमुक्तम्। सम्प्रति स्वरूपस्मरणमपि पदादेव नानुपपन्नमित्याह—

यथार्थेनाप्रमाणेन स्वपदं स्मार्यते क्वचित्।
पदेनाप्यप्रमाणेन तथार्थः स्मारयिष्यते ॥१४॥

न हि यत्प्रमाणं तदेव स्मरणकारणम्, अप्रमाणमेव हि तत्। **यस्य** तु **येन** सह कदाचित्प्रत्यासत्तिः प्रतीतपूर्वा सा तत्र संस्कारोद्बोधद्वारेण शक्नोत्येव स्मृतिं जनयितुम्। अस्ति च स्वरूपस्यापि तदभिधेयान्तर्गत्यां शब्देन प्रत्यासत्तिरिति शक्नोति तत्रापि शब्दः स्मृतिं जनयितुमर्थवत्। **यथा** निर्विकल्पकदशाप्रतीतमर्थस्वरूपमात्रमनभिधेमपि शब्दं स्मारयति, तथा शब्दोऽप्यर्थमिति किमनुपपन्नम्। एतेन **पदो**च्चारणानन्तर **पदार्थ-स्व**रूपप्रतीतिः समर्थिता। **अ**भिहितान्वयवादिनोऽपि सा न प्रमाणम्: **अ**भ्यधिकार्थपरिच्छेदाभाएात्। 'अनधिगतार्थगन्तृ प्रमाणमि'ति सिद्धान्ताभ्युपगमात्। तदुक्तम्—

'सर्वस्यानुपलब्धेऽर्थे प्रमाणं स्मृतिस्न्यथा ॥ इति।

(श्लो० वा० औ० सू० श्लो० ११)

अतएव स्मृतिरियम्। यदि पुनस्स्मृतिरेषा नाभ्युपेयेत, तदा प्रमाणस्मृतिसंशयविपर्ययेभ्यः प्रतिपत्त्यन्तरानभ्युपगमात् पदात् पदार्थ-प्रतीतिः क्वाप्यन्तर्भाव्यतामिति वाच्यम्। अतएवाभिहितान्वयवादेऽपि स्मारकत्वमेवास्मभ्यं रोचते ॥१४॥

इतरेतराश्रयमिदानीं परिहरति—

स्मृतिसन्निहितैरेवमर्थैरन्वितमात्मनः।
अर्थमाह पदं सर्वमिति नान्योन्यसंश्रयः ॥१५॥

स्वार्थस्वरूपमात्रस्मरणे हि न **पदं** पदान्तरमपेक्षते। स्मृतिसन्निहितमपीदं भवत्येव सन्निहितम्। नास्ति तेनेतरेतराश्रयत्वम्।

ननु वृद्धव्यवहारेण व्युत्पत्तिः, अन्वितार्थप्रतिपत्तिनिबन्धनश्च

वृद्धव्यवहारः अतस्तद्दर्शनात्, अन्वितप्रतिपत्तिरेवानुमातुं शक्या, नत्वनन्वितपदार्थमात्रस्मरणम् । उच्यते-व्यवहारानुमितान्वितप्रतिपत्त्यन्यथानुपपत्तिरेवानन्वितस्वार्थस्मरणसम्भवे प्रमाणम् । दर्शितं ह्येतत् नानन्वितप्रतिपत्तिमन्तरेणान्वितप्रतिपत्तिरुपपद्यत इति ।

अत्र कश्चिदाह – यदि स्मृतिसन्निहितमाश्रित्यान्विताभिधानं परैः क्रियते, तदा स्मरणस्य प्रत्यासत्तिनिबन्धनत्वात्, अनेकेषाञ्चार्थानां प्रत्यासत्तिसम्भवात् । तेषु स्मृतिसन्निहितेष्वगृह्यमाणविशेषत्वात् । 'उखायां पचती'ति नोखा पचत्यर्थान्वितैव केवलाऽभिधीयेत । सा हि कुलालाद्यन्विताऽपि प्रतिन्नैवेति, स्मरणात् तदन्विताप्युखाऽभिधीयेत । तथा पचत्यर्थोऽपि पिष्टकादिकरणोऽवगत इति तत्स्मरणान्नौदनान्वित एवाभिधीयेत । अभिहितान्वयवादे तु नायं दोषः । एकैकस्यार्थस्याभिधेयत्वात् इति ।

अत्रोच्यते । पदात्तावत् पदार्थप्रतीतिः स्मरणाद् भिन्ना वदितुं न शक्यते । तेन स्मृतानामेवान्वयबोधकत्वमित्याश्रयणीयम् तथा च तुल्यो दोषः । अथ शब्दैः स्मारितानामन्वयबोधकत्वं वृद्धव्यवहारे तथा दर्शनादित्यदोषः । मतान्तरेऽपि तुल्यमेतत् । न चायमेकान्तः, वृद्धव्यवहारेऽध्याहृतेनाप्यर्थेनान्विताभिधानदर्शनादित्युक्तम् । अथ शब्दैर्बहवोऽर्थास्स्मार्यन्ते, किन्तु तेषां कतमेनान्वयावबोधकत्वमिति न विद्मः । अभिहितान्वयवादे त्वभिहितेनैवान्वयबोधकत्व युक्तमेवेति, तदसत् । स्मारकत्वातिरेकिणी कान्याभिधायकता, या व्यवस्थानिबन्धनम् । अथोच्येत-स्मारकत्वं नाम प्रत्यासत्तिनिबन्धनम् तेन तदतिरेकिण्यभिधेयाभिधायकतालक्षणाप्रत्यासत्तिरङ्गीकरणीयेति । नैतदेवम् । स्मारकत्वेनैव वृद्धव्यवहारे दर्शनात् स्मारकत्वोपपत्तेः । प्रत्याय्यप्रत्यायकता हि वाच्यवाचकता, सा च यद्यप्यग्निधूमादीनां सम्बन्धान्तरपूर्विका दृष्टा । तथापि शब्दे तथा नाश्रीयते, किन्तु वाचकत्वावगमादेव वाचकत्वम्, एवं स्मारकत्वावगमादेव स्मारकत्वमिति, किं प्रत्यासत्यन्तराश्रयणेन ।

अपि चान्वितार्थवादिन एवेदं प्रतिनियतान्वयित्वमुपपद्यते यत्पदार्थान्तरान्विताभिधायकतया स्मार्यते, तदन्वितस्यैव वृद्धव्यवहारे वाच्यत्वदर्शनात् । यत्राप्यध्याहारः तत्रापि सन्निधापकवशेन विशेषान्विताभिधान-

लाभ इति लोकत एव ज्ञातमिति न कश्चिद्दोषः। अपि च ज्ञातं तावदेतद् यदनेन पदेनायमर्थोऽन्वितो वाच्य इति, तत्र यद्यन्येनाप्यन्विताभिधानं स्यात्, तदा वाक्यभेदो भवेत। न चासावेकवाक्यत्वसम्भवे न्याय्यः। तदुक्तम् "सम्भवत्येकवाक्यत्वे वाक्यभेदस्तु नेष्यते" ॥

इति [श्लो. वा. प्र. सू. श्लो. ६]

अत एव यथा कथञ्चिदेकवाक्यत्वोपपत्तौ वाक्यभेदस्यान्याय्यत्वम्. लोके च लक्षणा, गौणी च वृत्तिर्वाक्यभेदभयादेव। अन्यथा वाक्यं भित्त्वा किमित्यध्याहृत्य योग्यमर्थान्तरं सर्वपदान्येव मुख्यार्थानि नाश्रीयन्ते। वेदेऽप्येकवाक्यत्वबलादेवार्थं वादेषु गुणवादाद्याश्रयणम्, सम्मार्गाधिकरणे [मी. द. २.१.४] विभक्तिव्यत्ययवर्णनम्। उद्भिदाधिकरण पूर्वपक्षे [मी. द. १.४.२.] च कथञ्चित्पशुफलकत्वाश्रयणम्। चित्राधिकरणे [१.४.३.] रूढ़िपरित्यागेन 'पञ्चदशान्याज्यानि भवन्ति' [तां. ब्रा. २०.१.१] इति कथञ्चिनामधेयत्वाश्रयणम्। वाजपेयाधिकरणे [मी. द. १.४.६.] च वाक्यभेदभयादेव नामधेयत्वाश्रयणम्। पौर्णमास्यधिकरणे [मी. द. २.२.३.] चानेकगुणविधाने वाक्यभेदापत्तेस्समुदायानुवादकत्वसिद्धिः। प्रकरणान्तराधिकरणे [मी. द. २.३.११] च वाक्यभेददोषादेवाग्निहोत्रपदस्य गौणत्ववर्णनम् ग्रहाधिकरणे [मी. द. १.३.७] चैकत्वस्याविवक्षितत्वम्। अर्द्धमन्तर्वेदि मिनोति, अर्द्धं बहिर्वेदि' [मै. सं. ३.९.४.] इत्यत्र देशलक्षणापरत्वम् [मी.द. ३.७.६.] क्षौमाधिकरणे [६.१.५.] च पुंद्वयविधानहानम्। हविरार्त्यधिकरणे [६.४.६] चोभयपदस्याविवक्षा। 'वारुण्या निष्कासेन तुषैश्चावभृथं यन्ती'त्यत्र [७.३.५] निरपेक्षत्वत्यागः। पर्युदासाधिकरणे [१०.८.७] च नञर्थस्य लाक्षणिकत्वमित्यादि बहुतरं दृश्यते। तत्र यदि समभिव्याह्रियमाणस्य पदस्याभिधेयं परित्यज्य, अन्येन सहान्वयो लक्ष्यते तदा तदेकवाक्यता हीयेत। तदर्थमेवेदमुक्तं 'न्यायसम्पादितव्यक्ती'ति।

एकवाक्यत्वं हि न्यायः। तदनुसारेण योऽर्थः सोऽत्र वाक्यस्याश्रयणीयः। वृद्धव्यवहारव्युत्पत्तिनियन्त्रितायां शब्दार्थावगतौ ये न्यायाः वृद्धव्यवहारे वाक्यार्थावगतिहेतुतया विदिताः, तानपरिजहता वाक्यार्थो बोद्धव्या इति सर्वासामेवाऽनुपपत्तीनामनवकाशः।

भवतु तर्हि पदार्थान्तरेण तावदन्विताभिधानमेकवाक्यत्वबलात्, तत्स्मारितेन स्वयं स्मारितेन च तदेकवाक्यत्वानुगुणेनार्थान्तरेणापि किमित्यन्विताभिधानं न भवति। उच्यते, पदद्वयेनैवान्विताभिधानसिद्धेराकांक्षोपशान्तेः। अथ नोपशान्ताऽऽकांक्षा, तर्हि को नाम तत्रान्विताभिधानं वारयेत्। अत एवैकपदोच्चारणे तदर्थसम्बन्धमुखेन बहुष्वपि स्मृतिसन्निहितेषु यस्यार्थस्य केनचित्प्रकारेण विशेषो गृह्यते, तेनैवान्विताभिधानम्, अगृह्यमाणे तु विशेषेऽनध्यवसायादप्रतीतिरेव। अत एव विकृतिषु तत्सादृश्येन यदपूर्वं स्मर्यमाणं स्वोपकारकं स्मारयति, तदीयेनैवोपकारेण परिपूरणम्। अतो यत्र बहुतरधर्मसाधारण्यनिबन्धनं सादृश्यमत्यन्तोद्भटम्, तत्रैव शीघ्रं स्मृत्युपपत्तेस्तदीयोपकारपरिग्रह एव। दर्विहोमेषु तु सर्वापूर्वाणामविशेषाद् विशेषो ग्रहीतुमशक्य इत्यनध्यवसाय एव प्राकृतस्योपकारस्येति, तत्रैवोपकारकल्पना।

अपि च यथावृद्धव्यवहारावगमं वाक्यार्थावबोधः। तत्र यदेव पदेन अनपभ्रष्टसम्बन्धग्रहणसंस्कारस्य पुरुषस्य नियमेन स्मार्यते, तेनैवाऽन्विताभिधानं पदान्तरस्य दृश्यते, नान्येन। सर्वं पदं स्वार्थं हि नियमेन सम्बन्धग्रहणात्स्मारयति, नार्थान्तरम्। ततश्च तेनैवान्वितस्वार्थबोधकतेति न कश्चिद्दोषः।

किञ्च यद्यभिहितेनैवान्वितस्वार्थबोधनाभ्युपगम एव प्रतिनियतान्वयबोधो घटते, नान्यथा, तर्हि कल्प्यतां पदानामनन्विताभिधान शक्तिरपि। द्विरभिधानमापद्यत इति चेदापद्यताम्, न कश्चिद्दोषः। पूर्वं केवलं पदमनन्वितं स्वार्थमभिधत्ते, प्रतियोगिपदान्तराभिहितवस्त्वन्तरसहायप्राप्त्या तु तत्तदन्वितमर्थमाह इति न कश्चिद्दोषः। इत्थमपि चास्मन्मते शक्तिकल्पनालाघवमस्ति, पदार्थगतान्वयबोधनशक्त्याधानशक्तिकल्पनात्यागात्। तुल्यायामपि शक्तिकल्पनायाम् पदानामेवान्वितबोधनशक्तिराश्रयितुमुचिता, न पदार्थानाम्, प्रथमावगतत्वात् वाक्यार्थे च तात्पर्यस्योपगमात् इति ॥१५॥

कथं तर्हि इदं भाष्यम् 'पदानि हि' इत्यादि। तत्राह–

अन्बितेषु पदैरेवं बोध्यमानेषु शक्तिभिः ।
अन्वयार्थगृहीतत्वान्नान्यां शक्तिमपेक्षते ।।१६।।

आशङ्कितोत्तरमिदं भाष्यम् । किमाशङ्कितम् ? यद्यन्विताभिधायीनि पदानि तर्हि नान्वयाभिधायीनि । तत्सिद्ध्यर्थं पदानां शक्त्यन्तरं कल्प्यमिति । अत्रेदमुत्तरम् । यत्पदमन्विताभिधायकम्, तदन्वयाभिधायकमेव । अन्यथाऽन्वित एवासौ नाभिहितः स्यादिति, अन्वितरूपेणार्थेनान्वयः स्वीकृतः । तं विना तदसम्भवादिति नापरा तद्विषया पदानां शक्तिः कल्पनीया ।।१६।।

कथं पुनरसावर्थं गृहीत इत्यत्राऽऽह—

प्रतीयन्नन्वयं यस्मात्प्रतीयादन्वितं पुमान् ।
व्यक्तिं जातिमिवार्थेऽसाविति सम्परिकीर्त्यते ।।१७।।

अन्वयवानेव ह्यन्वितः । सोऽन्वयाप्रतीतौ न प्रतीत एव स्यात्, किन्तु स्वरूपमात्रमेव । न च तदन्वितमुच्यते । तस्मादन्वयं प्रतिपद्यमान एवान्वितं प्रतिपद्यते । यथा व्यक्तिं प्रतिपद्यमान एव जातिम् । अयन्तु विशेषः । अन्वयवानेवान्बित उच्यते इति अन्वयोऽप्यभिधानानुप्रविष्टः । व्यक्तिमत्तैव जातिस्वरूपं न भवति, किन्तु व्यक्तेराकारान्तरभूता जातिस्ततो भिन्ना । सा चेदाकृतिः शब्दाभिधेया न व्यक्तिरप्यभिधानानुप्रवेशिनी, किन्त्वाकारभूता जातिर्व्यक्तेर्व्यतिरिक्ताऽपि वस्तुस्वभावेन व्यक्तिमन्तरेण न प्रतीतिमनुभवति, एतावता च साम्येन दृष्टान्तः न सर्वात्मना ।

नन्वेकविज्ञानारूढा कथं व्यक्तिरनभिधेया । शब्दोत्थापितविज्ञानविषयता ह्यभिधेयता, अस्ति च व्यक्तेरपि तथा भाव इति कथमनभिधेयेति ? श्रूयतामवधानेन सर्वस्वं प्राभाकराणाम् । सत्यमेकसंवित्तिविषयता जातिव्यक्त्योः । तथापि चिन्तनीयमिदम्—कथमेषा संबित्तिरुभयबिषया जायत इति । किमस्योभयविषयत्वे शब्दमात्रस्यैव व्यापारः ? उत जातिमात्रविषयत्वे शब्दः स्वरूपमात्रेण व्याप्रियते ? व्यक्तिविषयत्वे जात्यनभिधायकतया जातेरन्यथा बोधयितुमशक्यत्वात् इति । तत्र तावदनन्तासु व्यक्तिषु सम्बन्धग्रहणाशक्ते, आकृत्युपलक्षितासु च यद्यपि सम्बन्धग्रहणं

सुकरम्, तथापि तद्रूपवत्त्वेनैव शब्दाद् व्यक्त्यवगमात्, उपलक्षणत्वे कारणाभावात्, चिह्नाभावेन च क्रियान्वयासम्भवादाकृतिविषयत्वं तावच्छब्दस्वरूपनिबन्धनम्। एवञ्चेत्तदभिधायकतयैव व्यक्तिविषयत्वे शब्दव्यापार इति निश्चीयते। तेनाकृतिर्न व्यक्तिं गमयति, किन्तु शब्द एव तदभिधायकतयेत्याकृतितो व्यक्तिरुच्यते। अतोऽन्विताभिधानायान्वयस्यार्थगृहीतत्वादसावन्वयो नाभिधीयते। तेन व्यतिषक्ताभिधानवन्न व्यतिषङ्गाभिधानं निष्कृष्टाभिधानन्तु न भवति। व्यतिषक्ततोऽवगतेर्व्यतिषङ्गस्य, व्यतिषक्तस्य व्यतिषङ्गं विनाभिधानानुपपत्तेः।

भाष्याक्षराणामयमर्थः—पदानि अन्वितमभिधाय निवृत्तव्यापाराणि नान्वयं पृथगभिदधति। अथेदानीमन्विताः प्रतिपन्ना अन्वयमपि प्रतीतं सम्पादयन्ति इति। लोके च पदार्थानां सम्बन्धग्रहणसमय एव विदितत्वात्, वाक्यान्तरे चान्वयान्तरस्यैव प्रतिपन्नत्वात् तत्परतंत्र वाक्यस्येति। वाक्यार्थशब्देन भाष्यकारोऽन्वयमाह। वेदेत्वपूर्वात्माऽन्वितो वाक्यार्थ इति वक्ष्यामः। तस्य च स्वरूपमनवगतमित्यस्यैव वाक्यार्थत्वम्। एवमुक्तेन न्यायेन विशेषेणैवान्विताभिधानं समर्थितम् ॥१७॥

येऽन्विताभिधानवादिन एवमाहुः—वृद्धव्यवहारप्रसिद्धसम्बन्धश्शब्दोऽर्थस्य वाचकः, अन्वयव्यतिरेकाभ्याञ्च सम्बन्धावधारणम्। न च विशेषान्वयविषयौ तौ संभवतः। क्रियापदं हि कारकसामान्याव्यभिचारिण्या क्रियया सहान्वयव्यतिरेकौ भजते, विशेषान्वयान्तरव्यभिचारात्। एवं कारकपदेऽपि योज्यम्। तन्निराकरणायाह—

सामान्येनान्वितं वाच्यं पदानां ये प्रचक्षते।
नियतेन विशेषेण तेषां स्यादन्वयः कथम् ॥१८॥

दर्शितमिदं विशेषान्वयेऽप्याकांक्षासन्निधियोग्यतोपाधिवशेन सम्बन्धग्रहणं सुकरमिति, तदभिधायकतैव युक्ता पदानाम्। यदि चासौ नेष्यते, तदा वाक्यार्थप्रतिपत्तिरेव नोपपद्यते विशेषान्वयरूपत्वाद्वाक्यार्थस्य ॥१८॥

ननु च सामान्यान्वयोऽभिहितो विशेषान्वयमाक्षेप्स्यति, निर्विशेषस्य सामान्यस्य प्रत्येतुमशक्तेर्विशेषान्वयप्रतिपत्तिरुपपन्नैवेत्यत्राह—

यद्यप्याक्षिप्यते नाम विशेषो व्यक्तिजातिवत् ।
निर्धारितविशेषस्तु तद्वदेव न गम्यते ॥१६॥

यथा जातिर्व्यक्तिमाक्षिपन्त्यपि न प्रतिनियतं विशेशमाक्षिपति, तथाऽत्राऽपि प्रतिनियतविशेषालाभान्नियतविशेषात्मकवाक्यार्थप्रतिपत्तिरनुपपन्ना ॥१६॥

अथ विशेषमात्राक्षेपेऽप्याकांक्षितस्सन्निहितो योग्यश्चयोगविशेषो यः पदान्तरेण समर्प्यते, स एव गृह्यते । तदतिक्रमे प्रमाणाभावादित्यत्राह—

यद्यप्याकांक्षितो योग्यो बिशेषः सन्निधौ श्रुतः ।
सम्बन्धबोधकाभावे गृह्यते न तथाऽप्यसौ ॥२०॥

सामान्यान्चिताभिधानवादिनो मते पदानि तावत् तन्मात्र एव पर्यवसितशक्तीनि, पदार्थानामप्यन्वयबोधवशक्तिर्नाऽङ्गीक्रियते । न च सामान्याक्षेपोऽपि नियतं विशेषमास्कन्दति । तेनाऽऽकांक्षिते योग्ये च विशेषे पदान्तरेण सन्निधापितेऽपि तदन्वयबोधकप्रमाणाभावात् तदन्वयो न प्रतीयेतैय । अत आकांक्षासन्निधियोग्यत्वान्यनुपयोगीन्येव । विशेषान्वयवादिनस्तु मते सम्बन्धग्रहणं प्रत्युपाधित्वेन प्रविष्टानि तानि वाक्यार्थप्रतिपत्तावुपयुज्यन्ते ॥२०॥

सम्बन्धबोधे व्युत्पत्तावुपाधित्वे सम।विशत् ।
विशेषान्वयवादे तु योग्य त्वाद्युपकारकम् ॥२१॥

पदानां पदार्थान्तरसम्बद्धः स्वार्थो बोध्य इत्यस्यां व्युत्पत्तावुपाधित्वेन योग्यत्वादिकमनुप्रविष्टं विशेषान्विताभिधानवादिपक्षे उपकारकम्, न तु सामान्यान्विताभिधाने इति दर्शितं प्राक् ॥२१॥

दूषणान्तञ्चाह—

किञ्च वस्तुबलेनैव सिद्धे सामान्यसङ्गमे ।
तस्य वाच्यत्वमिच्छद्भिर्वृथा शब्दः प्रयासितः ॥२२॥

क्रियाकारकस्वभावालोचनयापि कारकमात्रेण क्रियामात्रेण चान्वयावगमसिद्धेः, वृथा सामान्यान्वयाभिधायचता शब्दस्याङ्गीक्रियत इति ।

वाक्यमेकं न निर्भागं वाक्यान्त्यो वर्ण एव वा।
पदवृन्दं स्मृतिस्थं वा प्रथमं पदमेव वा॥
आख्यातपदमात्रं वा पादार्था वाप्यनन्विताः।
सामान्यान्वयबोधे वा हेतुर्वाक्यार्थबोधने॥
पदान्येव समर्थानि वाक्यार्थस्यावबोधने।
विशेषान्वयवादीनि भागशो भागशालिनः॥

॥ इतिसंग्रहश्लोकाः॥

तथा चोक्तम् 'अस्ति वा पदस्यार्थः? बाढमस्ति। कथं तर्हि वाक्यवाक्यार्थयोरौत्पत्तिकत्वं? वृद्धव्यवहारात्। सत्यम्। स तु भवयववश इत्युक्तम्'।

इति महामहोपाध्यायश्रीमच्छालिकनाथमिश्रप्रणीतायां वाक्यार्थमातृकावृत्तौ उपोद्घातो नाम प्रथमः परिच्छेदः समाप्तः।

द्वितीयः परिच्छेदः

उपोद्घातभूतमन्विताभिधानं प्रसाध्य, **अपूर्वं कार्यं** वेदवाक्यानामर्थ इति साधयितुकामः पूर्वपक्षं तावदाह—

ननु व्युत्पत्त्यपेक्षेषु शब्देष्वर्थाभिधायिषु ।
कथं मानान्तरावेद्यं कार्यमाहुर्लिङादयः ॥१॥

अपूर्वाधिकरणे (मी. द. २.१.२.) लिङ्ङ्यर्थोऽपूर्वमित्युक्तम् । प्रमाणान्तरायोग्यञ्चापूर्वमिष्यते । यच्च प्रमाणान्तरायोग्यम्, तत्र सम्बन्ध-ग्रहणमशक्यम्, सम्बन्धिग्रहणपूर्वकत्वात्तस्य । विशिष्टार्थव्यवहारदर्शनेन हि तद्विषया शब्दशक्तिरनुमीयते, तदेव च सम्बन्धग्रहणम् । यच्च प्रतीयते, न तद्विषयो व्यवहारोऽवसीयते । तदनवसाये च न तद्विषया बुद्धिरनुमीयते । तदननुमाने च कुतः शब्दस्य शक्तिः कल्प्यते । अपूर्वञ्च न प्रमाणान्तर-गोचरः । न च शब्दादेव तदवगम्य सम्बन्धावधारणम् इतरेतराश्रयप्रसङ्गात्, अवसितशक्तेरवबोधकत्वात्, अवबोधकत्वादेव शक्त्यवगमात् । स्यान्मतम् । लिङादेः शब्दस्यायं महिमा, यदनवसितशक्तिरपि स्वार्थमवगमयति इति । तदिदमप्रमाणम् । क्रियामात्रावबोधकत्वाङ्गीकारेण लिङादेर्लोकतो व्युत्पत्ति-सम्भवे शब्दान्तरवैलक्षण्येनागृहीतसम्बन्धस्यैव वाचकत्वकल्पनानुपपत्तेः ।

वेदवाक्यादपूर्वकार्यावगतेरेवं कल्प्यत इति चेन्न, तस्या एवासिद्ध-त्वात्, क्रियैव कार्यतया वेदवाक्येभ्योऽवगम्यत इति, व्युत्पत्तिबलेना-प्रामाणिकं मनोरथमात्रविजृम्भितन्त्वपूर्वं कार्यं प्रतीयत इति । तस्माद-गृहीतसम्बन्धो लिङादिः कथमपूर्वं कार्यमभिधत्ते, तथा च कथं तद्वाक्यार्थः । अभिधेय एव ह्यर्थो भवति वाक्यार्थः ॥१॥

एवञ्च—

शब्दान्तराण्यपि कथं तेनादृष्टेन कुत्रचिद् ।
वदिष्यन्त्यन्वितं स्वार्थं व्युत्पत्तिपथदूरगम् ॥२॥

तस्मिन्नप्रतीयमाने तदन्वितस्याप्रतीते,, तत्र सम्बन्धावधारणानुपपत्तेर्दूरनिरस्तं शब्दान्तराणां तदन्वितस्वार्थबोधकत्वमिति ।।२।।

राद्धान्तमुपक्रमते—

अत्रोच्यते यदा नाम वृद्धेनैकेन भाषिते ।
जलं चैत्राहरस्वेति चैत्र आहरते जलम् ।।३।।
तदा व्युत्पित्समानोऽन्यस्तत्रैवमवगच्छति ।

बुद्धिपूर्वा ममेवास्य प्रवृत्तिरियमीदृशी । लिङादियुक्तवाक्यश्रवणसमनन्तरं वृद्धस्य विशिष्टार्थविषयां प्रवृत्तिं दृष्ट्वा व्युत्पित्समानो बाल एवमाकलयति-येयं स्वाधीनास्य प्रवृत्तिः सा मद्वत् बुद्धिपूर्विकेति । पुनश्च तस्यायं विमर्शो जायते-अहं बुद्ध्वा प्रवृत्तो यथा, तद्वद् एषोऽपि । यस्याः प्रवृत्तेर्हेतुभूता बुद्धिः सा यद्विषयां सती मम प्रवृत्तिहेतुः, तद्विषयैवास्यापीति, पुनर्व्युत्पित्सोरनुमा जायते । तदेवमनुमानद्वयमेतद् वृद्धस्य स्वतन्त्रा प्रवृत्तिः धर्मिणी, बुद्धिपूर्विका इति साध्यो धर्मः, स्वतन्त्रप्रवृत्तित्वान्मदीयस्वतन्त्रप्रवृत्तिवदिति, तथा वृद्धस्य प्रवृत्तिहेतुभूता बुद्धिः धर्मिणी, यद्विषया बुद्धिर्मम प्रवृत्तिहेतुभूता तद्विषयैवास्यापि इति साध्योधर्मः प्रवृत्तिहेतुभूतबुद्धित्वात्, मदीयप्रवृत्तिहेतुभूतबुद्धिवत् इति । पुनश्च तस्यायं विमर्शः प्रवर्त्तते । पदस्य तु शब्देन बोध्यते । अनेन मम मानान्तेरण तु यद्विषया सा बुद्धिः प्रवृत्तिहेतुभूता तद्वस्त्वनेन शब्देन बोध्यते । तद्भावे सत्यवगमात्, मम तु मानान्तरेण तद् बोध्यत इति, अयमावयोर्विशेषः । तेन यद् बुद्ध्वा प्रवृत्तिर्मम तदस्यानेन शब्देन बोध्यत इति शब्दस्य प्रवृत्तिहेतुभूतार्थावबोधकतामवधारयति ।।३।।

पुनश्च कोऽसौ प्रवृत्तिहेतुभूतोऽर्थश्शब्दाभिधेय इति निर्धारयितुम्, स्वात्मनि प्रतिपन्नं प्रवृत्तिहेतुभूतमर्थमनुसन्धत्तेः—

तत्र बुद्ध्वा प्रवृत्तोऽहं किं तावत्स्वयमन्यदा ।।४।।

शब्दनिरपेक्षः स्वयमहं प्रवर्त्तमानः किं बुद्ध्वा प्रवृत्त इति जिज्ञासते । 'अन्यदा' इत्यनेन व्युत्पत्तितः प्रागवस्थेत्युच्यते । व्युत्पन्नेन

बालेन यदात्मनि प्रवृत्तिकारणतया प्रतीतम्, तदेव व्युत्पन्नस्यापीति कल्प्यते, नान्यदित्यर्थः ।

तेन शब्द एव प्रवृत्तिहेतुभूतो विधिः तद्व्यापारो वेति निरस्तं भवति। तयोर्बालेनात्मनि प्रवृत्तिकारणत्वेनादर्शनात् ।

अति मन्दतया चेमौ पक्षौ न साक्षादुपन्यस्य निरस्तौ। तथाहि लिङादिशब्दस्वरूपस्य प्रवर्त्तकत्वे सर्व एव तच्छ्रविणो नियमेन प्रवर्त्तेरन्, न चैवं दृश्यते, कस्यचित् कदाचित्प्रवृत्तेः । लिङादिव्यापारस्य तु प्रवृत्ति-हेतुत्वाश्रयणं देवाः प्रपद्यन्ताम्, पिशितचक्षुषो मानुषा वयं नेयतीं प्रमाण-भूमिमवगाहितुं क्षमाः ।

केयं शब्दभावनोच्यते – लिङादिव्यापाररूपा पुरुषप्रवृत्तिभवनानुकूला स्वज्ञानकरणिका अर्थवादोदितप्राशस्त्यलक्षणेतिकर्त्तव्यतायोगिनी प्रेरणा-त्मिका कल्प्यते । "स्वाध्यायाध्ययनविधिना हि सर्वे विधायकाः, स्वाध्याय-पदोपात्तश्चात्मा नियुज्यन्ते 'भावयेदिति" (तं० वा० पृ० ११४) । तत्र किमित्यपेक्षायां पुरुषप्रवृत्तिः सम्बद्ध्यते । केनेत्याकांक्षायां विधिज्ञानमेव योग्यतया करणत्वेनाङ्गीक्रियये । ज्ञाता हि शाब्दभावना प्रवृत्तिं प्रसूते, योग्यतयैवार्थवादसमुत्थप्राशस्त्यज्ञानमितिकर्तव्यतांशे निविशते । अवसी-दन्ती हि विधिशक्तिः प्राशस्त्य ज्ञानेनोत्तभ्यते । तस्याश्च पुरुषव्यापाररूपा स्वर्गादिभाव्यावच्छिन्ना भावार्थकरणिका श्रौतस्मार्त्त-आचारप्राप्तपदार्थ-जनितकरणोपकारवत्यार्थभावना समानप्रत्ययवाच्या विषयभूता इति ।

तन्न, लिङादेस्तादृशो व्यापारो विद्यत इत्यत्र न किञ्चन प्रमाणम् । लिङादिशब्दानन्तरभाविनी पुरुषप्रवृत्तिरेव प्रमाणमिति चेन्न, तन्निबन्धन-त्वेन प्रवृत्तेरन्यत्राऽदृष्टत्वात् । यन्निबन्धना हि प्रवृत्तिर्दृष्टा, तदेव तां दृष्ट्वा शक्यमनुमातुम्, न पुनरप्रतिपन्नपूर्वकारणभावः शब्दव्यापार-विशेषः । अथ लिङादिशब्द एव प्रमाणमिति साहसम्, अगृहीत सम्बन्ध-स्यावाचकत्वात् । अनवधारिते हि सम्बन्धिनि सम्बन्धबोधवैधुर्यात् । कथञ्च तत्र स्वाध्यायाध्ययनविधिना सर्वे विधायकाः स्वात्मा च विनियु-ज्यन्ते । पुरुषं विधिरार्थभावनायां प्रेरयति । यश्च येन प्रेर्यते, स तेन

नियुज्यते। न चाचेतनानां विधीनां नियोजकत्वमपि सम्भवति। अथ न नियोज्यन्ते, तदप्यनुपपन्नं शाब्दभावनासु सर्वशब्दानां स्वत एव कर्त्तृत्वात् विनियोगानपेक्षणात्। अथ न पुरुषाः प्रेरणे विनियुज्यन्ते, किन्त्वर्थावबोधने। तदपि न घटते। तत्रापि नियोज्यानपेक्षायास्तुल्यत्वात्। अध्ययनविधेश्च अक्षरसंस्काररूपाध्ययनविधायकत्वाभ्युपगमात्।

तथाचाहु :–

"द्रव्यादीनां पुनः कस्मिन्स्वाध्यायोऽन्तर्गतो भवेत्।
त्रेधापि प्रतिभात्यस्मिन् संस्कारत्वस्य निर्णयः॥
संस्कार्यंगणनायां च युक्तैवाक्षरसंस्क्रिया।
स्वाध्यायो हि स्फुटं कर्म साक्षात्संस्क्रियते हि सः॥" इति।

संस्कारविधिश्च न संस्कार्यं विनियुंक्ते, प्रमाणान्तरावसितोपयोगस्य शेषित्वात्। संस्कारपर्यवसायी तु संस्कारविधिर्न संस्कार्यस्य कार्यं कल्पयेत्। आत्मा चाऽध्ययनविधिना विनियज्यते, न विनियुज्यते वेति प्रतिपत्तिद्वयस्याऽप्यसम्भवादनुपपन्नम्।

कथञ्च पुरुषवृत्तिस्तस्या भाव्यम्, न तावदनन्तरनिष्पत्तेः, विधिज्ञानस्य करणत्वाभावप्रसङ्गात्। क्रियाफलं हि तथा पुरुषप्रवृत्तिः स्यात्। न च क्रिया फलप्रसवाय करणमपेक्षते। न च गमनं संयोगविभागारम्भे करणापेक्षम्। स्यान्मतम्। लिङादिशब्दो विधिज्ञानं जनयित्वा करणानुगृहीतः प्रेरणारूपं स्वव्यापारमारभते इति। न च करणत्वाभावः क्रियानिष्पत्तावेव करणत्वात्। तदिदमलौकिकम्। न हि कस्यचिद्वस्तुनः स्वज्ञानस्वज्ञानमुत्पादहेतुः प्रतीतम्।

एवमर्थवादोदित प्राशस्त्यस्यापि इतिकर्त्तव्यतात्वं विध्वस्तम्। योग्यतया हि तस्य तथाभावः। न च प्रेरणोत्पत्तौ शब्दकर्तृकाया करणीभूतज्ञानानुग्रहयोग्यता तस्य शक्यतेऽवगन्तुम्। पुरुषकर्तृकायां तु प्रवृत्तौ स्यात्तस्य योग्यताऽवगमः, प्रशस्ते पुरुषप्रवृत्तिदर्शनात्। स्यान्मतम्। अप्रशस्ते पुरुषप्रवृत्यसम्भवे प्रेरणैव नोपपद्यते। न फलसम्भवायत्ता क्रियानिष्पत्तिः, क्रियानिष्पत्त्यायत्तैव तु फलसिद्धिरिति लोके प्रतीतम्। अतएव तस्मिन्पक्षे

निष्फलेऽपि प्रेरणासिद्धेः स्यात्। अथ फलमपि इतिकर्त्तव्यतापदनिवेशि प्राशस्त्यवत, अतस्तदभावे न प्रेरणा निष्पद्यत इति। तर्हि फलमेवास्त्विति कर्त्तव्यतांशपूरकम्, किं प्राशस्त्येन। सत्यमेतद्, अस्ति तावद्, तदपीति न-त्यज्यते। एवं तर्ह्यश्रुते प्राशस्त्ये तदपेक्षा मा भूत्। ततश्च तदतिदेशादि-कल्पनमघटमानं केवलस्य विधेः दर्विहोमवत्करतिकर्तव्यता कल्पनाऽपि कल्पनामात्रमेव। दर्विहोमवदिति चासिद्धो दृष्टान्तः। तत्रापि श्रौत-द्रव्यदेवतास्मृत्याचारप्राप्ताचमनादीतिकर्तव्यतामात्रेणोपकारक्लृप्तेरभिम-तत्वात्। नह्येकस्यैव वस्तुनोऽनुग्राहकताऽनुग्राह्यता च स्वात्मन्युपपद्यते। अथ शब्दः प्रेरणां करोत्येव, प्रवृत्तिस्तु न तावन्मात्रेण, किन्तु तज्ज्ञाने सति। एवं तर्हि ज्ञानफलमेव प्रवृत्तिरस्तु, न प्रेरणाफलम्, तस्मिन्सति भावात्, असति चाभावात्। तथा च न शब्दभावना विधिरिति सिद्धम्।

किञ्च शब्दोऽम्बरगुण इति, प्राप्यकारीन्द्रियवादिनाभ्युपेयम्। अन्यथा नभसश्श्रोत्रभूतस्य शब्दस्य च प्राप्त्यसम्भवात्संयोगसमवाय-योरन्यतरस्य च प्राप्तिरूपत्वात्, संयोगस्याऽन्यतरकर्मजस्य उभयकर्मजस्य संयोगजस्य च द्रव्यत्वे सति शब्दस्य नभसा सहाऽसम्भवात्, तस्य च त्रैविध्यनियमात् पारिशेष्यात्समवायः प्राप्तिरिति। आकाशगुणः शब्दः। न च तस्य व्यापारसम्भवः द्रव्याश्रितत्वाद् व्यापाराणाम्।

कथं तर्हि शब्दस्याऽभिधानलक्षणो व्यापार आश्रीयते? यथा तत् तथा श्रूयताम्—यत्तावदात्मन्यर्थविषयज्ञानं शब्दविषयज्ञानानन्तरं जायते, तच्छब्दकर्त्तृकतया यदा विवक्ष्यते, तदा तदाभिधानिकमित्युच्यते। परस्थे-ऽपि व्यापारे भवत्येव कर्त्तृता, परिस्पन्द इवात्मन इति न कश्चिद्दोषः।

कथञ्चाऽसौ शब्दव्यापार आर्थभावनाविषयः? एक प्रत्ययवाच्य-त्वात् इति।

तदुक्तम्—'विधिभावनयोश्चैकप्रत्ययग्राह्यता कृतः।
धात्वर्थात्प्रथमं तावत्सम्बन्धोऽध्यवसीयते॥

तन्न।

प्रत्ययस्य भावनाभिधानमस्मिन्पक्षे दुर्घटं यतः। इति

ननु च सर्वाख्यातानां भावनावचनता करोतिसामानाधिकरण्या- दध्यवसीयते । तथाहि–भवत्यर्थस्य कर्त्तुः प्रयोजकव्यापारो भावना, सैव कृतिः । भाव्यमानस्यैव क्रियमाणत्वात्, तस्य कृतिकर्मत्वात् । किमकार्षीत् ? अपाक्षीत्; किं करोति ? पचति; किं करिष्यति ? पक्ष्यति इति प्रश्नोत्तर- दर्शनात् करोत्यर्थः सर्वाख्यातैरभिधीयत इति गम्यते । अन्यथा करोत्यर्थ- विषयप्रश्ने तदुत्तरानुपपत्तिः । तत्र सत्यामपि प्रकृतौ घञन्तादिषु करोत्यर्था- नवबोधात्, आख्यातप्रत्ययसन्निधाने च तदवगमात् आख्यातानामेव सोऽर्थ इति निश्चीयते ।

तदसत् । किं करोतीत्यस्य प्रश्नस्य यद्ययमर्थः यत् करोति तत् किमिति, तत्र चेत्पचतीत्युत्तरं स्यात्, तदा पाकं करोतीत्यस्मिन्नर्थे पचतीति वर्त्तते । तथा च सिद्ध्येदाख्यातानां करोत्यर्थता । न चैतदेवम् । अनवगते हि धातुवाच्ये व्यापारविशेषे तद्विशेष एवैवं पृच्छ्यते, तत्र पचतीत्युत्तरम् । तथा च न सिद्ध्यति धात्वर्थातिरिक्तकरोत्यर्थवचनताऽऽख्यातानाम् सर्वे धात्वर्थाश्च कस्यचिद् भूतस्य भवनेऽनुकूलतां भजन्तः करोत्यर्थतामापन्नाः करोतिना प्रष्टुम्, निर्देष्टुञ्च शक्यन्त इति, तद्विशेषप्रश्नोत्तरे एव ते । किञ्च धातुवाच्यव्यापारविशेषविषयत्वेनाऽपि प्रश्नोत्तरयचेरुपपत्तौ, तदतिरिक्त करोत्यर्थवाचकताऽऽख्यातानां न शक्यते वक्तुम् ।

अपि च सप्रयत्नक्रियेषु देवदत्तादिषु व्यापारभेदसम्भवात् घटेतां प्रश्नोत्तरे । व्यतिरिक्तकरोत्यर्थविषये 'किं करोति' इति प्रश्ने, 'गच्छति' इति चोत्तरे गमनातिरिक्तव्यापाराभावादनुपपत्तिरेव स्यात् । धात्वर्थयिषयत्वे तु तत्राप्युपपत्तिः । अथ संयोगविभागौ धात्वर्थः, परिस्पन्दस्तु विभक्त्यर्थ इति, तत्रापि धात्वर्थव्यतिरिक्तव्यापारसम्भवान्नानुपपत्तिः । तन्न परिस्पन्दस्यैव गमिवाच्यत्यात् । तथाहि न केवले संयोगे विभागे वा गमेः प्रयोगः, स्थाणौ स्येनेन वियुक्ते संयुक्ते वाऽप्रयोगात् । नापि द्वयोः उत्पत्य निपतिते श्येने स्थाणौ प्रयोगप्रसङ्गात् । एकक्रियाक्षणजन्यौ संयोगविभागौ गमिवाच्याविति यद्युच्येत, तर्हि क्रियैवास्तु वाच्या, किमसावुपाधिकोटौ निवेश्यते । एवं ह्युपाधिसमाश्रयणगौरवमेव परिहृतं भवति ।

अपि च वृद्धव्यवहाराच्छब्दार्थनिर्णयः । न चाख्यातानां भावना- वचनत्वमन्तरेण कस्यचिद् वृद्धव्यवहारस्यानुपपत्तिः । प्रश्नोत्तरे तु सम्बन्ध-

ज्ञानोत्तरकालभाविनी, अतो न तद्वशेन सम्बन्धिनिरूपणा । कर्त्रादि संख्यामात्रवाचितयाऽऽख्यातप्रयोगोपपत्तौ, नाधिकं वाच्यं शक्यं कल्पयितुम् । अपि च 'पाकं करोति देवदत्तः,' इत्यत्र तावत्पच्यर्थं पाकशब्दो ब्रवीति, तदनुगुणन्तु पुरुषप्रयत्नं करोतिराष्टे; आख्यातन्तु केवलकर्त्तृसंख्यां ब्रवीतीति सिद्धं तन्मात्रवाचित्वम् । अतोऽन्यत्रापि तत्रैव वर्त्तते इति युक्तम् । एवं 'पचति देवदत्तः' इत्यस्य यद् विवरणं 'पाकं करोति' इति, तदप्यनुपपन्नम् । पचतीत्यत्र यः पुरुषप्रयत्नः यत्सम्बन्धेन पच्यर्थः साध्यभूतः, तं करोतिना प्रकृतिभूतेनोपादाय विवरणोपपत्तेः । यत्रापि 'रथो गमनं करोति' इति न प्रयत्नोऽपरोऽस्ति, तत्रापि गमनस्य साध्यतां दर्शयितुं गौणः करोतिप्रयोगो द्रष्टव्यः । पक्षद्वयेऽपि तुल्यत्वात् ।

यस्तु 'देवदत्त ओदनं पचति इत्यादौ वृद्धव्यवहारे एव प्रकृत्यर्थातिरिक्ते प्रयत्ने प्रयोगादाख्यातानां तदर्थतामाह,' स इत्थं शिक्षितव्यः वत्स ? किं न वेत्सि 'अनन्यलभ्यः शब्दार्थः' इति । इह च प्रकृत्यर्थाक्षेपेणाऽपि प्रयत्नप्रतिपत्त्युपपत्तेः, न शक्यते तद्वाचकताऽऽख्यातानामाश्रयितुम् इति ।

ननु प्राभाकरा अपि भावनावाचकतां न कथमाख्यातप्रत्ययस्येच्छन्ति । उच्यते, न सर्वाख्यातप्रत्ययानां भावनावचनत्वमभ्युपेमः, किन्तु कार्याभिधायिनो लिङादयः कार्यस्यान्यथाऽनभिधानात् कृत्यभिधायिन इष्यन्ते । कृतिसम्बन्धि हि कार्यं कृत्यनभिधाने नाभिहितं स्यात् । नह्यस्ति सम्भवः, कृतिश्च नाभिधीयते, कार्यञ्चाभिधीयते इति ।

अथ मतम् । यथा दण्डीत्यत्र प्रत्ययेन दण्डो नाभिधीयते, अथ च तद्विशिष्टपुरुषप्रतीतिः, एवमिहापि भवेदिति, तन्न, तत्राप्यप्रतीते दण्डे न तद्वति प्रत्ययः । अस्ति च तत्र प्रकृतिभूतो दण्डशब्दः, स च तस्य प्रत्याययिता । न चेह तथा संभवति, प्रकृतीनां पुरुषव्यापाराभिधानानियमात् । पुरुषो हि चेतनः कार्यं लिङादिभिरवबुद्ध्यते । न चासौ परकृति सम्बन्धि स्वयं कार्यं बोद्धुमलमिति तदीयकृत्यभिधानमेषितव्यम् । तस्य च कृतिः प्रयत्नरूपा । न च सर्वथा तदननुभवे तदभिधायिन इति, न दण्डिन्यायस्याऽयं विषयः । स्यान्मतम् । यथा लिङां कर्त्रादिसंख्यामात्र-

वचनता, क्रियाक्षेपेण च कर्त्रादीनां प्रतीतिः। तथेहापि क्रिया प्रयत्न-माक्षिपति, मा भूत्तस्य लिङ्वाच्यता इति। तदसत्। यद्यपि प्रकृत्यर्थभूतया क्रियया प्रयत्न आक्षिप्यते। तथाऽपि तदायत्तसिद्धिकतया कथमपूर्वं गम्यते। प्रत्नाभिधाने तदवच्छिन्नतया प्रतीयमानं तदायत्तसिद्धिकं गम्यते, नान्यथा। न च कृत्यनवच्छिन्नस्वरूपमात्रेणापूर्वमभिहितं कृतिमाक्षेप्तु-मलम्। अवगतसम्बन्धं हि वस्त्वाक्षिप्यते। न च शब्दमन्तरेणापूर्वस्य प्रयत्नसम्बन्धावगमे कारणमस्ति। अतः कथं तत्प्रयत्नमाक्षिपेत्। तस्मादपूर्वकार्याभिधायिनां प्रयत्नाभिधानमवश्यमाश्रयणीयमिति, विषय-करणीये निपुणतरमुपपादितमित्यलमतिप्रसङ्गेन ॥४॥

तत्र न क्रियामात्रंतावदहं बुद्ध्वा प्रवृत्तः, नापि फलमात्रम्, न क्रिया-फल-सम्बन्धमात्रं वा। क्रियाफलयोः साध्यसाधनतावगमेऽपि न प्रवृत्तिरुप-पद्यते। तृप्तिहेतौ भोजनेऽतीते वर्त्तमाने वाऽप्रवृत्तेः, भविष्यत्यपि तत्साधने सामुद्रविदाख्यात इवाऽनुष्ठानाभावात्। पुरुषाशयावगमस्तु प्रवृत्ति-हेतुत्वेनाऽऽशङ्कितोऽपि, स्वतन्त्रप्रवृत्तौ व्युत्पित्सोर्दूरोत्सारितत्वात्। किन्तु कार्यतां बुद्ध्वा प्रवृत्तोऽहम् ममेदं कार्यमिति प्रतीत्य अहं सर्वत्र प्रवृत्तः। तथाहि—

आस्तां तावत्क्रिया लोके गमनागमनादिका।
अन्ततः स्तन्यपानादिः तृप्तिकारिण्यपि क्रिया ॥५॥
सा यावन्मम कार्येयमिति नैवावधार्यते।
तावत्कदापि मे तत्र प्रवृत्तिरभवन्नहि ॥६॥

अत्रापर आह—सत्यं कार्यवगमादेव प्रवृत्तिः। इष्टसाधनतैव तु कार्यता, न परा काचित्, सैवं प्रवृत्तिहेतु विधिरुच्यते। तदाह—

'अपेक्षितोपायतैव विधिरिष्टो मनीषिभिः।
अतो ह्यध्यवसायादिर्नाकस्मान्नाभिधानतः' ॥ इति।

तथा— (१. ब्रह्मसिद्धिः ३. १०३½—१०४½ पृ० ११५)

'पुंसो नेष्टाभ्युपायत्वात् क्रियास्वन्यः प्रवर्त्तकः।
प्रवृत्तिहेतुं धर्मञ्च प्रवदन्ति प्रवत्तनाम्'। इति।

"कर्तुरिष्टाभ्युपाये हि कर्त्तव्यमिति लोकधीः ।
विपरीते त्वकर्त्तव्यमिति तद्विषये ततः ॥"

(१. विधिविवेक का. २६ पृ० २४३
२. विधिविवेक ३० पृ० ३०२)

तत्र तावदिदमेव वक्तव्यम्—अतीतस्य वर्त्तमानस्य चेष्टसाधनताऽस्ति, न च तत्कार्यतावसीयते । तेनान्या कार्यता, अन्य चेष्टसाधनता इति । तथा प्रवृत्तिरपि तन्मात्रावगमायत्ता न भवतीत्युपेक्ष्यैव तावत्तं फलसाधनता-कार्यतयोः भेदं विनिर्दिशति—

फलसाधनता नाम या सा नैव च कार्यता ।
कार्यता कृतिसाध्यत्वं फलसाधनता पुनः ॥७॥
करणत्वं फलोत्पादे भिद्येते ते परस्परम् ।

यद्यप्येकवस्तुनिवेशिता द्वयोः तथापि स्वरूपभेदोऽस्त्येव । तदेव हि बस्तुफलं प्रत्युपायभावात्फलसाधनमित्युच्यते, कृत्यधीनात्मलाभतया च कार्यमिति ॥ ७½ ॥

किमितीस्टाभ्युपायेष्वेव कर्तव्यतावगमः, अन्यत्र नेत्याह—

किन्तु स्वयं क्लेशरूपं कर्म यत्कार्यतां व्रजेत् ॥८॥
फलसाधना तत्र कारणं तेन कार्यता ।
तद्भावभाविनी नित्यं तदा सैव प्रकाशते ॥९॥

स्वभावेन हि कर्माणि दुःखोत्पादहेतुभूतानि । तेषु कार्यत्वावगमः फलसाधनतावगमनिबन्धनः । कार्यता हि न कृत्यधीनसिद्धितामात्ररूपा, किन्तु कृतिं प्रति प्रधानभूतं सत् यत् तदधीनसत्ताकम्, तत्कार्यमुच्यते । तच्च कृतेः प्रधानम्, यदधिकृत्य कृतिः प्रवर्त्तते । न च दुःखं दुखहेतुर्वाऽधिकृत्य कृतेः प्रवृत्तिरुत्पन्ना, नाप्यदुःखम्, अदुःखहेतुं वा । किन्तु सुखं सुखहेतुं वा । तत्र न तावत्स्वयं सुखरूपं कर्म, सुखसाधनमपि चेन्न स्यात्, न तस्य कृतिं प्रति प्राधान्यावगमो घटते । अतः कर्मसु कार्यत्वावगमः

फलसाधनतावगमनिबन्धन इति. ज्ञापककोटिनिविष्टा फलसाधनता कार्यतामनुरुध्यते, नत्वसौ तदात्मैव। तथा चासाधनस्यापि सुखस्यैवास्ति कार्यता। सुखं हि सर्वः कार्यतयाऽवैति, न तस्य फलसाधनतामपेक्षते। तेन फलसाधनतोत्तीर्णकार्यतावगमेन मे प्रवृत्तिरिति निश्चित्य व्युत्पित्सुमानश्चैत्रं प्रवर्तमानं दृष्ट्वाऽनुमिनोति 'चैत्रोऽपि कार्यबोधात्प्रवर्तत' इति। 'चैत्रस्य प्रवृत्तिः धर्मिणी कार्यबोधपूर्विका' इति साध्यो धर्मः, बुद्धिपूर्वकत्वे सति प्रवृत्तित्वान्मदीयप्रवृत्तिवदिति। लिङादयश्च प्रवृत्तिहेतुभूतार्थाभिधायिनः कार्यमेवाऽभिदधते। तस्यैवावगतस्य प्रवृत्त्यनन्तरकारणत्वात् ॥९॥

इच्छा यद्यपि प्रवृत्तिहेतुः, तथापि सा लिङादिवाच्या न भवति, तदवगमस्य प्रवृत्तावनपेक्षितत्वात्। उत्पन्ना हि सा प्रवृत्तिकारणम्, नावगता।

नन्वेवमपि कथं लिङादीनां कार्ये व्युत्पत्तिरित्यत्राह—

शब्दान्तराणि स्वार्थेषु व्युत्पद्यन्ते यथैव हि।
आवापोद्वापभेदेन तथा कार्ये लिङादयः ॥१०॥

लिङादियुक्तवाक्यश्रवणे तद्भावभाविन्या प्रवृत्त्या विशिष्टकार्यावगतिमनुमाय वाक्यस्य हेतुतामध्यवस्यति। तत्रापि कोऽर्थः केन शब्देनाऽभिहित इति विवेचने लिङाद्यावापे कार्यावगतिदर्शनात्, तदुद्धारे चादर्शनात्, त एव कार्यावगतिं कुर्वन्तीति शब्दान्तरवल्लिङादीनां कार्यवाचकत्वव्युत्पत्तिसिद्धिः ॥ १० ॥

ननु लोकव्यवहारात् लिङादयो वाचकतया व्युत्पाद्यमाना प्रैषादिष्वेव वाचकतया व्युत्पत्तिमर्हन्ति। तत्रैव तेषां प्रयोगदर्शनादित्याशंक्याह—

कार्यमेव हि सर्वत्र प्रवृत्तावेककारणम्।
प्रवृत्त्यव्यभिचारित्वाल्लिङाद्यर्थोऽवधार्यते ॥१२॥

प्रवृत्तिर्हि बालेन स्वात्मनि कार्यावगमपूर्विका प्रतिपन्नेति, सर्वपुरुषानपि प्रवर्तमानान्दृष्ट्वा कार्यावगममेव बालः कल्पयति इति प्रैषादी-

नामपि प्रवृत्तिः कार्यावगमनिबन्धनेति कार्यमेव प्रैषादिव्यपदेशयोगीति सिद्धम् ।

वस्तुतस्तु प्रैषादीनामपि प्रवृत्त्यव्यभिचारित्वात्कार्यस्य च प्रवृत्तिषु सर्वासु हेतुभूतत्वात्प्रैषादिष्वपि लिङादीनां कार्यमेवार्थ इति निश्चीयते ॥ १२ ॥

केन पुनः प्रमाणेन बालः स्वयं कार्यमवगच्छति । यतः प्रवर्तत इत्यत्राह—

कृतिसाध्यं प्रधानं यत्तत्कार्यमभिधीयते ।
तच्च मानान्तरेणापि वेद्यमोदनपाकवत् ॥१३॥

कृतौ सत्यां भावात्, असत्याञ्चाऽभावादनुमानतः कृतिसाध्यता तावदवगम्यते । यदधिकृत्य कृतिः प्रव्रर्तते, तत्कृतेः प्रधानम्, प्रयत्नश्च कृतिः । स च मानसप्रत्यक्षवेद्य इति विशिष्टप्रयोजनतापि प्रयत्नस्य प्रत्यक्षवेद्यैव । तेन प्रत्यक्षानुमानाभ्यां कार्यमवगम्यते । यथा चोदनपाकयोरिति न किञ्चिदनुपन्नम् ।

उपसंहरति—

एवं कार्यात्मकेऽप्यर्थे व्युत्पद्यन्ते लिङादयः ।
तदन्वितेषु स्वार्थेषु तथा शब्दान्तरण्यपि ॥ १४ ॥

एवमपि कथं मानान्तरावेद्यकार्यवाचिता लिङादीनामित्याशंक्य मीमांसामवतारयति—

सम्प्रधार्यमिदन्त्वत्र तत्कार्यं किं क्रियात्मकम् ।
यद वा तद् व्यतिरेकीति

को नु निर्णय इत्यत्राह–

तत्र लोकानुसारतः ॥ १५ ॥

प्रमाणान्तरविज्ञेया क्रिया कार्येति यद्यपि ।

लोके हि लिङादियुक्तवाक्यश्रवणे विशिष्टक्रियानुष्ठानदर्शनात्तद्-विषया कार्यावगतिर्लिङादिभिः क्रियते इति युक्तम्, अवगतिप्रवृत्त्योरेक-

विषयत्वात् । नह्यन्यत्कार्यतयाऽवगम्याऽन्यत्र बालः प्रवर्त्तते । किञ्च क्रियायां कार्यभूतायां लिङादियुक्तवाक्यप्रतिपाद्यायामभ्युपगम्यमानायां शक्तिकल्पनालाघवं स्यादेव । तथा हि धातुरेव कार्यभूतं स्वार्थं ब्रवीतु, तथाभूतार्थवाचिनस्तु धातोः परे लिङादयो भवन्तीत्याश्रीयते । लिङादिश्रवणे तु तथाभूतार्थपरतया धातुः प्रयुक्त इत्यवगम्य कार्यभूतधात्वर्थावगमः सम्पद्यते । यथा लडादिभ्यो वर्त्तमानाद्यध्यवसायः, तेष्वपि वर्त्तमानेऽर्थे वर्त्तमानाद्धातोर्लडित्यैवसूत्रार्थः । कर्त्रादिसंख्यामात्रवाचित्वमेव केवलं लडादीनामिव लिङादीनामप्यर्थ इति, क्रियैव कार्यतया वेदेऽप्यवगम्यते इति, यद्यपि विवेकसमर्थानामवगतिर्भवति ।

तथापि वेदे षष्ठाद्यसिद्धान्तेऽवस्थिते सति ॥ १६ ॥
स्वर्गकामादयः कार्ये नियोज्यत्वेन सम्मताः ।
स्वर्गकामादिभिश्शब्दैर्वक्तव्या इत्यवस्थितम् ॥ १७ ॥

षष्ठाद्ये ह्येतदुक्तम्—लिङादिप्रयोगे तावत्कार्यावगतिरस्तीति निर्विवादम् । कृतिसाध्यञ्च कार्यं भवति । सति कर्त्तरि तस्यात्मलाभः । कर्त्तृलाभश्च स्वसम्बन्धिकार्यावबोधे सति भवति, नान्यथा । तेन यद्यपि लोकानुसारेण क्रियाया एव कार्यतया बोध्यमानाया वाक्यार्थत्वात्, तदन्वयित्वाच्चेतरेषामपि पदार्थानां कारकत्वादृते चान्यस्य क्रियान्वयित्वासम्भावल्लोहितोष्णीषन्यायेन विशेषणभूतस्वर्गकामनासमर्पणपरतया कर्त्रविशेषणत्वेन स्वर्गकामस्यान्वयोऽवगम्यते । तथापि स्वसम्बन्धिकार्यबोद्धृत्वेनैवान्वयो वर्णनीय इति नियोज्यसमर्पकत्वमेवाऽऽश्रीयते इति ॥१७॥

एवमपि किमित्याह—

नियोज्यः स च कार्यं यः स्वकीयत्वेन बुद्ध्यते ।

तथापि किमित्याह—

स्वर्गादिः कामयोगाच्च साध्यत्वेनैव गम्यते ॥१८॥

साध्यविषयस्यैव हि सर्वत्र कामना भवति, तेन तत्सम्बन्धात्साध्यभूतं स्वर्गादि काम्यमानयता पुरुषं विशिनष्टि—

तेन साध्यत्वपर्यन्तस्वर्गादीच्छाविशेषितः ।
तदेव शक्नुयात्कार्यं बोद्धुं यत्काम्यसाधनम् ॥१९॥

अत्र कश्चिदाह—यद्यपि मनोकामनायोगात्साध्यता स्वर्गादीनामवगम्यते तथापि प्रकृतकार्यसाध्यत्वावगमो निष्प्रमाणक एव अन्यसाध्यस्यापि साध्यत्वसम्भवात्। न च यत्काम्यते तस्यावश्यं साधनमस्ति। मनोरथपरम्पराहृतचेतसो हि तन्नास्ति यन्न कामनाविषयी भवति। न च तस्य सर्वस्य साधनं भवति, सर्वज्ञत्वमपि केचित् कामयन्ते, न च तस्योपायसम्भवः। अथ तदिच्छावतोऽतत्साधने कर्त्तृता नोपपद्यते। कथं नोपपद्यते। दृश्यन्ते हि ग्रामाभिगमनकामा अपि यादृच्छिकीषु क्रियासु प्रवर्त्तमानाः। अपि च सर्वोऽभ्युदयार्थ्येव पुरुषः, तथापि प्रायशस्तद्विरोधिष्वेवेन्द्रियार्थेषु प्रवर्त्तमानो दृश्यते।

अत्रोच्यते—स्वर्गादिकं कामयमानस्य तदेव कार्यतया बोद्धुमवकल्प्यते, यदेव तस्य काम्यमानस्य सिद्ध्यनुगुणम्। अन्यथा हि तत्कामिना सता तत्कार्यतयाऽनवबुद्धं स्यात्। अपरित्यक्ततत्कामना सम्बन्धो हि तत्साधनं कार्यतयाऽवबुद्ध्यते। तस्माद्यत्कामिनो यत्कार्यतयोपदिश्यते तत्तस्य काम्यस्य साधनमिति नियोज्यकार्यान्वियानुपपत्त्यैव गम्यते ॥१९॥

एवं सति किं फलमित्याह—

लिङादिस्तत्र कार्यञ्चेत् क्रियामेवाऽवबोधयेत्।
समन्वयो नियोज्येन तदानीमेव हीयते ॥२०॥

कथमित्याह—

क्रिया हि क्षणिकत्वेन न कालान्तरभाविनः।
स्वर्गादेः काम्यमानस्य समर्थाः जननं प्रति ॥२१॥
इष्टस्याऽजनिका सा च नियोज्येन फलार्थिना।
कार्यत्वेन न सम्बन्धमर्हति क्षणभङ्गिनी ॥२२॥

कार्यविरोधि कर्मेति प्रमाणान्तरसिद्धम्। परिस्पन्दो ह्युत्तरदेशसंयोगोदयापवर्गीत्याशुतरविनाशी, स्वर्गश्च नियतदेशान्तरकालान्तरभोग्यः।

ननु प्रीतिमात्रवचनः स्वर्गः इति षष्ठाद्ये साधितम्, प्रीतिसाधनेषु द्रव्येषु स्वर्गशब्दप्रयोगात्। नच तेषु स्वरूपनिबन्धन एव तत्प्रयोगः,

प्रीत्यपगमे तदभावात्। न च तत्साधनवचनता तदनभिधाने घटते, तदभिधानाभ्युपगमे तद्वाचकतैव। लक्षणया तत्साधने प्रयोगोपपत्तेः, तत्र शक्तिकल्पना परिक्षयात्। अखण्डशब्दतया च दण्डिन्यायस्यासम्भवात्त-दन्तर्गतस्य दण्डशब्दस्य दण्डप्रत्यायकत्वसम्भवात्। प्रीतेश्च कर्मान्तरभा-वित्वमपि न सम्भवत्येव।

उच्यते—न प्रीतिमात्रवचनतया ज्योष्टोमादिचोदनासु स्वर्गशब्दस्य प्रयोगोऽवकल्पते, अर्थवादेषु दुःखासम्भिन्नचिरतरोपभोग्याभिलाषोपनेय-प्रीतिश्रवणात्। तत्र यदि विध्युद्देशगतः स्वर्गशब्दः तथाविधप्रीतिपरतया न वर्ण्यते, तदाऽतिपरोक्षार्थवादपदानां वृत्तिरादृता न भवेदिति, तदानुगुण्येन तादृश्यामेव प्रीतौ स्वर्गशब्दः प्रयुक्त इति निश्चीयते। तथाभूता च सा नियतमेव देशान्तरभोग्या। अतो न कर्मानन्तरभाविनीति, न तत्र कर्मण आशुतरविनाशिनः साधनताऽवकल्पते। यस्मिन् हि पूर्ववर्त्तिनि यन्निष्पाद्यते तत्तस्य साधनमिति लोकप्रतीतिः। अत एव च विनष्टस्यापि कर्मणः शास्त्रेण साधनत्वं बोध्यते इति ये ब्रुवते तेऽपि निरस्ताः। एवं चाशुतर-विनाशिनी क्रिया स्वर्गकामिना नियोज्येन सह कार्यतया सम्बन्धुं नार्हति, स्वर्गं प्रति साधनत्वानुपपत्तेः ॥२०-२२॥

तस्मान्नियोज्यसम्बन्धसमर्थं विधिवाचिभिः।
कार्यं कालान्तरस्थायि क्रियातो भिन्नमुच्यते ॥२३॥

ननु क्रियैव कार्यतयोच्यताम्, अस्तु सैव फलसाधनम्। तेन तस्या अपिनियोज्यसम्बन्धो घटत एव। न त्वसौ क्षणभङ्गिनी देहान्तरोपभोग्य-स्वर्गसाधनतां कथमवलम्बिष्यते। उच्यते-वरं तस्या एव तदनुपपत्त्या चिरतरावस्थायिताकल्पना, न पुनरदृष्टस्याश्रुतस्य तदतिरेकिणोऽर्थस्य कल्पना।

यदि वा कर्मण एव शक्तिरवस्थायिनीत्यभ्युपगम्यताम्, तदिदमु-भयमपि प्रमाणान्तरविरोधान्न कल्पनामर्हति। अविरोधि हि प्रतीति-सिद्ध्यर्थं कल्पयितुं शक्यम्। कर्मणश्चाऽऽशुतरविनाशिनश्चिरतरावस्था-यिता प्रमाणान्तरविरुद्धा।

शक्तिमति चातीते शक्तिरप्यतीतेति प्रमाणान्तरसिद्धमिति, न सापि स्थायिनी शक्या कल्पयितुम्। अपि चाश्रये निवृत्ते किमाश्रया शक्तिरवतिष्ठताम्। आत्माश्रितेति चेत् नान्यदीया शक्तिरन्यत्र वर्त्तते, प्रमाणान्तरविरोधादेव। किञ्च शक्तिमत्यसति, शक्तेः फलं न युक्तम्। शक्तिमद्धि साधनम्, न शक्तिः केवला, अन्यथा शक्तित्वं न स्यात्।

ननु यागादिक्रिया देवताऽऽराधनोपायभूता सती कार्यतयोच्यताम्। सा तत्प्रत्यासत्तिद्वारेण कालान्तरेऽपि फलं जनयितुमलमेव। देवताफलदानसमर्था कर्मभिराराध्यते, साऽऽराधिता प्रसीदति, प्रसन्ना च कर्तृन्कालान्तरेऽपि फलेन योजयत्येव इति।

नतदेवम्। यागादीनां देवताराधनहेतुत्वे प्रमाणाभावात्। नहि देवताराधनोपायभूतो याग इत्यत्र किञ्चित्प्रमाणमस्ति। ननु देवपूजार्थः एव यजिः स्मर्यते। पूजा च सर्वा पूज्यमानाराधनार्थेत्यवगतम्। उच्यते-न स्मृतिः प्रमाण स्मृतित्वादेव। प्रमाणान्तरापेक्षया च स्मृतीनामर्थवर्णनम्, तदनुवर्त्तित्वात्तासाम्। न च प्रमाणान्तरेण देवताराधनोपायता यागस्यावगम्यत इत्युक्तम्। अतो देवतोद्देशेन द्रव्यत्यागो याग इति गौणं देवतापूजात्मकत्वमवगन्तव्यम्। पूजापि पूज्योद्देशेनैव हि प्रवर्त्तते इति। अपि च सा कर्मभिराराध्यते, याऽऽराधनं प्रतिपद्यते। नाना देशगामिना पुरुषेणानुष्ठीयमानयागात्मकपूजावगमश्च देवताया इति प्रमाणविरुद्धमेव, विग्रहवतश्च प्रतिपत्तियोगिता, तस्य च वेदेनानादिनाऽऽराध्यतया प्रतिपादनमपि प्रमाणान्तरविरुद्धमेव, तस्यानादित्वानुपपत्तेः। देवताधिकरणे च प्रपञ्चेनायमर्थो निरस्त इति नातीवात्र यतितव्यम्।

अथापि स्यात्पुरुषसंस्कारहेतुभूतैव क्रियाशब्देन कार्यतयोच्यते, तस्याश्च स्वर्गकामादिपुरुषसम्बन्धात्पुरुषसंस्कारादेव कालान्तरे फलं भविष्यति इति। तन्न पुरुषसंस्कारत्वे प्रमाणाभावात्। न हि प्रमाणान्तरतः शब्दतो वा पुरुषसंस्कारहेतुता यागादीनामवसीयते इति 'कर्मण्यारम्भभाव्यत्वादि' त्यत्रोक्तम्।

ननु क्रियैव कार्यतवोच्यताम्, फलसाधनता च तस्या एवाऽऽश्रीयताम्। तदन्यथानुपपत्त्या तु किञ्चिदप्यपरं तज्जन्यं फलोदयानुगुणं

कालान्तरस्थाय्यात्माश्रयं परिकल्प्यताम्, माभूत्तस्य लिङादिवाच्यता इति।

उच्यते-तद्धि तदनुपपत्त्या कल्प्यते, यद्यस्योपपादकम्। न च क्रिया-जन्येनान्येन फलजनकेन कल्पितेन क्रियायाः फलसाधनतोपपादिता भवति। न हि साधनसाधनं तस्य साधनं भवति, अवान्तरव्यापारो वा शक्तिर्वा तत्साधनतां निर्वाहयति। व्यापारयोगितयैव शक्तिमतां साधनता यतः। न चात्मसमवाय्यर्थान्तरं कर्मणामवान्तरव्यापारः, नापि शक्तिरिति, न तस्यार्थापत्तिगम्यता युक्ता। किंत्वन्विताभिधाने स्थिते नियोज्यानुगुण्या-च्छब्दवाच्यतैवोचितेति सूक्तम् 'नियोज्यसम्बन्धसमर्थं कालान्तरस्थायि कार्यं क्रियातिरिक्तं लिङादिभिरेवोच्यते" इति।

गुरुमतसर्वस्वम्—

अत्रैषा प्रक्रिया। चोदनासूत्रे कार्यार्थता प्रतिपादिता। षष्ठाद्ये कार्यस्य स्वसम्बन्धितया बोध्यः स्वर्गकामादिर्नियोज्य इति व्युत्पादितम्। स्वर्गकामना च नियोज्यविशेषणमित्येकादशाद्ये व्युत्पादितम् तस्य कार्यस्य नियोज्यविशेषणीभूत-काम्योत्पत्तिहेतुत्वमिति बादर्यधिकरणे राद्धान्तितम्। तच्च तथा भूतं कार्यं क्रियारूपं न भवति तस्या फलसाधनत्वायोगात्। देवताराधनमुखेन तावत् फलसाधनता नास्तीति 'कर्मण्यारम्भभाव्यत्वादि त्यत्रोक्तम्। कर्मणः तच्छक्तेर्वा स्थायिता नेति चापूर्वाधिकरणे प्रतिपा-दितम्। अनो नियोज्यान्वय मुखेन मानान्तरापूर्वमात्मसमवायिकार्यं लिङादिभिरभिधीयत इत्यनेकन्यायसाध्यम् कार्यञ्च कृतिसाध्यम्। कृतिश्च पुंसां प्रयत्न एव। न चासौ भावार्थमन्तरेणास्तीति, तत्सम्बद्ध एवोच्यते इति भावार्थाधिकरणे स्थितम्। स च भावार्थः सम्बध्यमानस्तमवच्छिन-त्तीति शब्दान्तराधिकरणे निर्णीतम्। विषयभूतश्च भावार्थः करणीभव-तीति बादर्यधिकरणे एवोक्तम्। स्वकार्यसाधने भावार्थे पुरुषस्यैश्वर्यमिति च तत्रैवोक्तम् ॥२३॥

कालान्तरावस्थायिनः कार्यस्य नियोज्यान्वययोग्यतामाह—

तद्धि कालान्तरस्थानाच्छक्तं स्वर्गादिसिद्धये।
सम्बन्धोऽप्युपपद्येत नियोज्येनास्य कामिना ॥२४॥

ननु भाष्यकारः प्रत्ययार्थमपूर्वं मित्याह, न क्रियादिभिन्नं कार्यमिति यो मन्यते, तं प्रत्याह—

क्रियादिभिन्नं यत्कार्यं वेद्यं मानान्तरैर्न तत् ।
अतो मानान्तरापूर्वमपूर्वमिति गीयते ॥२५॥

नन्वेवमपूर्वं वाक्यार्थः स्याद् न नियोगः । नियोगश्च वाक्यार्थ इति प्राभाकराणामुल्लाप इत्यत्राह—

कार्यत्वेन नियोज्यं च स्वात्मनि प्रेरयन्नसौ ।
नियोग इति मीमांसानिष्णातैरभिधीयते ॥२६॥

एवमपि कथं तस्य वाक्यार्थत्वमित्याह—

कार्यस्यैव प्रधानत्वाद्वाक्यार्थत्वञ्च युज्यते ।
वाक्यं तदेव हि प्राह नियोज्यविषयान्वितम् ॥२७॥

उक्तं ह्येतत्-यत् प्रधानतया प्रतिपाद्यते तद् वाक्यार्थः इति । कार्यञ्च प्रधानतयोच्यते इति तस्यैव वाक्यार्थत्वम् ।

नियोज्यान्विताभिधानं च प्रायिकम्, आधानाध्ययनाङ्गप्रधानोत्पत्तिनियोगानां नियोज्यशून्यानामभिधानाभ्युपगमात् । विवरणकारा ह्याधानविषयमपि नियोगान्तरमिच्छन्ति, क्रतुनियोगप्रत्यभिज्ञानाभावात् । असन्निधाने हि तन्नियोगप्रत्यभिज्ञानं नोपपद्यते । नापि पर्णतादिवदव्यभिचरितक्रतुसम्बन्धाग्निमुखेन प्रत्यभिज्ञोपपत्तिः । प्रागाधानादाहवनीयादिशब्दानामर्थापरिज्ञानात्क्रतुसम्बन्धानवगमात् । जुह्वादीनान्त्वाकृतिवचनत्वात्प्रागेव विधेर्नियोगप्रत्यभिज्ञासम्भवः ।

नन्वग्नीनामपि साध्यत्वात्, साध्यद्वयं कथमेकस्मिन् वाक्येऽन्वीयते ? उच्यते-नियोग एवात्रापि प्रधानं साध्यम्, अनीप्सितकर्मतात्वग्नीनाम् । अनीप्सितकर्मत्वेऽपि यत्तदाधानजन्यं फलमग्निसमवायि, तद्योगिन्याहवनीयादिशब्दप्रयोगात् । आहवनीयादीनाञ्च क्रतूपयोगित्वात्तत्सिद्ध्यर्थतयैव पुरुषप्रवृत्त्युपपत्तेरनुष्ठानलाभादलं नियोज्यान्विताभिधानेनेति ।

तथाध्ययनविधावप्याचार्यकरणविधिप्रयुक्त्यैवानुष्ठानलाभान्नियोज्य-शून्याभिधानमिति स्थितम्। प्रधानोत्पत्तिनियोगा अप्यधिकारनियोगाक्षिप्तस्त्रविषयानुष्ठानेनैव लब्धसिद्धय इति न तत्र नियोज्यान्विताभिधानान्वेषणम्।

अङ्गोत्पत्तिनियोगा अपि विनियुक्तप्रयाजादिविषयत्वादधिकारनियोगाङ्गतयैव सिद्धयन्तीति किं तेषु नियोज्यान्विताभिधानेन।

कथं तर्हि प्रयाजादिविधीनां विनियुक्त विषयत्वम्? उच्यते-साधिकारनियोगसन्निधौ प्रयाजादिवाक्यानि श्रुतानि न तावत्स्वविषयं नियोगान्तरमवगमयितुमीशते, अवघातादिवदनुवादकत्वसम्भवात्। किन्तु स्वरूपमात्रमेव योग्यस्वपदार्थविशिष्टमुपस्थापयन्ति। तच्च प्रयोजनाकांक्षितया प्रयोजनीभूतेन साधिकारेण नियोगेनान्वीयते इति, अधिकारवाक्यगत एव लिङ्शब्दः तदन्वितं स्वार्थमभिधत्ते। स चान्वयः प्रयाजादीनामैदमर्थ्यमात्रेण ग्राहकग्रहणमित्युच्यते। करणोपकारसाकांक्षस्य चापूर्वस्य यत्करणोपकारपरिकल्पनं स प्रकरणव्यापारः इति यत्तेषां करणोपकार जनकत्वकल्पनं तदौपादानिकम् इति।

नास्ति तर्हि प्रयाजादिषु नियोगान्तरम्? न नास्ति, क्षणिकानां तेषां सम्भूय करणोपकारकत्वानुपपत्तेर्नियोगान्तरस्याऽवश्याश्रयणीयत्वात्। योऽसौ लिङादिः प्रागनूद्यमानार्थकतया शंकितः स इदानीं नियोगान्तरमभिधत्ते। अत एव चावघातादिवत्तेषां 'यजि' आदि शब्दानामेवाङ्गवाक्यगतानामधिकारनियोगान्वितस्वार्थाभिधानं नाभ्युपगम्यते। तथा सत्युत्पत्तावेवाङ्गयाग स्वरूपस्यान्यतिरश्चीनस्य नियोगान्तराविषयत्वात्, नियोगान्तरविषयता न स्यात्। उत्पत्तिदशायां त्वनन्यतिरश्चीनतयाऽभिधानाद्युक्तं नियोगान्तरविषयत्वम्। कस्मात्पुनरन्यतिरश्चीनस्य नियोगान्तराविषयत्वम्, कार्यद्वयसम्बन्धावगमानुपपत्तेः नह्येकं वस्तु युगपत्कार्यद्वयसम्बन्धि शक्यमवगन्तुम्। यच्च नियोगान्तरं प्रयाजादिषु, तत्पश्चादभिधीयमानमधिकारनियोगाङ्गतयैव स्वशब्देनाभिधीयते। अन्यथा विषयद्वयविनियोगविरोधादित्यलमति प्रसङ्गेन ॥२७॥

ननु नियोगस्य फलसाधनत्वात्, तस्य च सेतिकर्त्तव्यताकरण-निबन्धनसिद्धित्वात्, तदनुष्ठानानन्तरं नियोगसिद्धेः फलस्यैव प्राधान्यात्, तस्यैव वाक्यार्थत्वं युक्तमित्यत आह—

आत्मसिद्ध्यनुकूलस्य नियोज्यस्य प्रसिद्धये।
कुर्वंत्स्वर्गादिकमपि प्रधानं कार्यमेव न ॥२८॥

यत्तपूर्वं कार्यम्, तस्य नियोज्यान्वयं विना कार्यत्वानुपपत्तेः, अनुष्ठानं विना तदसम्भवात् कर्त्रा च विना तदनुपपत्तेः, अधिकारेण च विना कर्त्तुरभावात्, नियोज्यत्वं विना तदयोगात् अकामसाधने च कामिनो नियोगानवगमादिति, आत्मसिद्ध्यर्थमेव नियोगः काम्यमान-फलसिद्धिहेतुत्वमवलम्बते स्वामिवत्। यथाऽऽत्मन एव संविदधानः स्वामी गर्भदासस्योपकरोति, तथा नियोगोऽपि नियोज्यस्येति न प्राधान्य-प्रच्युतिः ॥२८॥

ननु नियोगस्य फलसाधनत्वात्, तस्य च सेतिकर्त्तव्यताकरण-निबन्धनसिद्धित्वात्, तदनुष्ठानानन्तरं नियोगसिद्धेः फलसिद्धिः स्यात्, अनन्तरनियोगो न निष्पद्यते, तर्हि क्रियायामतीतायां कुतस्तत्सिद्धिरित्य-त्राह—

विषयानुष्ठितौ सत्यां सिद्धो न हि विधिः फलम्।
तदानीमेव कुरुते सहकारिव्यपेक्षया ॥२९॥

एषात्र दर्शन स्थितिः—प्रधानोत्पत्तिनियोगाः अङ्गोत्पत्तिनियोगाश्च यथायथं सन्निपत्योपकारकाङ्गयुक्तस्वविषयमात्रानुष्ठानेनैव सिद्ध्यन्ति। तत्र यान्यङ्गानि पूर्वाणि तानि सम्भूय प्रधानोत्पत्त्यपूर्वेषूपकुर्वन्ति, तस्माच्च परमापूर्वं निष्पद्यते। यान्यपि चाङ्गापूर्वाणि दीक्षिणीयानीनां तेषामप्यारा-दुपकारकातिदेशिकाङ्गभाजामेकमुत्पत्त्यपूर्वम्, अपरमप्यङ्गापूर्वं प्रधानवद्वे-दितव्यमिति। अनया दिशाऽन्यत्रापि सकलमूहनीयम्।

इत्थं यद्यपि कर्मानुष्ठानानन्तरमेव नियोगसिद्धिः, तथापि यत्फलस्यानन्तराभवनम्, तत् उपपत्त्या कल्प्यत इति।

नन्वेवं सति फलहेतुताऽपूर्वस्य वाध्येतेत्यत्राह—

सहकारिव्यपेक्षा च कारणत्वं न बाध्यते ।
मा बाधिष्टेति सर्वत्र तदनुग्रहकल्पना ।।३०।।

तथेत्यर्थः ।

'अतः पुरुषकारश्च दैवञ्च फलसाधनम्' इत्याचार्याः । दैवम्-अपूर्वम् । अपेक्षणीयं सहकारि च पुरुषकारपदवेद्यम् ।

नन्वेवं भवतु काम्येष्वपूर्वकार्याभिधानं लिङादीनाम्, नित्यनैमित्तिकनिषेधाधिकारेषु कथम् ? न हि तेषु फलोदयं प्राभाकरा अनुमन्यन्ते। नहि फलं फलतयाऽन्वीयते, किन्त्वधिकारिविशेषणतया । लब्धे तु जीवनादावधिकारिविशेषणे किं फलान्वेषणेन । न च फलमन्तरेण प्रवृत्त्यसम्भवः, स्व सम्बन्धिकार्यावगममात्रायत्तत्वात्प्रवृत्तेः । निरपेक्षाच्छब्दात्फलमन्तरेणापि स्वसम्बन्धिकार्यावगमः, तावन्मात्रस्य लोके प्रवृत्तिहेतुत्वागमात् । कार्यावगमोत्पादनायैव फलमुपयुज्यते इत्युक्तम् । ननु यथा शब्दात्कार्यावगतिः, तथा निष्फलत्वादनुमानेनाऽकार्यता प्रतीतिरपीति, कथं प्रवृत्त्युपपत्तिः ? न, आगमविरोधेनानुमानस्याऽऽत्मलाभाभावात् । एतावानेव प्रमाणव्यापारः, यत्प्रवृत्तियोग्यार्थोपदर्शनम् । अन्यथा यदि कश्चित्कल्पिते फले न प्रवर्त्तते तदा किं कर्त्तव्यम् ।।३०।।

ननु फलोदयानभ्युपगमे च प्राच्यमार्गासम्भवात्, नित्यादिष्वपूर्वकार्याभिधानमप्रमाणकं स्यात्, तत्राह—

एवं कामाधिकारार्थपर्यालोचयोत्थिता ।
व्युत्पत्तिः सर्ववाक्यार्थप्रतिपत्तिनिबन्धनम् ।।३१।।

उक्तमिदमन्याय्यञ्चानेकार्थत्वम् इति । तेन कामाधिकारे सिद्धेऽपूर्वकार्याभिधायकत्वे, नित्यादिष्वपि स एवार्थो विरोधाभावादाश्रीयते । नित्याधिकाराद्यनुगुण्येन तु क्रियाकार्यत्वाभिमानं काम्येष्वनुपपन्नमिति, सर्वत्रापूर्वमेव वाक्यार्थ इति ।।३१।।

नन्वेवं वेदादेव व्युत्पत्तिरास्थिता स्यादित्याशंक्याह—

व्युत्पत्तिरपि कार्येऽर्थे व्यवहारानुसारिणी ।
किन्तु निर्धारणामात्रं वेदवाक्यविमर्शजम् ।।३२।।

तत्रैतदेव तावद् वक्तव्यम्-न केवलं वेदे लोकव्यवहारादेव शब्दार्थावधारणम्, किन्तु प्रसिद्धार्थपदसम्बन्धादपि पदार्थान्तरान्वययोग्यार्थाभिधायकतेति स्थिते, तदनुरूपार्थाभिधायकता निर्णीयत एव। एतच्च यववराहाधिकरणे व्युत्पादितम्। व्यवहारत एव सम्बन्धावधारणादुभयथाऽपि व्यवहारदर्शनात्समा प्रतिपत्तिरिति पूर्वपक्षः। पदान्तरसम्बन्धादपि पदान्तरार्थाध्यवसानं भवत्येव, तेन वैदिकवाक्यशेषान्वयार्हतालोचनेन दीर्घशूकाद्यर्थत्वमेवेति राद्धान्तः।

तथा त्रिवृच्छब्दे यूपाहवनीयादिषु च शक्त्यवधारणात्। लोकेऽपि चायं व्यवहारो बहुलमुपलभ्यते। तथा सति वैदिकनियोज्यान्वययोग्यतया लिङादीनामपूर्वकार्याभिधायकत्वनिर्णतो नाऽनुपपन्नः।

अयं चापरो विशेषः यल्लिङादियुक्तानां वाक्यानां कार्यार्थत्वम्, तत्तावद्वृद्धव्यवहारादेवासिद्धम्, किन्तु लिङादिप्रत्ययानां यद्वाच्यं कार्यं तच्चापूर्वरूपमित्येतावन्मात्रं वैदिकपदसम्बन्धादवसीयते इति ॥ ३२ ॥

एकदेशिमतमधुना निराकर्त्तुमुपन्यस्यति—

व्यवहारत एवाहुर्व्युत्पत्तिमपरे पुनः।
कार्ये मानान्तरावेद्ये क्रियादिव्यतिरेकिणि ॥३३॥

अस्यार्थः—केचिदेवमाहुः-लिङादिक्तयुवाक्यश्रवणे प्रवृत्तिदर्शनात्, कार्यावगतिनिबन्धनत्वात्प्रवृत्तेः, कार्यमात्रमेव तेषामर्थः, न क्रिया। तस्यां शब्दस्य प्रवृत्त्यनुपयोगित्वादिति क्रियानिष्कृष्टकार्याभिधायिता लौकिकव्यवहारादेव निर्णीयत इति ॥३३॥

तदिदमयुक्तमिति प्रतिजानीते—

सितेतर इव त्वेष पक्षश्चित्तं न कर्षति।
चन्द्रातपामलन्यायप्रवासमलिनीकृतः ॥३४॥

कथमित्याह—

कार्ये मानान्तरावेद्ये पार्श्वस्थस्तन्निबन्धनम्।
व्यवहारं कथंकारं शब्दात्प्रागवबुध्यताम् ॥३५॥
व्यवहारमविज्ञाय तन्निबन्धनतद्गता।
प्रतिपत्तिः कथं ज्ञेया शब्दशक्तिः कथन्तराम् ॥३६॥

इदमत्राकूतम् । यद्यपि कार्यमात्रमेव प्रवृत्त्युपयोगीति तावन्मात्रमेव शब्दार्थः, तथापि तस्य लोके क्रियागतस्यैव प्रवर्त्तकत्वदर्शनात्; शक्यते क्रियाश्रितता प्रत्येतुम् । यथाऽऽकृतिमात्रस्य शब्दार्थत्वेऽपि व्यक्त्याश्रिततापि न प्रतिक्षिप्यते, तथा क्रियाश्रितत्वं प्रमाणान्तरप्रमितं न प्रतिक्षेपमर्हति । तेन क्रियातिरिक्त-कार्याभिधायतत्वमसिद्धम् । यदि पयं तन्निबन्धनव्यवहार एव स्यात्, तदा तद्दर्शनात्तद्धेतुभूतप्रतिपत्त्यन्यथानुपपत्त्याऽनुमानेन शब्दस्य वाचकत्वाध्यवसानं भवेत् । न चैतदस्ति, तस्य शब्दादन्यतः प्रागनवगमात्त-न्निबन्धनव्यवहाराप्रतिपत्तिः, तदप्रतिपत्तौ च तद्धेतुभूतप्रतिपत्त्यननुमानान्न शक्तिकल्पनोपपत्तिः ।।३४-३६।।

तत्राकूतं विवृणोति—

कार्यप्रतीतिमात्रञ्च प्रवृत्तेरनुमीयताम् ।
किन्तु कार्या क्रियैवेति लोकदृष्ट्याऽवसीयते ।।३६।।

लोकप्रतीतं क्रियारूपत्वञ्च न शक्यतेऽपह्नोतुमिति, कार्यमात्रार्थत्वे क्रियैव कार्यतया लिङाद्यर्थ इति निश्चीयते, न पुनः प्रमाणान्तरादपूर्वमिति ।।३७।।

अन्ये पुनः वेदार्थबोधकाचार्यवचननिबन्धनप्रवृत्तिदर्शनेनातीन्द्रिये कार्ये लिङादयो व्युत्पद्यन्त इत्याहुः । यद्याचार्यवचनादपि क्रियैव कार्यतयावगम्यते, तदा तस्याः स्वयं दुःखरूपत्वात्पुरुषार्थान्तरानुबन्धनं विना प्रवृत्त्यसंभवान्नियमेन सुखार्थिनः प्रवृत्तिर्न स्यात् । न च सन्ध्योपासनादौ पुरुषार्थोऽस्ति । तस्मात्क्रियातिरिक्तकार्यमाचार्यवचनेभ्योऽवगम्यते इति ।

तान्प्रत्याह—

वेदार्थाचार्यवाक्येषु प्रवृत्तिर्यापि दृश्यते ।
तत्राऽप्येषैव सम्बन्धपरिज्ञानविधा भवेत ।।३८।।

आचार्यवाक्यश्रवणादपि शिष्याणां या सन्ध्योपासनादौ प्रवृत्तिः, तत्रापि बालः स्वविषयनिरूपितं क्रियाकार्यत्वावगममेव कारणत्वेन परिकल्पयेत्, फलं विना च तदनुपपत्तेः फलावगममपि सम्भावयेत् ।

लोकव्युत्पत्त्यनुसारेण वेदार्थमपि प्रतिपद्यमानो नित्यनैमित्तिकनिषेधाधिकारेष्वपि फलं कल्पयेत्। स एव बाल्यदशायां व्युत्पन्नः स्वयमाचार्यपदवीमधिरूढो वेदार्थं प्रतीत्य शिष्येभ्य उपदिशन् क्रियामेव कार्यतया प्रतिपादयेत्, नाऽपूर्वं कार्यम् इति।

उपसंहरति—

तस्माल्लोकानुसारेण व्युत्पत्तिः कार्यमात्रके।
तस्य त्वपूर्वरूपत्वं वेदवाक्यानुसारतः ॥३९॥

एवमपूर्वकार्याभिधायित्वे सिद्धे चोदयति—

ननु लोकविरोधित्वं पक्षेऽस्मिन्नपि दृश्यते।
सर्वथैव यतो लोके क्रिया कार्यैव गम्यते ॥४०॥

परिहरति—

भवेदेवं विरुध्येते कार्येऽपूर्वेऽपि लौकिके।
प्रतिपत्तिप्रयोगौ चेत् क्रियाकार्यत्वगोचरौ ॥४१॥

यदि कार्याकार्यत्वगोचरौ लौकिकौ प्रतिपत्तिप्रयोगावपूर्वकार्याभिधायित्वपक्षाङ्गीकारे विरुध्येते, ततो लोकविरुद्धत्वं स्यादस्मत्पक्षस्य। न चैतदस्ति इत्याह—

अपूर्वं हि क्रिया साध्यं साधिता साधनं क्रिया।
तस्मादपूर्वकार्यत्वं क्रियाकार्यत्वसङ्गतम् ॥४२॥
प्रमाणान्तरगम्यं हि लोकश्शब्दैर्विवक्षति।
क्रियाकार्यत्व एवातः प्रयोगो लक्षणान्वितः ॥४३॥

प्रतिपत्तिप्रयोगौ हि नावश्यं श्रौतवृत्त्यनुसारिणावेव लक्षणयाऽपि लोके तद्दर्शनात्। तेन यद्यप्युक्तेन न्यायेनापूर्वमेव कार्यं लिङादीनामभिधेयम्, तथापि तस्य क्रियाकार्यत्वाव्यभिचारात्, तत्र लक्षणया तयोर्नानुपपत्तिः। यत्तु श्रौतपदार्थे कार्ये लोके लिङादि न प्रयुज्यते इति, तत्तस्याऽपूर्वात्मनः प्रमाणान्तराप्रतीतत्वात्, प्रतीतविषयत्वाच्च लौकिकप्रयोगस्य। क्रिया-

साध्यन्त्वपूर्वम् । साधिता च सती क्रिया साधनं भवतीत्यपूर्वेण सह क्रिया कार्यत्वं नित्यसम्बद्धमिति शक्यते तल्लक्षयितुम् ॥

यद्येषा लक्षणा किमिति तर्हि लोको नावगच्छतीत्याह–

लक्षणानभिमानस्तु मुख्यार्थानवधारणात् ।
ये तु मुख्यार्थकुशलास्तेषां लाक्षणिकत्वधीः ॥४४॥

मुख्यमर्थमविदित्वा लाक्षणिकमप्यर्थं श्रौतमिव मन्यन्ते, म्लेच्छा इव यववराहाद्यर्थम् । मुख्यार्थविवेकिनान्तु परीक्षमाणां लाक्षणिकत्वधीः । इति ॥४४॥

उपसंहरति—

तस्मात्मानान्तरावेद्यं कार्यमर्थान्तरान्वितम् ।
वेदवाक्यं ब्रवीतीति संक्षेपोऽयमुदाहृतः ॥४५॥

ग्रन्थस्य, कर्त्तुश्च संज्ञां प्रयोजनञ्चाह–

वाक्यार्थमातृकेयं प्रभाकरगुरोर्मतानुसारेण ।
अनसूयुबोधनार्थं शालिकनाथेन सङ्ग्रथिता ॥४६॥
रचिता सच्चरितानामनुग्रहं कर्त्तुकामेन ।
वाक्यार्थमातृमायाः वृत्तिरियं शालिकेनैव ॥

इति महामहोपाध्यायश्रीमच्छालिकनाथमिश्रप्रणीतायां सवृत्तौ वाक्यार्थमातृकायां द्वितीयः परिच्छेदः समाप्तः ।

समाप्ता च सवृत्तिवाक्यार्थमातृका ॥